NEW PERSPECTIVES ON
Microsoft® Access® 2013

BRIEF

Joseph J. Adamski
Grand Valley State University

Kathleen T. Finnegan

Sharon Scollard
Mohawk College

CENGAGE
Learning·

Australia • Brazil • Japan • Korea • Mexico • Singapore • Spain • United Kingdom • United States

CENGAGE
Learning®

New Perspectives on Microsoft Access 2013, Brief

Director of Development: Marah Bellegarde

Executive Editor: Donna Gridley

Associate Acquisitions Editor: Amanda Lyons

Product Development Manager: Leigh Hefferon

Senior Product Manager: Kathy Finnegan

Product Manager: Julia Leroux-Lindsey

Developmental Editor: Sasha Vodnik

Editorial Assistant: Melissa Stehler

Brand Manager: Elinor Gregory

Market Development Managers: Kristie Clark, Gretchen Swann

Senior Content Project Manager: Jennifer Goguen McGrail

Composition: GEX Publishing Services

Art Director: GEX Publishing Services

Text Designer: Althea Chen

Cover Art: © Janaka Dharmasena/Shutterstock

Copyeditor: Michael Beckett

Proofreader: Lisa Weidenfeld

Indexer: Alexandra Nickerson

Some of the product names and company names used in this book have been used for identification purposes only and may be trademarks or registered trademarks of their respective manufacturers and sellers.

Microsoft and the Office logo are either registered trademarks or trademarks of Microsoft Corporation in the United States and/or other countries. Cengage Learning is an independent entity from the Microsoft Corporation, and not affiliated with Microsoft in any manner.

Disclaimer: Any fictional data related to persons or companies or URLs used throughout this book is intended for instructional purposes only. At the time this book was printed, any such data was fictional and not belonging to any real persons or companies.

Library of Congress Control Number: 2013936663

ISBN-13: 978-1-285-09922-4

ISBN-10: 1-285-09922-2

Cengage Learning
200 First Stamford Place, 4th Floor
Stamford, CT 06902
USA

Cengage Learning is a leading provider of customized learning solutions with office locations around the globe, including Singapore, the United Kingdom, Australia, Mexico, Brazil, and Japan. Locate your local office at: **international.cengage.com/global**

Cengage Learning products are represented in Canada by Nelson Education, Ltd.

To learn more about Cengage Learning, visit **www.cengage.com.**

Purchase any of our products at your local college store or at our preferred online store **www.cengagebrain.com**

ProSkills Icons © 2014 Cengage Learning.

Printed in the United States of America
1 2 3 4 5 6 7 19 18 17 16 15 14 13

Preface

The New Perspectives Series' critical-thinking, problem-solving approach is the ideal way to prepare students to transcend point-and-click skills and take advantage of all that Microsoft Office 2013 has to offer.

In developing the New Perspectives Series, our goal was to create books that give students the software concepts and practical skills they need to succeed beyond the classroom. We've updated our proven case-based pedagogy with more practical content to make learning skills more meaningful to students.

With the New Perspectives Series, students understand *why* they are learning *what* they are learning, and are fully prepared to apply their skills to real-life situations.

"This text provides real-world examples that guide learners through the material with clear explanations and rich graphics. The progression of lessons allows students to incorporate new concepts into their existing knowledge and continuously build to a high level of achievement and understanding."

—Christine Yero
Madison Area Technical College

About This Book

This book provides essential coverage of Microsoft Access 2013, and includes the following:

- Detailed, hands-on instruction of Microsoft Access 2013 basics, including creating and maintaining a database, querying a database, and creating forms and reports
- Coverage of important database concepts, including guidelines for designing databases, setting field properties, and defining table relationships

New for this edition!

- Each tutorial has been updated with new case scenarios throughout, which provide a rich and realistic context for students to apply the concepts and skills presented.
- A new Troubleshoot type of Case Problem, in which certain steps of the exercise require students to identify and correct errors—which are intentionally placed in the files students work with—promotes problem solving and critical thinking.
- The new "Managing Your Files" tutorial at the beginning of the book provides students with a solid foundation in organizing their files and folders.

System Requirements

This book assumes a typical installation of Microsoft Access 2013 and Microsoft Windows 8 Professional. (You can also complete the material in this text using another version of Windows 8 or using Windows 7. You may see only minor differences in how some windows look.) The browser used for any steps that require a browser is Internet Explorer 10.

www.cengage.com/series/newperspectives

The New Perspectives Approach

"The clear step-by-step instructions, real-world data files, and helpful figures make New Perspectives texts excellent for courses taught in the classroom, the hybrid/blended format, or entirely online."
—Sylvia Amito'elau
Coastline Community College

Context
Each tutorial begins with a problem presented in a "real-world" case that is meaningful to students. The case sets the scene to help students understand what they will do in the tutorial.

Hands-on Approach
Each tutorial is divided into manageable sessions that combine reading and hands-on, step-by-step work. Colorful screenshots help guide students through the steps. **Trouble?** tips anticipate common mistakes or problems to help students stay on track and continue with the tutorial.

VISUAL OVERVIEW
Visual Overviews
Each session begins with a Visual Overview, a two-page spread that includes colorful, enlarged screenshots with numerous callouts and key term definitions, giving students a comprehensive preview of the topics covered in the session, as well as a handy study guide.

PROSKILLS
ProSkills Boxes and Exercises
ProSkills boxes provide guidance for how to use the software in real-world, professional situations, and related ProSkills exercises integrate the technology skills students learn with one or more of the following soft skills: decision making, problem solving, teamwork, verbal communication, and written communication.

KEY STEP
Key Steps
Important steps are highlighted in yellow with attached margin notes to help students pay close attention to completing the steps correctly and avoid time-consuming rework.

INSIGHT
InSight Boxes
InSight boxes offer expert advice and best practices to help students achieve a deeper understanding of the concepts behind the software features and skills.

TIP
Margin Tips
Margin Tips provide helpful hints and shortcuts for more efficient use of the software. The Tips appear in the margin at key points throughout each tutorial, giving students extra information when and where they need it.

REVIEW
APPLY
Assessment
Retention is a key component to learning. At the end of each session, a series of Quick Check questions helps students test their understanding of the material before moving on. Engaging end-of-tutorial Review Assignments and Case Problems have always been a hallmark feature of the New Perspectives Series. Colorful bars and headings identify the type of exercise, making it easy to understand both the goal and level of challenge a particular assignment holds.

REFERENCE
TASK REFERENCE
GLOSSARY/INDEX
Reference
Within each tutorial, Reference boxes appear before a set of steps to provide a succinct summary and preview of how to perform a task. In addition, a complete Task Reference at the back of the book provides quick access to information on how to carry out common tasks. Finally, each book includes a combination Glossary/Index to promote easy reference of material.

www.cengage.com/series/newperspectives

Our Complete System of Instruction

BRIEF

INTRODUCTORY

COMPREHENSIVE

Coverage To Meet Your Needs

Whether you're looking for just a small amount of coverage or enough to fill a semester-long class, we can provide you with a textbook that meets your needs.

- Brief books typically cover the essential skills in just 2 to 4 tutorials.
- Introductory books build and expand on those skills and contain an average of 5 to 8 tutorials.
- Comprehensive books are great for a full-semester class, and contain 9 to 12+ tutorials.

So if the book you're holding does not provide the right amount of coverage for you, there's probably another offering available. Go to our Web site or contact your Cengage Learning sales representative to find out what else we offer.

COURSECASTS

CourseCasts – Learning on the Go. Always available...always relevant.

Want to keep up with the latest technology trends relevant to you? Visit http://coursecasts.course.com to find a library of weekly updated podcasts, CourseCasts, and download them to your mp3 player.

Ken Baldauf, host of CourseCasts, is a faculty member of the Florida State University Computer Science Department where he is responsible for teaching technology classes to thousands of FSU students each year. Ken is an expert in the latest technology trends; he gathers and sorts through the most pertinent news and information for CourseCasts so your students can spend their time enjoying technology, rather than trying to figure it out. Open or close your lecture with a discussion based on the latest CourseCast.

Visit us at http://coursecasts.course.com to learn on the go!

Instructor Resources

We offer more than just a book. We have all the tools you need to enhance your lectures, check students' work, and generate exams in a new, easier-to-use and completely revised package. This book's Instructor's Manual, ExamView testbank, PowerPoint presentations, data files, solution files, figure files, and a sample syllabus are all available on a single CD-ROM or for downloading at http://www.cengage.com.

SAM: Skills Assessment Manager

Get your students workplace-ready with SAM, the premier proficiency-based assessment and training solution for Microsoft Office! SAM's active, hands-on environment helps students master computer skills and concepts that are essential to academic and career success.

Skill-based assessments, interactive trainings, business-centric projects, and comprehensive remediation engage students in mastering the latest Microsoft Office programs on their own, allowing instructors to spend class time teaching. SAM's efficient course setup and robust grading features provide faculty with consistency across sections. Fully interactive MindTap Readers integrate market-leading Cengage Learning content with SAM, creating a comprehensive online student learning environment.

www.cengage.com/series/newperspectives

Acknowledgments

The authors wish to thank the following reviewers for their helpful feedback, valuable insights, and dedication to this project: Cliff Brozo, Monroe College; Deborah Franklin, Bryant & Stratton College; Debi Griggs, Bellevue College; Karen Miller, Hohokus of Hackensack School; and Christine Yero, Madison Area Technical College. Many thanks to everyone on the New Perspectives team, especially Donna Gridley for her leadership and inspiration; Amanda Lyons and Melissa Stehler for their contributions and support; Julia Leroux-Lindsey for her outstanding management of this project, keeping us all on task and focused through many hoops and hurdles; and Jennifer Goguen McGrail for her tireless efforts and expertise in guiding us through the production process. Thanks as well to the following Manuscript Quality Assurance (MQA) staff members for their diligent efforts in ensuring the quality and accuracy of this text: Chris Scriver, MQA Project Leader; and John Freitas, Susan Pedicini, and Danielle Shaw, MQA Testers.

Special thanks go to Sasha Vodnik, Developmental Editor, for his incredible attention to detail, his willingness to go the extra mile, and, above all, his positive attitude and friendship, which helped to turn a challenging project into a fun endeavor. To my co-author, Sharon Scollard, more thanks than I can express for her expertise and guidance, but most especially for her true spirit of collaboration and teamwork, which made it a pleasure to complete this book. Many thanks to Cindi DelFavero for her special contributions to this text. Finally, I am extremely grateful for the love and support of my wonderful parents, Ed and Mary Curran, and for being lucky enough to have the two best sons in the world, Connor and Devon, who make this all worthwhile.
–Kathleen T. Finnegan

I would like to express my gratitude and appreciation to the people whose dedication was invaluable in producing this book. Sasha Vodnik, Developmental Editor, made countless positive contributions and always had words of encouragement right when I needed them. Kathy Finnegan, co-author and Senior Product Manager, regardless of the hat she wore, always had words of wisdom, and I don't think we've had a single conversation without sharing a good laugh. Many thanks also to Joe Adamski, whose love for teaching and technology shines through this material, which forms such a strong foundation. Finally, with all my heart, I'd like to thank my children, Angela, Robyn and Andrew. They keep me grounded, they keep me laughing, and they're the top three records in my database.
–Sharon Scollard

TABLE OF CONTENTS

OBJECTIVES

- Explore the differences between Windows 7 and Windows 8
- Plan the organization of files and folders
- Use File Explorer to view and manage libraries, folders, and files
- Open and save files
- Create folders
- Copy and move files and folders
- Compress and extract files

Managing Your Files

Organizing Files and Folders with Windows 8

Case | *Savvy Traveler*

After spending a summer traveling in Italy, Matt Marino started Savvy Traveler, a travel company that organizes small tours in Europe. To market his company, Matt created flyers, brochures, webpages, and other materials that describe the tours he offers. Matt uses the Savvy Traveler office computer to locate and store photos, illustrations, and text documents he can include in his marketing materials. He recently hired you to help manage the office. To keep Matt connected to the office while traveling, he just purchased a new laptop computer running Windows 8. He is familiar with Windows 7, so he needs an overview explaining how Windows 8 is different. Matt asks you to train him on using Windows 8 to organize his files and folders. Although he has only a few files, he knows it's a good idea to set up a logical organization now so he can find his work later as he stores more files and folders on the computer.

In this tutorial, you'll explore the differences between Windows 7 and Windows 8, especially those related to file management tools. You'll also work with Matt to devise a plan for managing his files. You'll learn how Windows 8 organizes files and folders, and then create files and folders yourself and organize them on Matt's computer. You'll also use techniques to display the information you need in folder windows, and explore options for working with compressed files.

STARTING DATA FILES

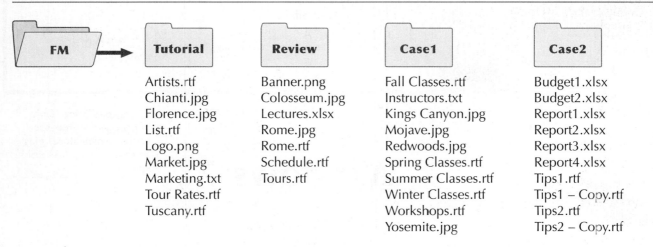

FM →	Tutorial	Review	Case1	Case2
	Artists.rtf	Banner.png	Fall Classes.rtf	Budget1.xlsx
	Chianti.jpg	Colosseum.jpg	Instructors.txt	Budget2.xlsx
	Florence.jpg	Lectures.xlsx	Kings Canyon.jpg	Report1.xlsx
	List.rtf	Rome.jpg	Mojave.jpg	Report2.xlsx
	Logo.png	Rome.rtf	Redwoods.jpg	Report3.xlsx
	Market.jpg	Schedule.rtf	Spring Classes.rtf	Report4.xlsx
	Marketing.txt	Tours.rtf	Summer Classes.rtf	Tips1.rtf
	Tour Rates.rtf		Winter Classes.rtf	Tips1 – Copy.rtf
	Tuscany.rtf		Workshops.rtf	Tips2.rtf
			Yosemite.jpg	Tips2 – Copy.rtf

Visual Overview:

You use the Change your view button to change the size of the icons in the window.

In Windows 7, you use **Windows Explorer** to navigate the contents of your computer.

Use the arrow buttons in the Address bar to navigate to other locations on your computer.

The **file path** is a notation that indicates a file's location on your computer.

Use the Search box to search for files in the current folder.

The Windows Explorer **toolbar** provides buttons for completing tasks.

Windows Explorer includes a **navigation pane**, which displays icons and links to resources and locations on your computer.

By default, Windows Explorer includes the **Details pane** at the bottom of the window, which displays the properties of the selected object.

Windows provides **libraries** so you can organize files by category—documents, music, pictures, and video.

A thumbnail image previews the file contents for certain types of files.

Windows 7

The zipped folder icon indicates a **compressed folder**, which stores files so they take up less disk space.

Comparing Windows 7 & Windows 8

The **View tab** on the ribbon contains options for specifying how the information displays in File Explorer.

Windows provides **libraries** so you can organize files by category—documents, music, pictures, and videos.

The **Quick Access toolbar** contains buttons for viewing properties and creating a folder.

Use the arrow buttons in the Address bar to navigate to other locations on your computer.

The **file path** in the Address bar shows a file's location on your computer.

In Windows 8, you use **File Explorer** to navigate the contents of your computer.

File Explorer includes a ribbon with tools organized on tabs for working with files and folders.

A thumbnail image previews the file contents for certain types of files.

A **filename** is the name you give to a file when you save it to identify the file's contents.

A **file icon** indicates the file type.

Clicking the Computer icon in the navigation pane shows the drives on your computer.

You can use the Large icons view button on the status bar or in the Layout group on the View tab to switch to Large icons view.

Data Files for this tutorial are stored on a removable disk on this computer.

File Explorer includes a **navigation pane**, which displays icons and links to resources and locations on your computer.

Windows 8

Exploring the Differences Between Windows 7 and Windows 8

Windows 8, the most recent version of the Microsoft operating system, is significantly different from Windows 7, the previous version. The major difference is that Windows 8 is designed for touchscreen computers such as tablets and laptops with touch-activated displays, though it runs on computers with more traditional pointing devices such as a mouse or a trackpad. This design change affects many of the fundamental Windows features you use to work on a computer. Figure 1 compares how to perform typical tasks in Windows 7 and Windows 8.

Figure 1   **Comparing Windows 7 and Windows 8**

Task	Windows 7 Method	Windows 8 Method
Start applications (sometimes called apps)	**Start menu** Open the Start menu by clicking the Start button.	**Start screen** The Start screen appears when you start Windows.
Access applications, documents, settings, and other resources	**Start menu** Use the Start menu, All Programs list, and Search box.	**Charms bar** The Charms bar appears when you point to the upper-right or lower-right corner of the screen, and displays buttons, called charms, for interacting with Windows 8 and accessing applications.
Select objects and commands	**Icons** Icons are small and detailed, designed for interaction with mechanical pointing devices.	**Icons and tiles** Icons and tiles are large and simplified, designed for interaction with your fingertips.
Open and work in applications	**Desktop** Applications all use a single desktop interface featuring windows and dialog boxes.	**Windows 8 and desktop** Applications use one of two interfaces: the Windows 8 interface (featuring tiles and a full-screen layout) or the desktop.
Display content out of view	**Vertical scrolling** Applications allow more vertical scrolling than horizontal scrolling.	**Horizontal scrolling** The Start screen and applications allow more horizontal scrolling than vertical scrolling to take advantage of wide-screen monitors.
Store files	**Physical storage devices** Windows primarily provides access to disks physically connected to the computer.	**Cloud storage locations** A Microsoft user account provides access to information stored online.
Enter text	**Physical keyboard** Type on the keyboard attached to the computer.	**On-screen keyboard** If your computer does not have a physical keyboard, type using the on-screen keyboard.

© 2014 Cengage Learning

Although Windows 7 introduced a few gestures for touchscreen users, Windows 8 expands the use of gestures and interactions. In Windows 8, you can use touch gestures to do nearly everything you can do with a pointing device. Figure 2 lists common Windows 8 interactions and their touch and mouse equivalents.

| Figure 2 | Windows 8 touch and mouse interactions |

Interaction	Touch Gesture	Mouse Action
Display a ScreenTip, text that identifies the name or purpose of the button	Touch and hold (or press) an object such as a button.	Point to an object such as a button.
Display an Apps bar, which displays options related to the current task and access to the Apps screen	Swipe from the top or bottom of the screen toward the center.	Right-click the bottom edge of the screen.
Display the Charms bar	Swipe from the right edge of the screen toward the center.	Point to the upper-right or lower-right corner of the screen.
Display thumbnails of open apps (the Switch List)	Swipe from the left edge of the screen toward the center.	Point to the upper-left corner of the screen, and then drag the pointer down.
Drag an object	Press and then drag.	Click, hold, and then drag.
Scroll the Start screen	Swipe from the right edge of the screen to the left.	Click the scroll arrows, or drag the scroll bar.
Select an object or perform an action such as starting an app	Tap the object.	Click the object.
Zoom	Pinch two fingers to zoom out or move the fingers apart to zoom in.	Click the Zoom button.

© 2014 Cengage Learning

Despite the substantial differences between how you interact with Windows 7 and Windows 8, the steps you follow to perform work in either operating system are the same. In a typical computer session, you start an application and open a **file**, often referred to as a document, which is a collection of data that has a name and is stored on a computer. You view, add, or change the file contents, and then save and close the file. You can complete all of these steps using Windows 7 or Windows 8. Because most of your work involves files, you need to understand how to save and organize files so you can easily find and open them when necessary.

Organizing Files and Folders

Knowing how to save, locate, and organize computer files makes you more productive when you are working with a computer. After you create a file, you can open it, edit its contents, print the file, and save it again—usually using the same application you used to create the file. You organize files by storing them in folders. A **folder** is a container for files. You need to organize files and folders so that you can find them easily and work efficiently.

A file cabinet is a common metaphor for computer file organization. As shown in Figure 3, a computer is like a file cabinet that has two or more drawers—each drawer is a storage device, or **disk**. Each disk contains folders that hold files. To make it easy to retrieve files, you arrange them logically into folders. For example, one folder might contain financial data, another might contain your creative work, and another could contain information you're gathering for an upcoming vacation.

Figure 3 **Computer as a file cabinet**

disks contain folders

folders contain files

each drawer is a storage device, or disk

© 2014 Cengage Learning

A computer can store folders and files on different types of disks, ranging from removable media—such as **USB drives** (also called USB flash drives) and digital video discs (DVDs)—to **hard disks**, or fixed disks, which are permanently housed in a computer. Hard disks are the most popular type of computer storage because they provide an economical way to store many gigabytes of data. (A **gigabyte**, or **GB**, is about 1 billion bytes, with each byte roughly equivalent to a character of data.)

To have your computer access a removable disk, you must insert the disk into a **drive**, which is a device that can retrieve and sometimes record data on a disk. A computer's hard disk is already contained in a drive inside the computer, so you don't need to insert it each time you use the computer.

A computer distinguishes one drive from another by assigning each a drive letter. The hard disk is assigned to drive C. The remaining drives can have any other letters, but are usually assigned in the order that the drives were installed on the computer— so your USB drive might be drive D or drive F.

Understanding How to Organize Files and Folders

Windows stores thousands of files in many folders on the hard disk of your computer. These are system files that Windows needs to display the Start screen and desktop, use drives, and perform other operating system tasks. To keep the system stable and to find files quickly, Windows organizes the folders and files in a hierarchy, or **file system**. At the top of the hierarchy, Windows stores folders and important files that it needs when you turn on the computer. This location is called the **root directory** and is usually drive C (the hard disk). As Figure 4 shows, the root directory contains all the other folders and files on the computer. The figure also shows that folders can contain other folders. An effectively organized computer contains a few folders in the root directory, and those folders contain other folders, also called **subfolders**.

Figure 4   **Organizing folders and files on a hard disk**

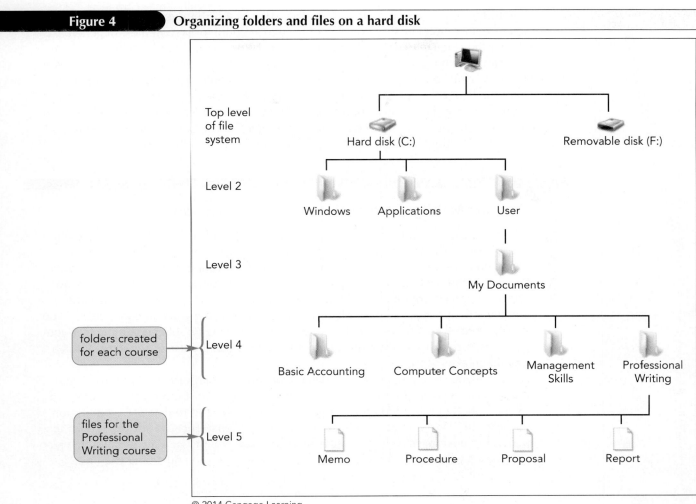

© 2014 Cengage Learning

The root directory is the top level of the hard disk and is for system files and folders only. You should not store your own work in the root directory because your files could interfere with Windows or an application. (If you are working in a computer lab, you might not be allowed to access the root directory.)

Do not delete or move any files or folders from the root directory of the hard disk; doing so could disrupt the system so that you can't start or run the computer. In fact, you should not reorganize or change any folder that contains installed software because Windows 8 expects to find the files for specific applications within certain folders. In Figure 4, folders containing software are stored at Level 2 of the file system. If you reorganize or change these folders, Windows 8 can't locate and start the applications stored in those folders. Likewise, you should not make changes to the folder (usually named Windows) that contains the Windows 8 operating system.

Level 2 of the file system also includes a folder for your user account, such as the User folder. This folder contains all of your system settings, preferences, and other user account information. It also contains subfolders, such as the My Documents folder, for your personal files. The folders in Level 3 of the file system are designed to contain subfolders for your personal files. You can create as many subfolders at Level 4 of the file system as you need to store other folders and files and keep them organized.

Figure 4 shows how you could organize your files on a hard disk if you were taking a full semester of business classes. To duplicate this organization, you would open the main folder for your documents, such as My Documents, create four folders— one each for the Basic Accounting, Computer Concepts, Management Skills, and Professional Writing courses—and then store the writing assignments you complete in the Professional Writing folder.

If you store your files on removable media, such as a USB drive, you can use a simpler organization because you do not have to account for system files. In general, the larger the storage medium, the more levels of folders you should use because large media can store more files and, therefore, need better organization. For example, if you were organizing your files on a 12 GB USB drive, you could create folders in the top level of the USB drive for each general category of documents you store—one each for Courses, Creative, Financials, and Vacation. The Courses folder could then include one folder for each course (Basic Accounting, Computer Concepts, Management Skills, and Professional Writing), and each of those folders could contain the appropriate files.

PROSKILLS

Decision Making: Determining Where to Store Files

When you create and save files on your computer's hard disk, you should store them in subfolders. The top level of the hard disk is off-limits for your files because they could interfere with system files. If you are working on your own computer, store your files within the My Documents folder in the Documents library, which is where many applications save your files by default. When you use a computer on the job, your employer might assign a main folder to you for storing your work. In either case, if you simply store all your files in one folder, you will soon have trouble finding the files you want. Instead, you should create subfolders within a main folder to separate files in a way that makes sense for you.

Even if you store most of your files on removable media, such as USB drives, you still need to organize those files into folders and subfolders. Before you start creating folders, whether on a hard disk or removable disk, you need to plan the organization you will use. Following your plan increases your efficiency because you don't have to pause and decide which folder to use when you save your files. A file organization plan also makes you more productive in your computer work—the next time you need a particular file, you'll know where to find it.

Exploring Files and Folders

As shown in the Visual Overview, you use File Explorer in Windows 8 to explore the files and folders on your computer. File Explorer displays the contents of your computer by using icons to represent drives, folders, and files. When you open File Explorer, it shows the contents of the Windows built-in libraries by default. Windows provides these libraries so you can organize files by category—documents, music, pictures, and video. A library can display these categories of files together, no matter where the files are actually stored. For example, you might keep some music files in a folder named Albums on your hard disk. You might also keep music files in a Songs folder on a USB drive. Although the Albums and Songs folders are physically stored in different locations, you can set up the Music library to display both folders in the same File Explorer window. You can then search and arrange the files as a single collection to quickly find the music you want to open and play. In this way, you use libraries to organize your files into categories so you can easily locate and work with files.

The File Explorer window is divided into two sections, called panes. The left pane is the navigation pane, which contains icons and links to locations on your computer. The right pane displays the contents of the location selected in the navigation pane. If the navigation pane showed all the contents on your computer at once, it could be a very long list. Instead, you open drives and folders only when you want to see what they contain. For example, to display the hierarchy of the folders and other locations on your computer, you select the Computer icon in the navigation pane, and then select the icon for a drive, such as Local Disk (C:) or Removable Disk (F:). You can then open and explore folders on that drive.

If a folder contains undisplayed subfolders, an expand icon appears to the left of the folder icon. (The same is true for drives.) To view the folders contained in an object, you click the expand icon. A collapse icon then appears next to the folder icon; click the collapse icon to hide the folder's subfolders. To view the files contained in a folder, you click the folder icor, and the files appear in the right pane. See Figure 5.

| Figure 5 | Viewing files in File Explorer |

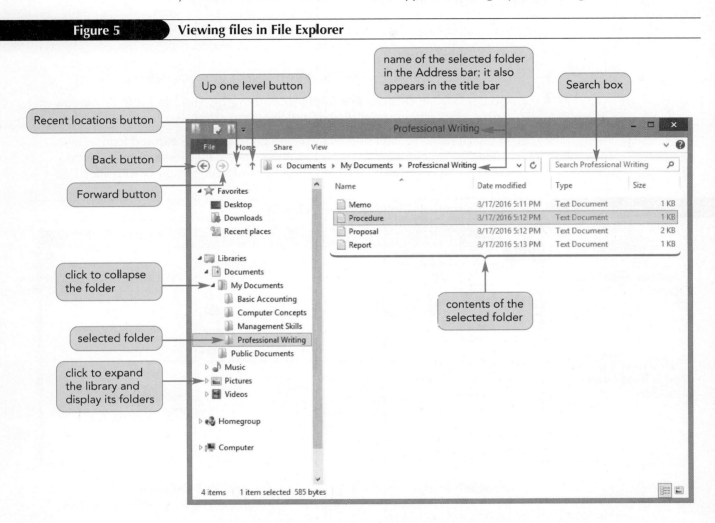

Using the navigation pane helps you explore your computer and orients you to your current location. As you move, copy, delete, and perform other tasks with the files and folders in the right pane of File Explorer, you can refer to the navigation pane to see how your changes affect the overall organization of the selected location.

In addition to using the navigation pane, you can explore your computer in File Explorer using the following navigation techniques:

- Opening drives and folders in the right pane—To view the contents of a drive or folder, double-click the drive or folder icon in the right pane of File Explorer.
- Using the Address bar—You can use the Address bar to navigate to a different folder. The Address bar displays the file path for your current folder. (Recall that a file path shows the location of a folder or file.) Click a folder name such as My Documents in the Address bar to navigate to that folder, or click an arrow button to navigate to a different location in the folder's hierarchy.
- Clicking the Back, Forward, Recent locations, and Up to buttons—Use the Back, Forward, and Recent locations buttons to navigate to other folders you have already opened. Use the Up to button to navigate up to the folder containing the current folder.
- Using the Search box—To find a file or folder stored in the current folder or its subfolders, type a word or phrase in the Search box. The search begins as soon as you

start typing. Windows finds files based on text in the filename, text within the file, and other properties of the file.

You'll practice using some of these navigation techniques later in the tutorial. Right now, you'll show Matt how to open File Explorer. Your computer should be turned on and displaying the Start screen.

To open File Explorer:

▶ **1.** On the Start screen, click the **Desktop** tile to display the desktop.

▶ **2.** On the taskbar, click the **File Explorer** button 🗎. The File Explorer window opens, displaying the contents of the default libraries.

▶ **3.** In the Libraries section of the navigation pane, click the **expand** icon ▷ next to the Documents icon. The folders in the Documents library appear in the navigation pane; see Figure 6. The contents of your computer will differ.

| Figure 6 | Viewing the contents of the Documents library |

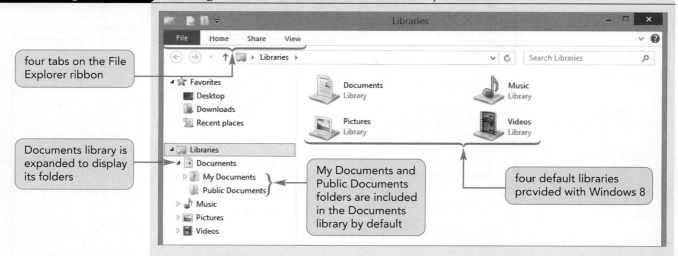

Trouble? If your window displays icons in a size or arrangement different from the one shown in the figure, you can still explore files and folders. The same is true for all the figures in this tutorial.

▶ **4.** In the navigation pane, click the **My Documents** folder to display its contents in the right pane.

TIP

When you are working in the navigation pane, you only need to click a folder to open it; you do not need to double-click it.

As Figure 6 shows, the File Explorer window includes a ribbon, which is collapsed by default so it displays only tab names, such as File, Home, Share, and View. The Visual Overview shows the expanded ribbon, which displays the options for the selected tab. You'll work with the ribbon and learn how to expand it later in the tutorial.

Navigating to Your Data Files

To navigate to the files you want, it helps to know the file path because the file path tells you exactly where the file is stored in the hierarchy of drives and folders on your computer. For example, Matt has a file named "Logo," which contains an image of the company's logo. If Matt stored the Logo file in a folder named "Marketing" and saved that folder in a folder named "Savvy Traveler" on drive F (a USB drive) on his computer, the Address bar would show the following file path for the Logo file:

Computer ▸ Removable Disk (F:) ▸ Savvy Traveler ▸ Marketing ▸ Logo.png

This path has five parts, with each part separated by an arrow button:

- Computer—The main container for the file, such as "Computer" or "Network"
- Removable Disk (F:)—The drive name, including the drive letter followed by a colon, which indicates a drive rather than a folder
- Savvy Traveler—The top-level folder on drive F
- Marketing—A subfolder in the Savvy Traveler folder
- Logo.png—The name of the file

Although File Explorer uses arrow buttons to separate locations in a file path, printed documents use backslashes (\ ). For example, if you read an instruction to open the Logo file in the Savvy Traveler\Marketing folder on your USB drive, you know you must navigate to the USB drive attached to your computer, open the Savvy Traveler folder, and then open the Marketing folder to find the Logo file.

File Explorer displays the file path in the Address bar so you can keep track of your current location as you navigate between drives and folders. You can use File Explorer to navigate to the Data Files you need for this tutorial. Before you perform the following steps, you should know where you stored your Data Files, such as on a USB drive. The following steps assume that drive is Removable Disk (F:), a USB drive. If necessary, substitute the appropriate drive on your system when you perform the steps.

To navigate to your Data Files:

1. Make sure your computer can access your Data Files for this tutorial. For example, if you are using a USB drive, insert the drive into the USB port.

   Trouble? If you don't have the starting Data Files, you need to get them before you can proceed. Your instructor will either give you the Data Files or ask you to obtain them from a specified location (such as a network drive). If you have any questions about the Data Files, see your instructor or technical support person for assistance.

2. In the navigation pane of File Explorer, click the **expand** icon ▷ next to the Computer icon to display the drives on your computer, if necessary.

3. Click the **expand** icon ▷ next to the drive containing your Data Files, such as Removable Disk (F:). A list of the folders on that drive appears below the drive name.

4. If the list of folders does not include the FM folder, continue clicking the **expand** icon ▷ to navigate to the folder that contains the FM folder.

5. Click the **expand** icon ▷ next to the FM folder to expand the folder, and then click the **FM** folder so that its contents appear in the navigation pane and in the right pane of the folder window. The FM folder contains the Case1, Case2, Review, and Tutorial folders, as shown in Figure 7. The other folders on your computer might vary.

| Figure 7 | Navigating to the FM folder |

file path displayed in the Address bar

the name of the selected folder appears in the File Explorer title bar

FM

File   Home   Share   View

← → ▾ ↑   ▸ Computer ▸ Removable Disk (F:) ▸ FM   ∨ ↻   Search FM   ⌕

	Name		Date modified	Type	Size
🔲 Libraries					
	📁 Case1		12/3/2016 1:49 PM	File folder	
📇 Homegroup	📁 Case2		12/3/2016 1:49 PM	File folder	
	📁 Review		12/3/2016 1:49 PM	File folder	
🖥 Computer	📁 Tutorial		12/3/2016 1:49 PM	File folder	
🖴 Local Disk (C:)					
▴ 🖴 Removable Disk (F:)					

contents of the FM folder; your Date modified information might differ

your Data Files might be stored on a different drive

selected FM folder is expanded in the navigation pane

▴ 📁 FM
  📁 Case1
  📁 Case2
  📁 Review
  📁 Tutorial ◂

Tutorial folder

▸ **6.** In the navigation pane, click the **Tutorial** folder. The files it contains appear in the right pane.

You can change the appearance of the File Explorer window to suit your preferences. You'll do so next so you can see more details about folders and files.

Changing the View

File Explorer provides eight ways to view the contents of a folder: Extra large icons, Large icons, Medium icons, Small icons, List, Details, Tiles, and Content. For example, the files in the Tutorial folder are currently displayed in Details view, which is the default view for all folders except those stored in the Pictures library. Details view displays a small icon to identify each file's type and lists file details in columns, such as the date the file was last modified, the file type, and the size of the file. Although only Details view lists the file details, you can see these details in any other view by pointing to a file to display a ScreenTip.

To change the view of File Explorer to any of the eight views, you use the View tab on the ribbon. To switch to Details view or Large icons view, you can use the view buttons on the status bar.

REFERENCE

Changing the View in File Explorer

• Click a view button on the status bar.

or

• Click the View tab on the ribbon.
• In the Layout group, click the view option; or click the More button, if necessary, and then click a view option.

You'll show Matt how to change the view of the Tutorial folder in the File Explorer window.

To change the view of the Tutorial folder in File Explorer:

▶ **1.** On the ribbon, click the **View** tab.

▶ **2.** In the Layout group, click **Medium icons**. The files appear in Medium icons view in File Explorer. See Figure 8.

Figure 8   Files in the Tutorial folder in Medium icons view

View tab on the ribbon

icons are displayed in Medium icons view

Tutorial folder is selected in the navigation pane

Expand the Ribbon button

thumbnail image previews the file contents for certain file types

file icon identifies the file type; your icons might be different

Details view button

9 items

Photos courtesy of Lisa Ruffolo

Because the icons used to identify types of files depend on the applications installed on your computer, the file icons that appear in your window might be different.

TIP

When you change the view, it only changes the view for the currently selected folder.

▶ **3.** On the status bar, click the **Large icons view** button 🖼. The window shows the files with large icons and no file details.

When you clicked the View tab in the previous steps, the ribbon expanded so you could select an option and then collapsed after you clicked the Medium icons option. You can keep the ribbon expanded in the File Explorer window so you can easily access all of its options. You'll show Matt how to expand the ribbon and then use the View tab to switch to Details view.

To expand the ribbon in File Explorer:

▶ **1.** Click the **Expand the Ribbon** button ⌄ to expand the ribbon. The Expand the Ribbon button changes to the Minimize the Ribbon button, which you could click if you wanted to collapse the ribbon.

▶ **2.** On the View tab, in the Layout group, click **Details**. The window shows the files with small icons and lists the file details.

No matter which view you use, you can sort the file list by the name of the files or another detail, such as size, type, or date. When you **sort** files, you list them in ascending order (A to Z, 0 to 9, or earliest to latest date) or descending order (Z to A, 9 to 0, or latest to earliest date) by a file detail. If you're viewing music files, you can sort by details such as contributing artists or album title; and if you're viewing picture files, you can sort by details such as date taken or size. Sorting can help you find a particular file in a long file listing. For example, suppose you want to work on a document that you know you edited on June 4, 2016, but you can't remember the name of the file. You can sort the file list by date modified to find the file you want.

When you are working in Details view in File Explorer, you sort by clicking a column heading that appears at the top of the file list. In other views, you use the View tab on the ribbon to sort. In the Current view group, click the Sort by button, and then click a file detail.

TIP

To sort by a file detail that does not appear as a column heading, right-click any column heading and then select a file detail.

To sort the file list by date modified:

▶ **1.** At the top of the file list, click the **Date modified** column heading button. The down arrow that appears above the label of the Date modified button indicates that the files are sorted in descending (newest to oldest) order by the date the file was modified. At the top of the list is the List file, which was modified on June 18, 2016.

Trouble? If your folder window does not contain a Date modified column, right-click any column heading, click Date modified on the shortcut menu, and then repeat Step 1.

▶ **2.** Click the **Date modified** column heading button again. The up arrow on the Date modified button indicates that the sort order is reversed, with the files listed in ascending (oldest to newest) order.

▶ **3.** Click the **Name** column heading button to sort the files in alphabetical order by name. The Artists file is now listed first.

Now that Matt is comfortable working in File Explorer, you're ready to show him how to manage his files and folders.

Managing Files and Folders

As discussed earlier, you manage your personal files and folders by storing them according to a logical organization so that they are easy to find later. You can organize files as you create, edit, and save them, or you can do so later by creating folders, if necessary, and then moving and copying files into the folders.

To create a file-organization plan for Matt's files, you can review Figure 8 and look for files that logically belong together. In the Tutorial folder, Chianti, Florence, Logo, and Market are all graphics files that Matt uses for marketing and sales. He created the Artists and Tuscany files to describe Italian tours. The Marketing and Tour Rates files relate to business finances. Matt thinks the List file contains a task list for completing a project, but he isn't sure of its contents. He does recall creating the file using WordPad.

If the List file does contain a project task list, you can organize the files by creating four folders—one for graphics, one for tours, another for the financial files, and a fourth folder for projects. When you create a folder, you give it a name, preferably one that describes its contents. A folder name can have up to 255 characters, and any character is allowed, except / \ : * ? " < > and |. Considering these conventions, you could create four folders to contain Matt's files, as follows:

- Marketing Graphics folder—Chianti, Florence, Logo, and Market files
- Tours folder—Artists and Tuscany files
- Financial folder—Marketing and Tour Rates files
- Projects folder—List file

Before you start creating folders according to this plan, you need to verify the contents of the List file. You can do so by opening the file.

Opening a File

TIP

To select the default application for opening a file, right-click the file in File Explorer, point to Open with, and then click Choose default application. Click an application in the list that opens, and then click OK.

You can open a file from a running application or from File Explorer. To open a file in a running application, you select the application's Open command to access the Open dialog box, which you use to navigate to the file you want, select the file, and then open it. In the Open dialog box, you use the same tools that are available in File Explorer to navigate to the file you want to open. If the application you want to use is not running, you can open a file by double-clicking it in the right pane of File Explorer. The file usually opens in the application that you used to create or edit it.

Occasionally, File Explorer will open the file in an application other than the one you want to use to work with the file. For example, double-clicking a digital picture file usually opens the picture in a picture viewer application. If you want to edit the picture, you must open the file in a graphics editing application. When you need to specify an application to open a file, you can right-click the file, point to Open with on the shortcut menu, and then click the name of the application that you want to use.

Matt says that he might want to edit the List file to add another task. You'll show him how to use File Explorer to open the file in WordPad, which he used to create the file, and then edit it.

To open and edit the List file:

1. In the right pane of File Explorer, right-click the **List** file, and then point to **Open with** on the shortcut menu to display a list of applications that can open the file. See Figure 9.

   Trouble? If a list does not appear when you point to Open with on the shortcut menu, click Open with to display a window asking how you want to open this file.

| Figure 9 | Shortcut menu for opening a file |

List is the selected file

Open with command

applications on this computer that can open the List file

TIP

In File Explorer, you can also double-click a file to open it in the default application for that file type.

2. Click **WordPad** to open the List file in WordPad. The file contains a task list for the marketing project, which includes three items.

   Trouble? If you had to click Open with instead of pointing to it, in the window that asks how you want to open this file, click Keep using WordPad.

3. Press the **Ctrl+End** keys to move the insertion point to the end of the document, press the **Enter** key if necessary to start a new line, and then type **4. Review the Tours in Italy webpage.**

Now that you've added text to the List file, you need to save it to preserve the changes you made.

Saving a File

As you are creating or editing a file, you should save it frequently so you don't lose your work. When you save a file, you need to decide what name to use for the file and where to store it. Most applications provide a default location for saving a file, which makes it easy to find the file again later. However, you can select a different location depending on where you want to store the file.

Besides a storage location, every file must have a filename, which provides important information about the file, including its contents and purpose. A filename such as Italian Tours.docx has the following three parts:

• Main part of the filename—When you save a file, you need to provide only the main part of the filename, such as "Italian Tours."

• Dot—The dot (.) separates the main part of the filename from the extension.

• Extension—The **extension** includes the three or four characters that follow the dot in the filename and identify the file's type.

Similar to folder names, the main part of a filename can have up to 255 characters. This gives you plenty of room to name your file accurately enough so that you'll recognize the contents of the file just by looking at the filename. You can use spaces and certain punctuation symbols in your filenames. However, filenames cannot contain the symbols / \ : * ? " < > or | because these characters have special meanings in Windows 8.

Windows and other software add the dot and the extension to a filename, though File Explorer does not display them by default. Instead, File Explorer shows the file icon associated with the extension or a thumbnail for some types of files, such as graphics. For example, in a file named Italian Tours.docx, the docx extension identifies the file as one created in Microsoft Word, a word-processing application. File Explorer displays this file using a Microsoft Word icon and the main part of its filename. For a file named Italian Tours.png, the png extension identifies the file as one created in a graphics application such as Paint. In Details view or List view, File Explorer displays this file using a Paint icon and the main part of its filename. In other views, File Explorer does not use an icon, but displays the file contents in a thumbnail. File Explorer treats the Italian Tours.docx and Italian Tours.png files differently because their extensions distinguish them as different types of files, even though the main parts of their filenames are identical.

When you save a new file, you use the Save As dialog box to provide a filename and select a location for the file. You can create a folder for the new file at the same time you save the file. When you edit a file you saved previously, you can use the application's Save command to save your changes to the file, keeping the same name and location. If you want to save the edited file with a different name or in a different location, however, you need to use the Save As dialog box to specify the new name or location.

As with the Open dialog box, you specify the file location in the Save As dialog box using the same navigation techniques and tools that are available in File Explorer. You might need to click the Browse Folders button to expand the Save As dialog box so it displays these tools. In addition, the Save As dialog box always includes a File name box where you specify a filename.

INSIGHT

Saving Files on SkyDrive

Some Windows 8 applications, such as Microsoft Office, include SkyDrive as a location for saving and opening files. **SkyDrive** is a Microsoft service that provides up to 7 GB of online storage space for your files at no charge. You can purchase additional space if you need it. For example, if you create a document in Microsoft Word, your SkyDrive appears as a location for saving the document. (Your SkyDrive appears with your username, such as Matt's SkyDrive.) If you have a Microsoft account, you can select a folder on your SkyDrive to save the document online. (If you don't have a Microsoft account, you can sign up for one by visiting the SkyDrive website.) Because the file is stored online, it takes up no storage space on your computer and is available from any computer with an Internet connection. You access the document by opening it in Word or by visiting the SkyDrive website, and then signing in to your Microsoft account. To share the document with other people, you can send them a link to the document via email. They can use the link to access the document even if they do not have a Microsoft account.

One reason that Matt had trouble remembering the contents of the List file is that "List" is not a descriptive name. A better name for this file is Task List. You will save this document in the Tutorial subfolder of the FM folder provided with your Data Files. You will also use the Save As dialog box to specify a new name for the file as you save it.

To save the List file with a new name:

▶ 1. On the ribbon in the WordPad window, click the **File** tab to display commands for working with files.

▶ 2. Click **Save as** to open the Save As dialog box, as shown in Figure 10. The Tutorial folder is selected as the storage location for this file because you opened the file from this folder.

| Figure 10 | Saving a file using the Save As dialog box |

use the navigation pane or the Address bar to navigate to a different location for saving the file

the Save As dialog box displays the original location of the file as the default storage location

type the name for the file in the File name box

clicking the Hide Folders button collapses the dialog box

Save as type box

Trouble? If the navigation pane does not appear in the Save As dialog box, click the Browse Folders button. The Browse Folders button toggles to become the Hide Folders button.

TIP

To change the file type, click the Save as type box, and then click a file type such as Text Document.

▶ 3. With the current filename selected in the File name box, type **Task List**. The Save as type box shows that WordPad will save this file as a Rich Text Format (RTF) file, which is the default file type for WordPad files.

Trouble? If the current filename is not selected in the File name box, drag to select the text in the File name box and then type Task List.

▶ 4. Click the **Save** button. The Save As dialog box closes, WordPad saves the Task List file in the Tutorial folder, and the new filename appears in the WordPad title bar.

▶ 5. On the title bar, click the **Close** button ⊠ to close WordPad.

Now you're ready to start creating the folders you need to organize Matt's files.

Creating Folders

You originally proposed creating four new folders for Matt's files: Marketing Graphics, Tours, Financial, and Projects. Matt asks you to create these folders now. After that, you'll move his files to the appropriate folders. You create folders in File Explorer using one of three methods: using the New folder button in the New group on the Home tab; using the New folder button on the Quick Access Toolbar; or right-clicking to display a shortcut menu that includes the New command.

INSIGHT

Guidelines for Creating Folders

Consider the following guidelines as you create folders:

- Keep folder names short yet descriptive of the folder's contents. Long folder names can be more difficult to display in their entirety in folder windows, so use names that are short but clear. Choose names that will be meaningful later, such as project names or course numbers.
- Create subfolders to organize files. If a file list in File Explorer is so long that you must scroll the window, you should probably organize those files into subfolders.
- Develop standards for naming folders. Use a consistent naming scheme that is clear to you, such as one that uses a project name as the name of the main folder, and includes step numbers in each subfolder name (for example, 1-Outline, 2-First Draft, 3-Final Draft, and so on).

In the following steps, you will create the four folders for Matt in your Tutorial folder. Because it is easier to work with files using large file icons, you'll switch to Large icons view first.

To create the folders:

1. On the status bar in the File Explorer window, click the **Large icons view** button 🖼 to switch to Large icons view.

2. Click the **Home** tab to display the Home tab on the ribbon.

3. In the New group, click the **New folder** button. A folder icon with the label "New folder" appears in the right pane of the File Explorer window. See Figure 11.

Figure 11   **Creating a new folder in the Tutorial folder**

Photos courtesy of Lisa Ruffolo

Trouble? If the "New folder" name is not selected, right-click the new folder, click Rename on the shortcut menu, and then continue with Step 4.

Windows uses "New folder" as a placeholder, and selects the text so that you can replace it immediately by typing a new name. You do not need to press the Backspace or Delete key to delete the text.

▶ **4.** Type **Marketing Graphics** as the folder name, and then press the **Enter** key. The new folder is named Marketing Graphics and is the selected item in the right pane. To create a second folder, you can use a shortcut menu.

▶ **5.** In the right pane, right-click a blank area, point to **New** on the shortcut menu, and then click **Folder**. A folder icon appears in the right pane with the "New folder" text selected.

▶ **6.** Type **Tours** as the name of the new folder, and then press the **Enter** key. To create the third folder, you can use the Quick Access Toolbar.

▶ **7.** On the Quick Access Toolbar, click the **New folder** button 🗀, type **Financial**, and then press the **Enter** key to create and name the folder.

▶ **8.** Create a new folder in the Tutorial folder named **Projects**.

After creating four folders, you're ready to organize Matt's files by moving them into the appropriate folders.

Moving and Copying Files and Folders

You can either move or copy a file from its current location to a new location. **Moving** a file removes it from its current location and places it in a new location that you specify. **Copying** a file places a duplicate version of the file in a new location that you specify, while leaving the original file intact in its current location. You can also move and copy folders. When you do, you move or copy all the files contained in the folder. (You'll practice copying folders in a Case Problem at the end of this tutorial.)

In File Explorer, you can move and copy files by using the Move to or Copy to buttons in the Organize group on the Home tab; using the Copy and Cut commands on a file's shortcut menu; or using keyboard shortcuts. When you copy or move files using these methods, you are using the **Clipboard**, a temporary storage area for files and information that you copy or move from one location to place in another.

You can also move files by dragging the files in the File Explorer window. You will now organize Matt's files by moving them to the appropriate folders you have created. You'll start by moving the Marketing file to the Financial folder by dragging the file.

To move the Marketing file by dragging it:

1. In File Explorer, point to the **Marketing** file in the right pane, and then press and hold the mouse button.

2. While still pressing the mouse button, drag the **Marketing** file to the **Financial** folder. See Figure 12.

Figure 12   Dragging a file to move it to a folder

Marketing file is selected

Financial folder

Move to Financial ScreenTip

14 items   1 item selected 1.42 KB

TIP

If you drag a file or folder to a location on a different drive, the file is copied, not moved, to preserve the file in its original location.

3. When the Move to Financial ScreenTip appears, release the mouse button. The Marketing file is removed from the main Tutorial folder and stored in the Financial subfolder.

   Trouble? If you released the mouse button before the Move to Financial ScreenTip appeared, press the Ctrl+Z keys to undo the move, and then repeat Steps 1–3.

   Trouble? If you moved the Market file instead of the Marketing file, press the Ctrl+Z keys to undo the move, and then repeat Steps 1–3.

4. In the right pane, double-click the **Financial** folder to verify that it contains the Marketing file.

Trouble? If the Marketing file does not appear in the Financial folder, you probably moved it to a different folder. Press the Ctrl+Z keys to undo the move, and then repeat Steps 1–3.

▶ **5.** Click the **Back** button ⊝ on the Address bar to return to the Tutorial folder.

You'll move the remaining files into the folders using the Clipboard.

To move files using the Clipboard:

▶ **1.** Right-click the **Artists** file, and then click **Cut** on the shortcut menu. Although the file icon still appears selected in the right pane of File Explorer, Windows removes the Artists file from the Tutorial folder and stores it on the Clipboard.

▶ **2.** In the right pane, right-click the **Tours** folder, and then click **Paste** on the shortcut menu. Windows pastes the Artists file from the Clipboard to the Tours folder. The Artists file icon no longer appears in the File Explorer window, which is currently displaying the contents of the Tutorial folder.

▶ **3.** In the navigation pane, click the **expand** icon ▷ next to the Tutorial folder, if necessary, to display its contents, and then click the **Tours** folder to view its contents in the right pane. The Tours folder now contains the Artists file. See Figure 13.

| Figure 13 | Artists file in its new location |

Next, you'll use the Clipboard again to move the Tuscany file from the Tutorial folder to the Tours folder. But this time, you'll access the Clipboard using the ribbon.

▶ **4.** On the Address bar, point to the **Up to** button ⬆ to display its ScreenTip (Up to "Tutorial"), click the **Up to** button ⬆ to return to the Tutorial folder, and then click the **Tuscany** file to select it.

▶ **5.** On the Home tab, in the Clipboard group, click the **Cut** button to remove the Tuscany file from the Tutorial folder and temporarily store it on the Clipboard.

▶ **6.** In the Address bar, click the **arrow** button ▶ to the right of "Tutorial" to display a list of subfolders in the Tutorial folder, and then click **Tours** to display the contents of the Tours folder in File Explorer.

▶ **7.** In the Clipboard group, click the **Paste** button to paste the Tuscany file in the Tours folder. The Tours folder now contains the Artists and Tuscany files.

Finally, you'll move the Task List file from the Tutorial folder to the Projects folder using the Move to button in the Organize group on the Home tab. This button and the Copy to button are ideal when you want to move or copy files without leaving the current folder. When you select a file and then click the Move to or Copy to button, a list of locations appears, including all of the Windows libraries and one or more folders you open frequently. You can click a location in the list to move the selected file to that library or folder. You can also select the Choose location option to open the Move Items or Copy Items dialog box, and then select a location for the file, which you'll do in the following steps.

To move the Task List file using the Move to button:

▶ **1.** In the Address bar, click **Tutorial** to return to the Tutorial folder, and then click the **Task List** file to select it.

▶ **2.** On the Home tab, in the Organize group, click the **Move to** button to display a list of locations to which you can move the selected file. The Projects folder is not included on this list because you haven't opened it yet.

▶ **3.** Click **Choose location** to open the Move Items dialog box. See Figure 14.

Figure 14 ▶ **Move Items dialog box**

locations on your computer; yours might differ

▶ **4.** If necessary, scroll the list of locations, and then click the **expand** icon ▷ next to the drive containing your Data Files, such as Removable Disk (F:).

▶ **5.** Navigate to the FM ▶ Tutorial folder, and then click the **Projects** folder to select it.

▶ **6.** Click the **Move** button to close the dialog box and move the Task List file to the Projects folder.

▶ **7.** Open the Projects folder to confirm that it contains the Task List file.

One way to save steps when moving or copying multiple files or folders is to select all the files and folders you want to move or copy, and then work with them as a group. You can use several techniques to select multiple files or folders at the same time, which are described in Figure 15.

Figure 15   **Selecting multiple files or folders**

Items to Select in the Right Pane of File Explorer	Method
Files or folders listed together	Click the first item, press and hold the Shift key, click the last item, and then release the Shift key. *or* Drag the pointer to create a selection box around all the items you want to include.
Files or folders not listed together	Press and hold the Ctrl key, click each item you want to select, and then release the Ctrl key.
All files and folders	On the Home tab, in the Select group, click the Select all button.

Items to Deselect in the Right Pane of File Explorer	Method
Single file or folder in a selected group	Press and hold the Ctrl key, click each item you want to remove from the selection, and then release the Ctrl key.
All selected files and folders	Click a blank area of the File Explorer window.

© 2014 Cengage Learning

Next, you'll copy the four graphics files from the Tutorial folder to the Marketing Graphics folder using the Clipboard. To do this efficiently, you will select multiple files at once.

To copy multiple files at once using the Clipboard:

▶ **1.** Display the contents of the Tutorial folder in File Explorer.

▶ **2.** Click the **Chianti** file, press and hold the **Shift** key, click the **Market** file, and then release the **Shift** key.

▶ **3.** Press and hold the **Ctrl** key, click the **List** file to deselect it, and then release the **Ctrl** key. Four files—Chianti, Florence, Logo, and Market—are selected in the Tutorial folder window.

▶ **4.** Right-click a selected file, and then click **Copy** on the shortcut menu. Windows copies the selected files to the Clipboard.

▶ **5.** Right-click the **Marketing Graphics** folder, and then click **Paste** on the shortcut menu.

▶ **6.** Open the **Marketing Graphics** folder to verify it contains the four files you copied, and then return to the Tutorial folder.

7. Right-click the **Tour Rates** file, and then click **Copy** on the shortcut menu.

8. In the right pane, double-click the **Financial** folder to open it, right-click a blank area of the right pane, and then click **Paste** on the shortcut menu.

INSIGHT

Duplicating Your Folder Organization

If you work on two computers, such as one computer at an office or school and another computer at home, you can duplicate the folders you use on both computers to simplify the process of transferring files from one computer to another. For example, if you have four folders in your My Documents folder on your work computer, create these same four folders on a USB drive and in the My Documents folder of your home computer. If you change a file on the hard disk of your home computer, you can copy the most recent version of the file to the corresponding folder on your USB drive so the file is available when you are at work. You also then have a **backup**, or duplicate copy, of important files. Having a backup of your files is invaluable if your computer has a fatal error.

All the files that originally appeared in the Tutorial folder are now stored in appropriate subfolders. You can streamline the organization of the Tutorial folder by deleting the duplicate files you no longer need.

Deleting Files and Folders

TIP

In most cases, a file deleted from a USB drive does not go into the Recycle Bin. Instead, it is deleted when Windows 8 removes its icon, and the file cannot be recovered.

You should periodically delete files and folders you no longer need so that your main folders and disks don't get cluttered. In File Explorer, you delete a file or folder by deleting its icon. When you delete a file from a hard disk, Windows 8 removes the file from the folder but stores the file contents in the Recycle Bin. The Recycle Bin is an area on your hard disk that holds deleted files until you remove them permanently. When you delete a folder from the hard disk, the folder and all of its files are stored in the Recycle Bin. If you change your mind and want to retrieve a deleted file or folder, you can double-click the Recycle Bin on the desktop, right-click the file or folder you want to retrieve, and then click Restore. However, after you empty the Recycle Bin, you can no longer recover the files it contained.

Because you copied the Chianti, Florence, Logo, Market, and Tour Rates files to the subfolders in the Tutorial folder, you can safely delete the original files. You can also delete the List file because you no longer need it. You can delete a file or folder using various methods, including using a shortcut menu or selecting one or more files and then pressing the Delete key.

To delete files in the Tutorial folder:

1. Display the Tutorial folder in the File Explorer window.

2. In the right pane, click **Chianti**, press and hold the **Shift** key, click **Tour Rates**, and then release the **Shift** key. All files in the Tutorial folder are now selected. None of the subfolders should be selected.

Make sure you have copied the selected files to the Marketing Graphics and Financial folders before completing this step.

3. Right-click the selected files, and then click **Delete** on the shortcut menu. A message box appears, asking if you're sure you want to permanently delete these files.

4. Click the **Yes** button to confirm that you want to delete the files.

Renaming Files

After creating and naming a file or folder, you might realize that a different name would be more meaningful or descriptive. You can easily rename a file or folder by using the Rename command on the file's shortcut menu.

Now that you've organized Matt's files into folders, he reviews your work and notes that the Artists file was originally created to store text specifically about Florentine painters and sculptors. You can rename that file to give it a more descriptive filename.

TIP

To rename a file, you can also click the file, pause, click it again to select the filename, and then type to enter a new filename.

To rename the Artists file:

1. In the right pane of the File Explorer window, double-click the **Tours** folder to display its contents.

2. Right-click the **Artists** file, and then click **Rename** on the shortcut menu. The filename is highlighted and a box appears around it.

3. Type **Florentine Artists**, and then press the **Enter** key. The file now appears with the new name.

   Trouble? If you make a mistake while typing and you haven't pressed the Enter key yet, press the Backspace key until you delete the mistake and then complete Step 3. If you've already pressed the Enter key, repeat Steps 2 and 3 to rename the file again.

   Trouble? If your computer is set to display filename extensions, a message might appear asking if you are sure you want to change the filename extension. Click the No button, and then repeat Steps 2 and 3.

Working with Compressed Files

You compress a file or a folder of files so it occupies less space on the disk. It can be useful to compress files before transferring them from one location to another, such as from your hard disk to a removable disk or vice versa, or from one computer to another via email. You can then transfer the files more quickly. Also, if you or your email contacts can send and receive files only up to a certain size, compressing large files might make them small enough to send and receive. Compare two folders—a folder named Photos that contains files totaling about 8.6 MB, and a compressed folder containing the same files but requiring only 6.5 MB of disk space. In this case, the compressed files use about 25 percent less disk space than the uncompressed files.

You can compress one or more files in File Explorer using the Zip button, which is located in the Send group on the Share tab of the ribbon. Windows stores the compressed files in a special type of folder called an **archive**, or a compressed folder. File Explorer uses an icon of a folder with a zipper to represent a compressed folder. To compress additional files or folders, you drag them into the compressed folder. You can open a file directly from a compressed folder, although you cannot modify the file. To edit and save a compressed file, you must extract it first. When you **extract** a file, you create an uncompressed copy of the file in a folder you specify. The original file remains in the compressed folder.

Matt suggests that you compress the files and folders in the Tutorial folder so that you can more quickly transfer them to another location.

To compress the folders and files in the Tutorial folder:

TIP

Another way to compress files is to select the files, right-click the selection, point to Send to on the shortcut menu, and then click Compressed (zipped) folder.

1. In File Explorer, navigate to the Tutorial folder, and then select all the folders in the Tutorial folder.

2. Click the **Share** tab on the ribbon.

3. In the Send group, click the **Zip** button. After a few moments, a new compressed folder appears in the Tutorial window with the filename selected. By default, File Explorer uses the name of the first selected item as the name of the compressed folder. You'll replace the name with a more descriptive one.

4. Type **Savvy Traveler**, and then press the **Enter** key to rename the compressed folder. See Figure 16.

Figure 16	Compressing files and folders

5. Double-click the **Savvy Traveler** compressed folder to open it, open the **Tours** folder, and then note the size of the compressed Tuscany file, which is 1,815 KB.

6. Navigate back to the Tutorial folder.

You can move and copy the files and folders from an opened compressed folder to other locations, although you cannot rename the files. More often, you extract all of the files from the compressed folder to a new location that you specify, preserving the files in their original folders as appropriate.

To extract the compressed files:

1. Click the **Savvy Traveler** compressed folder to select it, and then click the **Compressed Folder Tools Extract** tab on the ribbon.

2. In the Extract all group, click the **Extract all** button. The Extract Compressed (Zipped) Folders Wizard starts and opens the Select a Destination and Extract Files dialog box.

3. Press the **End** key to deselect the path in the box and move the insertion point to the end of the path, press the **Backspace** key as many times as necessary to delete the Savvy Traveler text, and then type **Backups**. The final three parts of the path in the box should be \FM\Tutorial\Backups. See Figure 17.

| Figure 17 | Extracting files from a compressed folder |

your path might differ, but should end with FM\Tutorial\Backups

check box should be selected

> **Extract Compressed (Zipped) Folders**
>
> **Select a Destination and Extract Files**
>
> Files will be extracted to this folder:
>
> F:\FM\Tutorial\Backups   [Browse...]
>
> ☑ Show extracted files when complete
>
>   [Extract] [Cancel]

4. Make sure the Show extracted files when complete check box is checked, and then click the **Extract** button. Windows extracts the files and then opens the Backups folder, showing the Financial, Marketing Graphics, Projects, and Tours folders.

5. Open each folder to make sure it contains the files you worked with in this tutorial. When you open the Tours folder, note the uncompressed size of the Tuscany file, which is about four times as large as its compressed version.

6. Close all open windows.

In this tutorial, you examined the purpose of organizing files and folders, and you planned and created an organization for a set of related files and folders. You also explored your computer using File Explorer and learned how to navigate to your Data Files using the navigation pane. You used File Explorer to manage files and folders by opening and saving files; creating folders; and selecting, moving, and copying files. You also renamed and deleted files according to your organization plan. Finally, you compressed and extracted files.

REVIEW

Quick Check

1. You organize files by storing them in _____.
2. What is the purpose of the Address bar in File Explorer?
3. A filename _____ identifies the file's type and indicates the application that created the file.
4. Explain how to use File Explorer to navigate to a file in the following location: E: ▸ Courses ▸ Computer Basics ▸ Operating Systems.txt.
5. One way to move files and folders is to use the _____, a temporary storage area for files and information that you copied or moved from one place and plan to use somewhere else.
6. What happens if you click the first file in a folder window, press the Shift key, click the last file, and then release the Shift key?
7. When you delete a file from a hard disk, Windows removes the file from the folder but stores the file contents in the _____.
8. Describe how to compress a file or folder.
9. What are the benefits of compressing files and folders?

Review Assignments

Data Files needed for the Review Assignments: Banner.png, Colosseum.jpg, Lectures.xlsx, Rome.jpg, Rome.rtf, Schedule.rtf, Tours.rtf

Matt has saved a few files from his old computer to a removable disk. He gives you these files in a single, unorganized folder, and asks you to organize them logically into subfolders. To do this, you will need to devise a plan for managing the files, and then create the subfolders you need. Next, you will rename, copy, move, and delete files, and then perform other management tasks to make it easy for Matt to work with these files and folders. Complete the following steps:

1. Use File Explorer to navigate to and open the FM ▸ Review folder provided with your Data Files. Examine the seven files in this folder and consider the best way to organize the files.
2. Open the **Rome** text file in WordPad, and then add the following tip to the end of the document: **Dine on the Italian schedule, with the main meal in the middle of the day.**
3. Save the document as **Rome Dining Tips** in the Review folder. Close the WordPad window.
4. In the Review folder, create three folders: **Business**, **Destinations**, and **Supplements**.
5. To organize the files into the correct folders, complete the following steps:
   • Move the Banner and Schedule files from the Review folder to the Business folder.
   • Move the Colosseum and Rome JPEG image files and the Rome Dining Tips and Tours text files to the Destinations folder.
   • Copy the Lectures file to the Supplements folder.
6. Copy the Tours file in the Destinations folder to the Business folder.
7. Rename the Schedule file in the Business folder as **2016 Schedule**. Rename the Lectures file in the Supplements folder as **On-site Lectures**.
8. Delete the Lectures file and the Rome text file from the Review folder.
9. Create a compressed (zipped) folder in the Review folder named **Rome** that contains all the files and folders in the Review folder.
10. Extract the contents of the Rome compressed folder to a new folder named **Rome Backups** in the Review folder. (*Hint:* The file path will end with \FM\Review\Rome Backups.)
11. Close the File Explorer window.

Case Problem 1

APPLY

See the Starting Data Files section at the beginning of this tutorial for the list of Data Files needed for this Case Problem.

Bay Shore Arts Center   Casey Sullivan started the Bay Shore Arts Center in Monterey, California, to provide workshops and courses on art and photography. Attracting students from the San Francisco and San José areas, Casey's business has grown and she now holds classes five days a week. She recently started a course on fine art landscape photography, which has quickly become her most popular offering. Casey hired you to help her design new classes and manage other parts of her growing business, including maintaining electronic business files and communications. Your first task is to organize the files on her new Windows 8 computer. Complete the following steps:

1. Open File Explorer. In the FM ▸ Case1 folder provided with your Data Files, create three folders: **Classes**, **Landscapes**, and **Management**.
2. Move the Fall Classes, Spring Classes, Summer Classes, and Winter Classes files from the Case1 folder to the Classes folder.
3. Rename the four files in the Classes folder by deleting the word "Classes" from each filename.
4. Move the four JPEG image files from the Case1 folder to the Landscapes folder.
5. Copy the remaining two files to the Management folder.
6. Copy the Workshops file to the Classes folder.
7. Delete the Instructors and Workshops files from the Case1 folder.
8. Make a copy of the Landscapes folder in the Case1 folder. The name of the duplicate folder appears as Landscapes – Copy. Rename the Landscapes – Copy folder as **California Photos**.
9. Copy the Workshops file from the Classes folder to the California Photos folder. Rename this file **California Workshops**.
10. Compress the graphics files in the California Photos folder in a new compressed folder named **Photos**.
11. Move the compressed Photos folder to the Case1 folder.
12. Close File Explorer.

Case Problem 2

See the Starting Data Files section at the beginning of this tutorial for the list of Data Files needed for this Case Problem.

Charlotte Area Business Incubator   Antoine Jackson is the director of the Charlotte Area Business Incubator, a service run by the University of North Carolina in Charlotte to consult with new and struggling small businesses. You work as an intern at the business incubator and spend part of your time organizing client files. Since Antoine started using Windows 8, he has been having trouble finding files on his computer. He sometimes creates duplicates of files and then doesn't know which copy is the most current. Complete the following steps:

1. Navigate to the FM ▶ Case2 folder provided with your Data Files, and then examine the files in this folder. Based on the filenames and file types, begin to create an organization plan for the files.

⚙ **Troubleshoot** 2. Open the Tips1 and the Tips1 – Copy files and consider the problem these files could cause. Close the files and then fix the problem, renaming one or more files as necessary to reflect the contents.

⚙ **Troubleshoot** 3. Open the Tips2 and the Tips2 – Copy files and compare their contents. Change the filenames to clarify the purpose and contents of the files.

4. Complete the organization plan for Antoine's files. In the FM ▶ Case2 folder, create the subfolders you need according to your plan.

5. Move the files in the Case2 folder to the subfolders you created. When you finish, the Case2 folder should contain at least two subfolders containing files.

6. Rename the spreadsheet files in each subfolder according to the following descriptions.
   - Budget1: **Website budget**
   - Budget2: **Marketing budget**
   - Report1: **Travel expense report**
   - Report2: **Project expense report**
   - Report3: **Balance sheet**
   - Report4: **Event budget**

⚙ **Troubleshoot** 7. Make sure all files have descriptive names that accurately reflect their contents.

⚙ **Troubleshoot** 8. Based on the work you did in Steps 6 and 7, move files as necessary to improve the file organization.

9. Close File Explorer.

OBJECTIVES

Session 1.1
- Learn basic database concepts and terms
- Start and exit Access
- Explore the Microsoft Access window and Backstage view
- Create a blank database
- Create and save a table in Datasheet view
- Enter field names and records in a table datasheet
- Open a table using the Navigation Pane

Session 1.2
- Open an Access database
- Copy and paste records from another Access database
- Navigate a table datasheet
- Create and navigate a simple query
- Create and navigate a simple form
- Create, preview, navigate, and print a simple report
- Use Help in Access
- Learn how to compact, back up, and restore a database

Creating a Database

Tracking Patient, Visit, and Billing Data

ACCESS

Case | *Chatham Community Health Services*

Chatham Community Health Services, a nonprofit health clinic located in Hartford, Connecticut, provides a range of medical services to patients of all ages. The clinic specializes in the areas of pulmonology, cardiac care, and chronic disease management. Cindi Rodriguez, the office manager for Chatham Community Health Services, oversees a small staff and is responsible for maintaining the medical records of the clinic's patients.

In order to best manage the clinic, Cindi and her staff rely on electronic medical records for patient information, billing, inventory control, purchasing, and accounts payable. Several months ago, the clinic upgraded to **Microsoft Access 2013** (or simply **Access**), a computer program used to enter, maintain, and retrieve related data in a format known as a database. Cindi and her staff want to use Access to store information about patients, billing, vendors, and products. She asks for your help in creating the necessary Access database.

STARTING DATA FILES

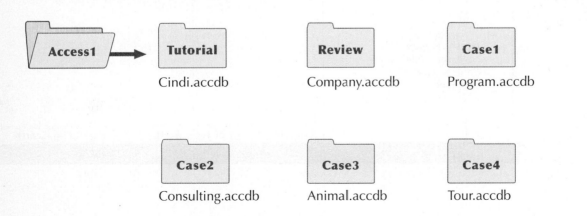

Access1 → Tutorial
Cindi.accdb

Review
Company.accdb

Case1
Program.accdb

Case2
Consulting.accdb

Case3
Animal.accdb

Case4
Tour.accdb

Session 1.1 Visual Overview:

The **Quick Access Toolbar** provides one-click access to commonly used commands, such as Save.

The **Shutter Bar Open/Close Button** allows you to close and open the Navigation Pane; you might want to close the pane so that you have more room on the screen to view the object's contents.

Access assigns the default name "Table1" to the first new table you create. When you save the table, you can give it a more meaningful name.

By default, Access creates the **ID field** as the primary key field for all new tables.

The **Click to Add column** provides another way for you to add new fields to a table.

The **Navigation Pane** lists all the objects (tables, reports, and so on) in the database, and it is the main control center for opening and working with database objects.

The **Add & Delete group** contains options for adding different types of fields, including Short Text and Number, to a table.

The **FIELDS tab** provides options for adding, removing, and formatting the fields in a table.

Datasheet view shows the table's contents as a datasheet.

The Access Window

The **Access window** is the program window that appears when you create a new database or open an existing database.

You use the window buttons to minimize, maximize, and close the Access window.

The **Sign in link** lets you sign into your Office account. If you have already signed in, your name might appear here instead of this link.

TABLE TOOLS

FIELDS   TABLE

Chatham : Database- E:\Access1\Tutorial\Chatham.accdb...   ?   –   □   ✕

Sign in

ion

Modify Lookups   Modify Expression   Memo Settings ▾

$ % ,   ←.0 .00   .00 →.0

Properties

Data Type:

Format: Formatting ▾

Formatting

☐ Required

☐ Unique

☐ Indexed

Validation ▾

Field Validation

The **ribbon** provides the main Access commands organized by task into tabs and groups.

✕

The **title bar** displays the name of the open file and the program.

A **datasheet** displays the table's contents in rows and columns, similar to a table that you create in a Word document or an Excel spreadsheet. Each row will be a separate record in the table, and each column will contain the field values for one field in the table.

The **status bar** provides information about the program or open file, as well as buttons for working with the file. At the far left, the status bar indicates the current view, in this case, Datasheet view.

Filter   Search

Introduction to Database Concepts

Before you begin using Access to create the database for Cindi, you need to understand a few key terms and concepts associated with databases.

Organizing Data

Data is a valuable resource to any business. At Chatham Community Health Services, for example, important data includes patients' names and addresses, visit dates, and billing information. Organizing, storing, maintaining, retrieving, and sorting this type of data are critical activities that enable a business to find and use information effectively. Before storing data on a computer, however, you must organize the data.

Your first step in organizing data is to identify the individual fields. A **field** is a single characteristic or attribute of a person, place, object, event, or idea. For example, some of the many fields that Chatham Community Health Services tracks are patient ID, first name, last name, address, phone number, visit date, reason for visit, and invoice amount.

Next, you group related fields together into tables. A **table** is a collection of fields that describes a person, place, object, event, or idea. Figure 1-1 shows an example of a Patient table that contains the following four fields: PatientID, FirstName, LastName, and Phone. Each field is a column in the table, with the field name displayed as the column heading.

Figure 1-1	Data organization for a table of patients

fields

Patient table

PatientID	FirstName	LastName	Phone
22501	Edward	Darcy	860-305-3985
22504	Lilian	Aguilar	860-374-5724
22510	Thomas	Booker	860-661-2539
22512	Lisa	Chang	860-226-6034
22529	Robert	Goldberg	860-552-2873
22537	Amrita	Mehta	860-552-0375

records

© 2014 Cengage Learning

The specific content of a field is called the **field value**. In Figure 1-1, the first set of field values for PatientID, FirstName, LastName, and Phone are, respectively: 22501; Edward; Darcy; and 860-305-3985. This set of field values is called a **record**. In the Patient table, the data for each patient is stored as a separate record. Figure 1-1 shows six records; each row of field values in the table is a record.

Databases and Relationships

A collection of related tables is called a **database**, or a **relational database**. In this tutorial, you will create the database for Chatham Community Health Services, and within that database, you'll create a table named Visit to store data about patient visits. Later on, you'll create two more tables, named Patient and Billing, to store related information about patients and their invoices.

As Cindi and her staff use the database that you will create, they will need to access information about patients and their visits. To obtain this information, you must have a way to connect records in the Patient table to records in the Visit table. You connect the records in the separate tables through a **common field** that appears in both tables.

In the sample database shown in Figure 1-2, each record in the Patient table has a field named PatientID, which is also a field in the Visit table. For example, Robert Goldberg is the fifth patient in the Patient table and has a PatientID field value of 22529. This same PatientID field value, 22529, appears in two records in the Visit table. Therefore, Robert Goldberg is the patient who made these two visits.

Figure 1-2	Database relationship between tables for patients and visits

© 2014 Cengage Learning

Each PatientID value in the Patient table must be unique so that you can distinguish one patient from another. These unique PatientID values also identify each patient's specific visits in the Visit table. The PatientID field is referred to as the primary key of the Patient table. A **primary key** is a field, or a collection of fields, whose values uniquely identify each record in a table. No two records can contain the same value for the primary key field. In the Visit table, the VisitID field is the primary key because Chatham Community Health Services assigns each visit a unique identification number.

When you include the primary key from one table as a field in a second table to form a relationship between the two tables, it is called a **foreign key** in the second table, as shown in Figure 1-2. For example, PatientID is the primary key in the Patient table and a foreign key in the Visit table. The PatientID field must have the same characteristics in both tables. Although the primary key PatientID contains unique values in the Patient table, the same field as a foreign key in the Visit table does not necessarily contain unique values. The PatientID value 22529, for example, appears two times in the Visit table because Robert Goldberg made two visits to the clinic. Each foreign key value, however, must match one of the field values for the primary key in the other table. In the example shown in Figure 1-2, each PatientID value in the Visit table must match a PatientID value in the Patient table. The two tables are related, enabling users to connect the facts about patients with the facts about their visits to the clinic.

Storing Data in Separate Tables

When you create a database, you must create separate tables that contain only fields that are directly related to each other. For example, in the Chatham database, the patient and visit data should not be stored in the same table because doing so would make the data difficult to update and prone to errors. Consider the patient Robert Goldberg and his visits to the clinic, and assume that he has many more than just two visits. If all the patient and visit data were stored in the same table, so that each record (row) contained all the information about each visit and the patient, the patient data would appear multiple times in the table. This causes problems when the data changes. For example, if Robert Goldberg's phone number changed, you would have to update the multiple occurrences of the phone number throughout the table. Not only would this be time-consuming, it would increase the likelihood of errors or inconsistent data.

Relational Database Management Systems

To manage its databases, a company uses a database management system. A **database management system (DBMS)** is a software program that lets you create databases and then manipulate the data they contain. Most of today's database management systems, including Access, are called relational database management systems. In a **relational database management system**, data is organized as a collection of tables. As stated earlier, a relationship between two tables in a relational DBMS is formed through a common field.

A relational DBMS controls the storage of databases and facilitates the creation, manipulation, and reporting of data, as illustrated in Figure 1-3.

Figure 1-3	Relational database management system

© 2014 Cengage Learning

Specifically, a relational DBMS provides the following functions:

- It allows you to create database structures containing fields, tables, and table relationships.
- It lets you easily add new records, change field values in existing records, and delete records.
- It contains a built-in query language, which lets you obtain immediate answers to the questions (or queries) you ask about your data.
- It contains a built-in report generator, which lets you produce professional-looking, formatted reports from your data.
- It protects databases through security, control, and recovery facilities.

An organization such as Chatham Community Health Services benefits from a relational DBMS because it allows users working in different groups to share the same data. More than one user can enter data into a database, and more than one user can retrieve and analyze data that other users have entered. For example, the database for Chatham Community Health Services will contain only one copy of the Visit table, and all employees will use it to access visit information.

Finally, unlike other software programs, such as spreadsheet programs, a DBMS can handle massive amounts of data and can be used to create relationships among multiple tables. Each Access database, for example, can be up to two gigabytes in size, can contain up to 32,768 objects (tables, reports, and so on), and can have up to 255 people using the database at the same time. For instructional purposes, the databases you will create and work with throughout this text contain a relatively small number of records compared to databases you would encounter outside the classroom, which would likely contain tables with very large numbers of records.

Starting Access and Creating a Database

Now that you've learned some database terms and concepts, you're ready to start Access and create the Chatham database for Cindi.

To start Access:

▶ **1.** Display the Windows Start screen, if necessary.

   Using Windows 7? To complete Step 1, click the Start button on the taskbar.

▶ **2.** Click the **Access 2013** tile. Access starts and displays the Recent screen in Backstage view. See Figure 1-4.

Figure 1-4   **Recent screen in Backstage view**

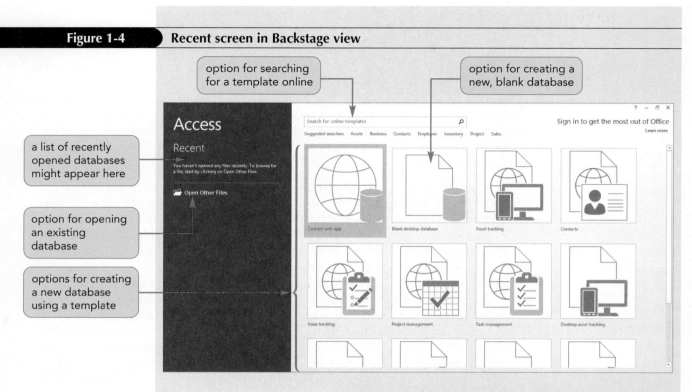

option for searching for a template online

option for creating a new, blank database

a list of recently opened databases might appear here

option for opening an existing database

options for creating a new database using a template

Trouble? If you don't see the Access 2013 tile on your Start screen, type Access to display the Apps screen with the Access 2013 tile highlighted, and then click the tile.

Using Windows 7? To complete Step 2, point to All Programs on the Start menu, click Microsoft Office 2013, and then click Access 2013.

When you start Access, the first screen that appears is Backstage view, which is the starting place for your work in Access. **Backstage view** contains commands that allow you to manage Access files and options. The Recent screen in Backstage view provides options for you to create a new database or open an existing database. To create a new database that does not contain any data or objects, you use the Blank desktop database option. If the database you need to create contains objects that match those found in common databases, such as databases that store data about contacts or tasks, you can use one of the templates provided with Access. A **template** is a predesigned database that includes professionally designed tables, reports, and other database objects that can make it quick and easy for you to create a database. You can also search for a template online using the Search box.

In this case, the templates provided do not match Cindi's needs for the clinic's database, so you need to create a new, blank database from scratch.

To create the new Chatham database:

1. Make sure you have the Access starting Data Files on your computer.

   Trouble? If you don't have the starting Data Files, you need to get them before you can proceed. Your instructor will either give you the Data Files or ask you to obtain them from a specified location (such as a network drive). If you have any questions about the Data Files, see your instructor or technical support person for assistance.

2. Click the **Blank desktop database** option (see Figure1-4). The Blank desktop database screen opens.

Be sure to type **Chatham** or you'll create a database named Database1.

3. In the File Name box, type **Chatham** to replace the selected database name provided by Access, Database1. Next you need to specify the location for the file.

4. Click the **Browse** button 🗀 to the right of the File Name box. The File New Database dialog box opens.

5. Navigate to the drive and folder where you are storing your files, as specified by your instructor.

6. Make sure the "Save as type" box displays "Microsoft Access 2007 – 2013 Databases."

Trouble? If your computer is set up to show filename extensions, you will see the Access filename extension ".accdb" in the File name box.

TIP

If you don't type the filename extension, Access adds it automatically.

7. Click the **OK** button. You return to the Blank desktop database screen, and the File Name box now shows the name Chatham.accdb. The filename extension ".acccb" identifies the file as an Access 2007 - 2013 database.

8. Click the **Create** button. Access creates the new database, saves it to the specified location, and then opens an empty table named Table1.

Trouble? If you see only ribbon tab names and no buttons, click the HOME tab to expand the ribbon, and then in the bottom-right corner of the ribbon, click the Pin the ribbon button 📌.

Refer back to the Session 1.1 Visual Overview and spend some time becoming familiar with the components of the Access window.

INSIGHT

Understanding the Database File Type

Access 2013 uses the .accdb file extension, which is the same file extension used for databases created with Microsoft Access 2007 and 2010. To ensure compatibility between these earlier versions and the Access 2013 software, new databases created using Access 2013 have the same file extension and file format as Access 2007 and Access 2010 databases. This is why the File New Database dialog box provides the Microsoft Access 2007 - 2013 Databases option in the "Save as type" box. In addition, the notation "(Access 2007 - 2013 file format)" appears in the title bar next to the name of an open database in Access 2013, confirming that database files with the .accdb extension can be used in Access 2007, Access 2010, and Access 2013.

Working in Touch Mode

TIP

On a touch device, you *tap* instead of *click*.

If you are working on a touch device, such as a tablet, you can switch to Touch Mode in Access to make it easier for you to tap buttons on the ribbon and perform other touch actions. Your screens will not match those shown in the book exactly, but this will not cause any problems.

Note: The following steps assume that you are using a mouse. If you are instead using a touch device, please read these steps but don't complete them, so that you remain working in Touch Mode.

To switch to Touch Mode:

1. On the Quick Access Toolbar, click the **Customize Quick Access Toolbar** button . A menu opens listing buttons you can add to the Quick Access Toolbar as well as other options for customizing the toolbar.

   Trouble? If the Touch/Mouse Mode command on the menu has a checkmark next to it, press the Esc key to close the menu, and then skip to Step 3.

2. Click **Touch/Mouse Mode**. The Quick Access Toolbar now contains the Touch/Mouse Mode button , which you can use to switch between Mouse Mode, the default display, and Touch Mode.

3. On the Quick Access Toolbar, click the **Touch/Mouse Mode** button . A menu opens with two commands: Mouse, which shows the ribbon in the standard display and is optimized for use with the mouse; and Touch, which provides more space between the buttons and commands on the ribbon and is optimized for use with touch devices. The icon next to Mouse is shaded red to indicate that it is selected.

   Trouble? If the icon next to Touch is shaded red, press the Esc key to close the menu and skip to Step 5.

4. Click **Touch**. The display switches to Touch Mode with more space between the commands and buttons on the ribbon. See Figure 1-5.

| Figure 1-5 | Ribbon displayed in Touch Mode |

Touch/Mouse Mode button on Quick Access Toolbar

ribbon includes more space around buttons and options

The figures in this text show the standard Mouse Mode display, and the instructions assume you are using a mouse to click and select options, so you'll switch back to Mouse Mode.

Trouble? If you are using a touch device and want to remain in Touch Mode, skip Steps 5 and 6.

5. On the Quick Access Toolbar, click the **Touch/Mouse Mode** button , and then click **Mouse**. The ribbon returns to the standard display, as shown in the Session 1.1 Visual Overview.

6. On the Quick Access Toolbar, click the **Customize Quick Access Toolbar** button , and then click **Touch/Mouse Mode** to deselect it. The Touch/Mouse Mode button is removed from the Quick Access Toolbar.

Creating a Table in Datasheet View

Tables contain all the data in a database and are the fundamental objects for your work in Access. There are different ways to create a table in Access, including entering the fields and records for the table directly in Datasheet view.

REFERENCE

Creating a Table in Datasheet View

- On the ribbon, click the CREATE tab.
- In the Tables group, click the Table button.
- Rename the default ID primary key field and change its data type, if necessary; or accept the default ID field with the AutoNumber data type.
- In the Add & Delete group on the FIELDS tab, click the button for the type of field you want to add to the table (for example, click the Short Text button), and then type the field name; or, in the table datasheet, click the Click to Add column heading, click the type of field you want to add from the list that opens, and then press the Tab or Enter key to move to the next column in the datasheet. Repeat this step to add all the necessary fields to the table.
- In the first row below the field names, enter the value for each field in the first record, pressing the Tab or Enter key to move from one field to the next.
- After entering the value for the last field in the first record, press the Tab or Enter key to move to the next row, and then enter the values for the next record. Continue this process until you have entered all the records for the table.
- On the Quick Access Toolbar, click the Save button, enter a name for the table, and then click the OK button.

For Chatham Community Health Services, Cindi needs to track information about each patient visit at the clinic. She asks you to create the Visit table according to the plan shown in Figure 1-6.

Figure 1-6   **Plan for the Visit table**

Field	Purpose
VisitID	Unique number assigned to each visit; will serve as the table's primary key
PatientID	Unique number assigned to each patient; common field that will be a foreign key to connect to the Patient table
VisitDate	Date on which the patient visited the clinic
Reason	Reason/diagnosis for the patient visit
WalkIn	Whether the patient visit was a walk-in or a scheduled appointment

© 2014 Cengage Learning

As shown in Cindi's plan, she wants to store data about visits in five fields, including fields to contain the date of each visit, the reason for the visit, and if the visit was a walk-in or scheduled appointment. These are the most important aspects of a visit and, therefore, must be tracked. Also, notice that the VisitID field will be the primary key for the table; each visit at Chatham Community Health Services has a unique number assigned to it, so this field is the logical choice for the primary key. Finally, the PatientID field is needed in the Visit table as a foreign key to connect the information about visits to patients. The data about patients and their bills will be stored in separate tables, which you will create later.

Notice the name of each field in Figure 1-6. You need to name each field, table, and other object in an Access database.

Decision Making: Naming Fields in Access Tables

One of the most important tasks in creating a table is deciding what names to specify for the table's fields. Keep the following guidelines in mind when you assign field names:

- A field name can consist of up to 64 characters, including letters, numbers, spaces, and special characters, except for the period (.), exclamation mark (!), grave accent (`), and square brackets ([ ]).
- A field name cannot begin with a space.
- Capitalize the first letter of each word in a field name that combines multiple words, for example VisitDate.
- Use concise field names that are easy to remember and reference, and that won't take up a lot of space in the table datasheet.
- Use standard abbreviations, such as Num for Number, Amt for Amount, and Qty for Quantity, and use them consistently throughout the database. For example, if you use Num for Number in one field name, do not use the number sign (#) for Number in another.
- Give fields descriptive names so that you can easily identify them when you view or edit records.
- Although Access supports the use of spaces in field names (and in other object names), experienced database developers avoid using spaces because they can cause errors when the objects are involved in programming tasks.

By spending time obtaining and analyzing information about the fields in a table, and understanding the rules for naming Access fields, you can create a well-designed table that will be easy for others to use.

Renaming the Default Primary Key Field

As noted earlier, Access provides the ID field as the default primary key for a new table you create in Datasheet view. Recall that a primary key is a field, or a collection of fields, whose values uniquely identify each record in a table. However, according to Cindi's plan, the VisitID field should be the primary key for the Visit table. You'll begin by renaming the default ID field to create the VisitID field.

TIP

A **shortcut menu** opens when you right-click an object and provides options for working with that object.

To rename the ID field to the VisitID field:

1. Right-click the **ID** column heading to open the shortcut menu, and then click **Rename Field**. The column heading ID is selected, so that whatever text you type next will replace it.

2. Type **VisitID** and then click the row below the heading. The column heading changes to VisitID, and the insertion point moves to the row below the heading. See Figure 1-7.

   Trouble? If you make a mistake while typing the field name, use the Backspace key to delete characters to the left of the insertion point or the Delete key to delete characters to the right of the insertion point. Then type the correct text. To correct a field name by replacing it entirely, press the Esc key, and then type the correct text.

Figure 1-7   **ID field renamed to VisitID**

TABLE TOOLS contextual tab is active

AutoNumber data type assigned to the default primary key field (ID)

VisitID field name entered in the column heading

option for specifying the data type for a field

The **insertion point** is a flashing cursor that shows where text you type will be inserted. In this case, it is hidden within the selected field value (New).

Notice that the TABLE TOOLS tab is active on the ribbon. This is an example of a **contextual tab**, which is a tab that appears and provides options for working with a specific object that is selected—in this case, the table you are creating. As you work with other objects in the database, other contextual tabs will appear with commands and options related to each selected object.

INSIGHT

Buttons and Labels on the Ribbon

Depending on the size of the monitor you are using and your screen resolution settings, you might see more or fewer buttons on the ribbon, and you might not see labels next to certain buttons. The screenshots in these tutorials were created using a screen resolution setting of 1366 x 768 with the program window maximized. If you are using a smaller monitor or a lower screen resolution, some buttons will appear only as icons, with no labels next to them, because there is not enough room on the ribbon to display the labels.

You have renamed the default primary key field, ID, to VisitID. However, the VisitID field still retains the characteristics of the ID field, including its data type. Your next task is to change the data type of this field.

Changing the Data Type of the Default Primary Key Field

Notice the Formatting group on the FIELDS tab. One of the options available in this group is the Data Type option (see Figure 1-7). Each field in an Access table must be assigned a data type. The **data type** determines what field values you can enter for the field. In this case, the AutoNumber data type is displayed. Access assigns the AutoNumber data type to the default ID primary key field because the **AutoNumber** data type automatically inserts a unique number in this field for every record, beginning with the number 1 for the first record, the number 2 for the second record, and so on. Therefore, a field using the AutoNumber data type can serve as the primary key for any table you create.

Visit numbers at Chatham Community Health Services are specific, four-digit numbers, so the AutoNumber data type is not appropriate for the VisitID field, which is the primary key field in the table you are creating. A better choice is the **Short Text** data type, which allows field values containing letters, digits, and other characters, and which is appropriate for identifying numbers, such as visit numbers, that are never used in calculations. So, Cindi asks you to change the data type for the VisitID field from AutoNumber to Short Text.

To change the data type for the VisitID field:

1. Make sure that the VisitID column is selected. A column is selected when you click a field value, in which case the background color of the column heading changes to orange (the default color) and the insertion point appears in the field value. You can also click the column heading to select a column, in which case the background color of both the column heading and the field value changes (the default colors are gray and blue, respectively).

2. In the Formatting group on the FIELDS tab, click the **Data Type arrow**, and then click **Short Text**. The VisitID field is now a Short Text field. See Figure 1-8.

Figure 1-8 Short Text data type assigned to the VisitID field

Note the Unique check box in the Field Validation group. This check box is selected because the VisitID field assumed the characteristics of the default primary key field, ID, including the fact that each value in the field must be unique. Because this check box is selected, no two records in the Visit table will be allowed to have the same value in the VisitID field.

With the VisitID field created and established as the primary key, you can now enter the rest of the fields in the Visit table.

Adding New Fields

When you create a table in Datasheet view, you can use the options in the Add & Delete group on the FIELDS tab to add fields to your table. You can also use the Click to Add column in the table datasheet to add new fields. (See Figure 1-8.) You'll use both methods to add the four remaining fields to the Visit table. The next field you need to add is the PatientID field. Similar to the VisitID field, the PatientID field will contain numbers that will not be used in calculations, so it should be a Short Text field.

To add the rest of the fields to the Visit table:

1. In the Add & Delete group on the FIELDS tab, click the **Short Text** button. Access adds a new field named "Field1" to the right of the VisitID field. See Figure 1-9.

Figure 1-9   New Short Text field added to the table

The text "Field1" is selected, so you can simply type the new field name to replace it.

2. Type **PatientID**. The second field is added to the table. Next, you'll add the VisitDate field. Because this field will contain date values, you'll add a field with the **Date/Time** data type, which allows field values in a variety of date and time formats.

3. In the Add & Delete group, click the **Date & Time** button. Access adds a third field to the table, this time with the Date/Time data type.

4. Type **VisitDate** to replace the highlighted name "Field1." The fourth field in the Visit table is the Reason field, which will contain brief descriptions of the reason for the visit to the clinic. You'll add another Short Text field—this time using the Click to Add column.

5. Click the **Click to Add** column heading. Access displays a list of available data types from which you can choose the data type for the new field you're adding.

6. Click **Short Text** in the list. Access adds a fourth field to the table.

7. Type **Reason** to replace the highlighted name "Field1," and then press the **Enter** key. The Click to Add column becomes active and displays the list of field data types.

The fifth and final field in the Visit table is the WalkIn field, which will indicate whether or not the visit was a walk-in (that is, the patient did not have a scheduled appointment). The **Yes/No** data type is suitable for this field because it is used to define fields that store values representing one of two options—true/false, yes/no, or on/off.

TIP
You can also type the first letter of a data type to select it and close the Click to Add list.

8. Click **Yes/No** in the list, and then type **WalkIn** to replace the highlighted name "Field1."

Trouble? If you pressed the Tab or Enter key after typing the WalkIn field name, press the Esc key to close the Click to Add list.

9. Click in the row below the VisitID column heading. All five fields are now entered for the Visit table. See Figure 1-10.

Figure 1-10   **Table with all fields entered**

The table contains three Short Text fields (VisitID, PatientID, and Reason), one Date/Time field (VisitDate), and one Yes/No field (WalkIn). You'll learn more about field data types in the next tutorial.

As noted earlier, Datasheet view shows a table's contents in rows (records) and columns (fields). Each column is headed by a field name inside a field selector, and each row has a record selector to its left (see Figure 1-10). Clicking a **field selector** or a **record selector** selects that entire column or row (respectively), which you then can manipulate. A field selector is also called a **column selector**, and a record selector is also called a **row selector**.

Entering Records

With the fields in place for the table, you can now enter the field values for each record. Cindi requests that you enter eight records in the Visit table, as shown in Figure 1-11.

Figure 1-11   **Visit table records**

VisitID	PatientID	VisitDate	Reason	WalkIn
1550	22549	12/1/2015	Influenza	Yes
1527	22522	11/9/2015	Allergies - environmental	Yes
1555	22520	12/7/2015	Annual wellness visit	No
1542	22537	11/24/2015	Influenza	Yes
1530	22510	11/10/2015	Seborrheic dermatitis	No
1564	22512	1/5/2016	Annual wellness visit	No
1575	22513	1/13/2016	Broken leg	Yes
1538	22500	11/17/2015	Migraine	Yes

© 2014 Cengage Learning

To enter records in a table datasheet, you type the field values below the column headings for the fields. The first record you enter will go in the first row (see Figure 1-10).

Be sure to type the numbers "0" and "1" and not the letters "O" and "I" in the field value.

To enter the first record for the Visit table:

1. In the first row for the VisitID field, type **1550** (the VisitID field value for the first record), and then press the **Tab** key. Access adds the field value and moves the insertion point to the right, into the PatientID column. See Figure 1-12.

Figure 1-12   First field value entered

pencil symbol

star symbol

first VisitID field value entered

insertion point positioned in the PatientID field

Trouble? If you make a mistake when typing a value, use the Backspace key to delete characters to the left of the insertion point or the Delete key to delete characters to the right of the insertion point. Then type the correct value. To correct a value by replacing it entirely, press the Esc key, and then type the correct value.

Notice the pencil symbol that appears in the row selector for the new record. The **pencil symbol** indicates that the record is being edited. Also notice the star symbol that appears in the row selector for the second row. The **star symbol** identifies the second row as the next row available for a new record.

2. Type **22549** (the PatientID field value for the first record), and then press the **Tab** key. Access enters the field value and moves the insertion point to the VisitDate column.

3. Type **12/1/15** (the VisitDate field value for the first record), and then press the **Tab** key. Access displays the year as "2015" even though you entered only the final two digits of the year. This is because the VisitDate field has the Date/Time data type, which automatically formats dates with four-digit years.

   Trouble? Depending on your Windows date setting, your VisitDate field values might be displayed in a different format. This difference will not cause any problems.

4. Type **Influenza** (the Reason field value for the first record), and then press the **Tab** key to move to the WalkIn column.

   Recall that the WalkIn field is a Yes/No field. Notice the check box displayed in the WalkIn column. By default, the value for any Yes/No field is "No"; therefore, the check box is initially empty. For Yes/No fields with check boxes, you press the Tab key to leave the check box unchecked, or you press the spacebar to insert a checkmark in the check box. The record you are entering in the table is for a walk-in visit, so you need to insert a checkmark in the check box to indicate "Yes."

TIP

You can also click a check box in a Yes/No field to insert or remove a checkmark.

5. Press the **spacebar** to insert a checkmark, and then press the **Tab** key. The first record is entered into the table, and the insertion point is positioned in the VisitID field for the second record. The pencil symbol is removed from the first row because the record in that row is no longer being edited. The table is now ready for you to enter the second record. See Figure 1-13.

Figure 1-13 **Datasheet with first record entered**

next row available for a new record

value displayed with a four-digit year

field values for the first record entered

Now you can enter the remaining seven records in the Visit table.

To enter the remaining records in the Visit table:

TIP

You can also press the Enter key instead of the Tab key to move from one field to another, and to the next row.

1. Referring to Figure 1-11, enter the values for records 2 through 8, pressing the **Tab** key to move from field to field and to the next row for a new record. Keep in mind that you do not have to type all four digits of the year in the VisitDate field values; you can enter only the final two digits and Access will display all four. Also, for any WalkIn field values of "No," be sure to press the Tab key to leave the check box empty.

   Trouble? If you enter a value in the wrong field by mistake, such as entering a Reason field value in the VisitDate field, a menu might open with options for addressing the problem. If this happens, click the "Enter new value" option in the menu. You'll return to the field with the incorrect value highlighted, which you can then replace by typing the correct value.

   Notice that not all of the Reason field values are fully displayed. To see more of the table datasheet and the full field values, you'll close the Navigation Pane and resize the Reason column.

2. At the top of the Navigation Pane, click the **Shutter Bar Open/Close Button** ⟪. The Navigation Pane closes, and only the complete table datasheet is displayed.

3. Place the pointer on the vertical line to the right of the Reason field name until the pointer changes to a ✛ shape, and then double-click the vertical line. All the Reason field values are now fully displayed. See Figure 1-14.

| Figure 1-14 | Datasheet with eight records entered |

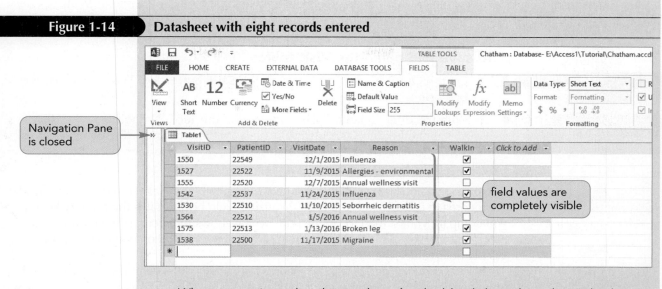

Navigation Pane
is closed

field values are
completely visible

When you resize a datasheet column by double-clicking the column dividing
line, you are sizing the column to its **best fit**—that is, so the column is just
wide enough to display the longest visible value in the column, including the
field name.

Carefully compare your
VisitID and PatientID
values with those in the
figure, and correct any
errors before continuing.

4. Compare your table to the one in Figure 1-14. If any of the field values in your
table do not match those shown in the figure, you can correct a field value by
clicking to position the insertion point in the value, and then using the Backspace
key or Delete key to delete incorrect text. Then type the correct text and press
the Enter key. To correct a value in the WalkIn field, simply click the check box
to add or remove the checkmark as appropriate. Also, be sure the spelling
and capitalization of field names in your table match those shown in the figure
exactly, and that there are no spaces between words. To correct a field name,
double-click it to select it, and then type the correct name; or use the Rename
Field option on the shortcut menu to rename a field with the correct name.

Saving a Table

The records you enter are immediately stored in the database as soon as you enter
them; however, the table's design—the field names and characteristics of the fields
themselves, plus any layout changes to the datasheet—are not saved until you save the
table. When you save a new table for the first time, you should give it a name that best
identifies the information it contains. Like a field name, a table name can contain up to
64 characters, including spaces.

REFERENCE

Saving a Table

- Make sure the table you want to save is open.
- On the Quick Access Toolbar, click the Save button. The Save As dialog box opens.
- In the Table Name box, type the name for the table.
- Click the OK button.

According to Cindi's plan, you need to save the table with the name "Visit."

To save and name the Visit table:

TIP

You can also use the Save command in Backstage view to save and name a new table.

1. On the Quick Access Toolbar, click the **Save** button 🖫. The Save As dialog box opens.

2. With the default name Table1 selected in the Table Name box, type **Visit**, and then click the **OK** button. The tab for the table now displays the name "Visit," and the Visit table design is saved in the Chatham database.

Notice that after you saved and named the Visit table, Access sorted and displayed the records in order by the values in the VisitID field because it is the primary key. If you compare your screen to Figure 1-11, which shows the records in the order you entered them, you'll see that the current screen shows the records in order by the VisitID field values.

Cindi asks you to add two more records to the Visit table. When you add a record to an existing table, you must enter the new record in the next row available for a new record; you cannot insert a row between existing records for the new record. In a table with just a few records, such as the Visit table, the next available row is visible on the screen. However, in a table with hundreds of records, you would need to scroll the datasheet to see the next row available. The easiest way to add a new record to a table is to use the New button, which scrolls the datasheet to the next row available so you can enter the new record.

To enter additional records in the Visit table:

1. If necessary, click the first record's VisitID field value (**1527**) to make it the current record.

2. On the ribbon, click the **HOME** tab.

3. In the Records group, click the **New** button. The insertion point is positioned in the next row available for a new record, which in this case is row 9. See Figure 1-15.

Figure 1-15   **Entering a new record**

4. With the insertion point in the VisitID field for the new record, type **1548** and then press the **Tab** key.

5. Complete the entry of this record by entering each value shown below, pressing the **Tab** key to move from field to field:

   PatientID = **22519**

   VisitDate = **11/30/2015**

   Reason = **Hypertension**

   WalkIn = **No (unchecked)**

6. Enter the values for the next new record, as follows, and then press the **Tab** key after entering the WalkIn field value:

   VisitID = **1560**

   PatientID = **22514**

   VisitDate = **12/15/2015**

   Reason = **Influenza**

   WalkIn = **Yes (checked)**

   Your datasheet should now look like the one shown in Figure 1-16.

Figure 1-16   **Datasheet with additional records entered**

The new records you added appear at the end of the table, and are not sorted in order by the primary key field values. For example, VisitID 1548 should be the fifth record in the table, placed between VisitID 1542 and VisitID 1550. When you add records to a table datasheet, they appear at the end of the table. The records are not displayed in primary key order until you either close and reopen the table or switch between views.

7. Click the **Close** button on the object tab (see Figure 1-16 for the location of this button). The Visit table closes, and the main portion of the Access window is now blank because no database object is currently open. The Chatham database file is still open, as indicated by the filename in the Access window title bar.

Opening a Table

The tables in a database are listed in the Navigation Pane. You open a table, or any Access object, by double-clicking the object name in the Navigation Pane. Next, you'll open the Visit table so you can see the order of all the records you've entered.

To open the Visit table:

▶ **1.** On the Navigation Pane, click the **Shutter Bar Open/Close Button** ⏩ to open the pane. Note that the Visit table is listed.

▶ **2.** Double-click **Visit** to open the table in Datasheet view. See Figure 1-17.

Figure 1-17   **Table with 10 records entered and displayed in primary key order**

Visit table object in the Chatham database

two records added now appear in primary key order

records listed in order by the values in the primary key field

Current Record box indicates the table contains 10 records

The two records you added, with VisitID field values of 1548 and 1560, now appear in the correct primary key order. The table now contains a total of 10 records, as indicated by the Current Record box at the bottom of the datasheet. The **Current Record box** displays the number of the current record as well as the total number of records in the table.

Each record contains a unique VisitID value because this field is the primary key. Other fields, however, can contain the same value in multiple records; for example, note the three values of "Influenza" in the Reason field.

Closing a Table and Exiting Access

When you are finished working in an Access table, it's a good idea to close the table so that you do not make unintended changes to the table data. You can close a table by clicking its Close button on the object tab, as you did earlier. Or, if you want to close the Access program as well, you can click the program's Close button. When you do, any open tables are closed, the active database is closed, and you exit the Access program.

TIP

To close a database without exiting Access, click the FILE tab to display Backstage view, and then click Close.

To close the Visit table and exit Access:

1. Click the **Close** button ☒ on the program window title bar. Access closes the Visit table and the Chatham database, and then the Access program closes.

INSIGHT

Saving a Database

Unlike the Save buttons in other Office programs, the Save button on the Quick Access Toolbar in Access does not save the active document (database). Instead, you use the Save button to save the design of an Access object, such as a table (as you saw earlier), or to save datasheet format changes, such as resizing columns. Access does not have a button or option you can use to save the active database.

Access saves changes to the active database automatically when you change or add a record or close the database. If your database is stored on a removable medium, such as a USB drive, you should never remove the drive while the database file is open. If you do, Access will encounter problems when it tries to save the database, which might damage the database. Make sure you close the database first before removing the drive.

Now that you've become familiar with database concepts and Access, and created the Chatham database and the Visit table, Cindi wants you to add more records to the table and work with the data stored in it to create database objects including a query, form, and report. You'll complete these tasks in the next session.

REVIEW

Session 1.1 Quick Check

1. A(n) _____ is a single characteristic of a person, place, object, event, or idea.
2. You connect the records in two separate tables through a(n) _____ that appears in both tables.
3. The _____, whose values uniquely identify each record in a table, is called a(n) _____ when it is placed in a second table to form a relationship between the two tables.
4. The _____ is the area of the Access window that lists all the objects in a database, and it is the main control center for opening and working with database objects.
5. What is the name of the field that Access creates, by default, as the primary key field for a new table in Datasheet view?
6. Which group on the FIELDS tab contains the options you use to add new fields to a table?
7. What does a pencil symbol at the beginning of a record represent? What does a star symbol represent?
8. Explain how the saving process in Access is different from saving in other Office programs.

Session 1.2 Visual Overview:

The **CREATE tab** provides options for creating various database objects, including tables, forms, and reports. The options appear on the tab grouped by object type.

The **Query Wizard button** opens a dialog box with different types of wizards that guide you through the steps to create a query. One of these, the **Simple Query Wizard**, allows you to select records and fields quickly to display in the query results.

You use the options in the Tables group to create a table in Datasheet view or in Design view.

The Forms group contains options for creating a **form**, which is a database object you use to enter, edit, and view records in a database.

The **Form tool** quickly creates a form containing all the fields in the table (or query) on which you're basing the form.

The **Form Wizard** guides you through the process of creating a form.

The Queries group contains options for creating a **query**, which is a question you ask about the data stored in a database. In response to a query, Access displays the specific records and fields that answer your question.

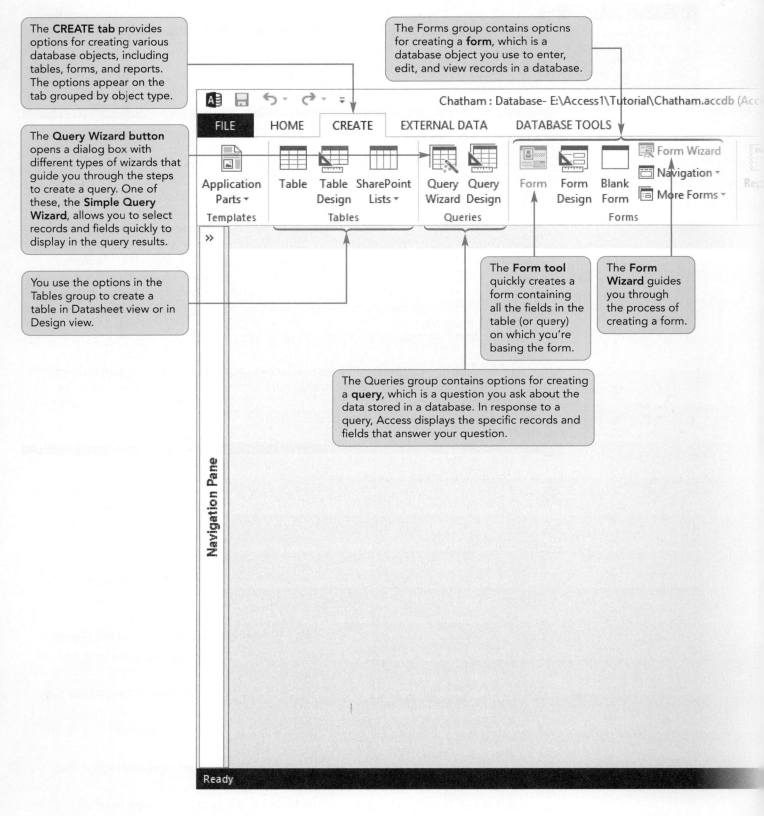

Chatham : Database- E:\Access1\Tutorial\Chatham.accdb (Acc

FILE   HOME   CREATE   EXTERNAL DATA   DATABASE TOOLS

Application Parts ▼ | Table | Table Design | SharePoint Lists ▼ | Query Wizard | Query Design | Form | Form Design | Blank Form | Form Wizard | Navigation ▼ | More Forms ▼ | Rep

Templates | Tables | Queries | Forms

Navigation Pane

Ready

The CREATE Tab Options

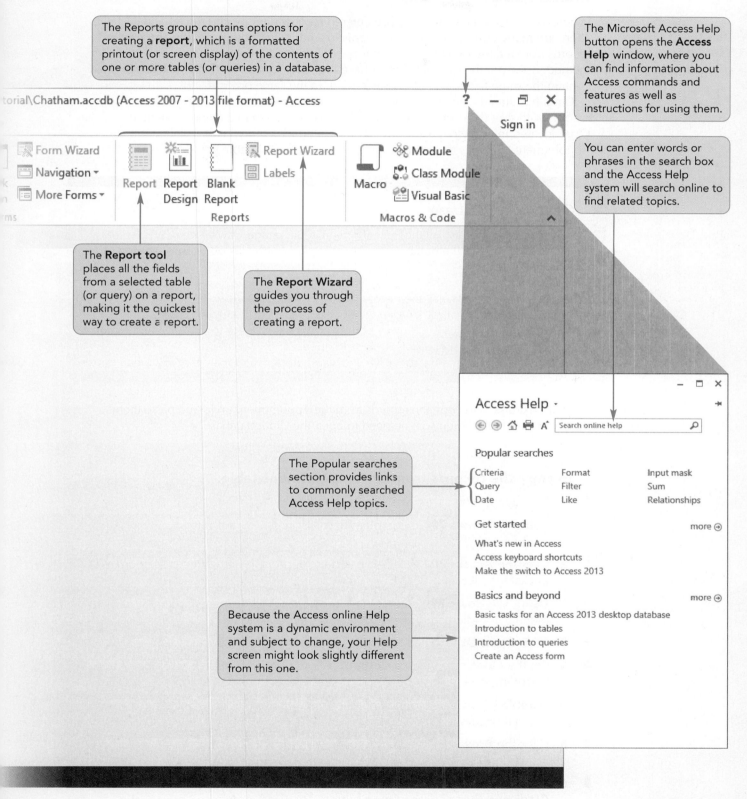

The Reports group contains options for creating a **report**, which is a formatted printout (or screen display) of the contents of one or more tables (or queries) in a database.

The Microsoft Access Help button opens the **Access Help** window, where you can find information about Access commands and features as well as instructions for using them.

torial\Chatham.accdb (Access 2007 - 2013 file format) - Access

Sign in

You can enter words or phrases in the search box and the Access Help system will search online to find related topics.

Form Wizard
Navigation ▾
More Forms ▾

Report   Report   Blank
Design   Report

Report Wizard
Labels

Reports

Macro

Module
Class Module
Visual Basic

Macros & Code

The **Report tool** places all the fields from a selected table (or query) on a report, making it the quickest way to create a report.

The **Report Wizard** guides you through the process of creating a report.

Access Help ▾

Search online help

Popular searches

Criteria	Format	Input mask
Query	Filter	Sum
Date	Like	Relationships

The Popular searches section provides links to commonly searched Access Help topics.

Get started   more ➔

What's new in Access
Access keyboard shortcuts
Make the switch to Access 2013

Basics and beyond   more ➔

Basic tasks for an Access 2013 desktop database
Introduction to tables
Introduction to queries
Create an Access form

Because the Access online Help system is a dynamic environment and subject to change, your Help screen might look slightly different from this one.

Copying Records from Another Access Database

When you created the Visit table, you entered records directly into the table datasheet. There are many other ways to enter records in a table, including copying and pasting records from a table into the same database or into a different database. To use this method, however, the two tables must have the same structure—that is, the tables must contain the same fields, with the same design, in the same order.

Cindi has already created a table named Appointment that contains additional records with visit data. The Appointment table is contained in a database named Cindi located in the Access1 ► Tutorial folder included with your Data Files. The Appointment table has the same table structure as the Visit table you created.

REFERENCE

Opening a Database

- Start Access and display the Recent screen in Backstage view.
- Click the name of the database you want to open in the list of recently opened databases.

or

- Start Access and display the Recent screen in Backstage view.
- In the navigation bar, click Open Other Files to display the Open screen.
- Click Computer, click the Browse button, and then navigate to the drive and folder containing the database file you want to open.
- Click the name of the database file you want to open, and then click the Open button.

Your next task is to copy the records from the Appointment table and paste them into your Visit table. To do so, you need to open the Cindi database.

To copy the records from the Appointment table:

1. Display the Windows Start screen, if necessary.

   Using Windows 7? To complete Step 1, click the Start button on the taskbar.

2. Click the **Access 2013** tile. Access starts and displays the Recent screen in Backstage view.

   Using Windows 7? To complete Step 2, click All Programs on the Start menu, click Microsoft Office 2013, and then click Access 2013.

3. Click **Open Other Files** to display the Open screen in Backstage view.

4. On the Open screen, click **Computer**. The right side of the screen now shows folder information for your computer.

   Trouble? If you are storing your files on SkyDrive, click SkyDrive, and then log in if necessary.

5. Click the **Browse** button, and then navigate to the drive that contains your Data Files.

6. Navigate to the **Access1 ► Tutorial** folder, click the database file named **Cindi**, and then click the **Open** button. The Cindi database opens in the Access program window. Note that the database contains only one object, the Appointment table.

Trouble? If a security warning appears below the ribbon indicating that some active content has been disabled, click the Enable Content button next to the warning. Access provides this warning because some databases might contain content that could harm your computer. Because the Cindi database does not contain objects that could be harmful, you can open it safely. If you are accessing the file over a network, you might also see a dialog box asking if you want to make the file a trusted document; click Yes.

▶ **7.** In the Navigation Pane, double-click **Appointment** to open the Appointment table in Datasheet view. The table contains 76 records and the same five fields, with the same characteristics, as the fields in the Visit table. See Figure 1-18.

Figure 1-18   **Appointment table in the Cindi database**

Cindi wants you to copy all the records in the Appointment table. You can select all the records by clicking the **datasheet selector**, which is the box to the left of the first field name in the table datasheet (see Figure 1-18).

▶ **8.** Click the **datasheet selector** to the left of the VisitID field, as shown in Figure 1-18. Access selects all the records in the table.

▶ **9.** In the Clipboard group on the HOME tab, click the **Copy** button. All the records are copied to the Clipboard.

▶ **10.** Click the **Close 'Appointment'** button ☒ on the object tab. A dialog box opens asking if you want to save the data you copied to the Clipboard. This dialog box opens only when you copy a large amount of data to the Clipboard.

▶ **11.** Click the **Yes** button. The dialog box closes, and then the Appointment table closes.

With the records copied to the Clipboard, you can now paste them into the Visit table. First you need to close the Cindi database while still keeping the Access program open, and then open the Chatham database.

To close the Cindi database and then paste the records into the Visit table:

▶ **1.** Click the **FILE** tab to display Backstage view, and then click **Close** in the navigation bar to close the Cindi database. You return to the HOME tab in the Access program window.

▶ **2.** Click the **FILE** tab to return to Backstage view, and then click **Open** in the navigation bar. The Recent section of the Open screen shows a list of the recently opened database files. This list should include the Chatham database.

▶ **3.** In the Recent section of the screen, click **Chatham** to open the Chatham database file.

   Trouble? If the Chatham database file is not listed in the Recent section on your computer, click Computer, and then click Browse. In the Open dialog box, navigate to the drive and folder where you are storing your files, and then open the Chatham database file.

   Trouble? If the security warning appears below the ribbon, click the Enable Content button, and then, if necessary, click Yes to make the file a trusted document.

▶ **4.** In the Navigation Pane, double-click **Visit** to open the Visit table in Datasheet view.

▶ **5.** On the Navigation Pane, click the **Shutter Bar Open/Close Button** ⧏ to close the pane.

▶ **6.** Position the pointer on the star symbol in the row selector for row 11 (the next row available for a new record) until the pointer changes to a ➡ shape, and then click to select the row.

▶ **7.** In the Clipboard group on the HOME tab, click the **Paste** button. The pasted records are added to the table, and a dialog box opens asking you to confirm that you want to paste all the records (76 total).

   Trouble? If the Paste button isn't active, click the ➡ pointer on the row selector for row 11, making sure the entire row is selected, and then repeat Step 7.

▶ **8.** Click the **Yes** button. The dialog box closes, and the pasted records are highlighted. See Figure 1-19. Notice that the table now contains a total of 86 records—10 records that you entered and 76 records that you copied and pasted.

| Figure 1-19 | Visit table after copying and pasting records |

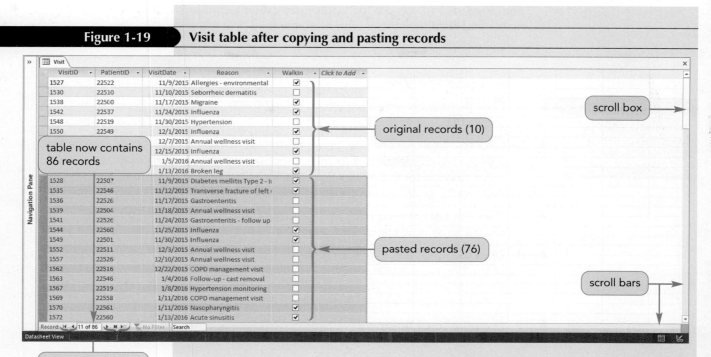

Not all the Reason field values are completely visible, so you need to resize this column to its best fit.

9. Place the pointer on the vertical line to the right of the Reason field name until the pointer changes to a ↔ shape, and then double-click the vertical line. The Reason field values are now fully displayed.

Navigating a Datasheet

The Visit table now contains 86 records, but only some of the records are visible on the screen. To view fields or records not currently visible on the screen, you can use the horizontal and vertical scroll bars shown in Figure 1-19 to navigate the data. The **navigation buttons**, shown in Figure 1-19 and also described in Figure 1-20, provide another way to move vertically through the records. The Current Record box appears between the two sets of navigation buttons and displays the number of the current record as well as the total number of records in the table. Figure 1-20 shows which record becomes the current record when you click each navigation button. Note the New (blank) record button, which works in the same way as the New button on the HOME tab you used earlier to enter a new record in the table.

| Figure 1-20 | Navigation buttons |

Navigation Button	Record Selected	Navigation Button	Record Selected
◄	First record	►|	Last record
◄	Previous record	►※	New (blank) record
►	Next record		

Cindi suggests that you use the various navigation techniques to move through the Visit table and become familiar with its contents.

To navigate the Visit datasheet:

1. Click the first record's VisitID field value (**1527**). The Current Record box shows that record 1 is the current record.

2. Click the **Next record** navigation button ▶. The second record is now high-lighted, which identifies it as the current record. Also, notice that the second record's value for the VisitID field is selected, and the Current Record box displays "2 of 86" to indicate that the second record is the current record.

3. Click the **Last record** navigation button ▶|. The last record in the table, record 86, is now the current record.

4. Drag the scroll box in the vertical scroll bar (see Figure 1-19) up to the top of the bar. Notice that record 86 is still the current record, as indicated in the Current Record box. Dragging the scroll box changes the display of the table datasheet, but does not change the current record.

5. Drag the scroll box in the vertical scroll bar back down until you can see the end of the table and the current record (record 86).

6. Click the **Previous record** navigation button ◀. Record 85 is now the current record.

7. Click the **First record** navigation button |◀. The first record is now the cur-rent record and is visible on the screen.

   As you moved through the datasheet, you might have noticed that not all the Reason field values are fully displayed. When you resize a column to its best fit, the column expands to fully display only the field values that are visible on the screen at that time. To make sure all field values are displayed for the entire table, you need to scroll through the datasheet and repeat the resizing process.

8. Drag the scroll box down to display more of the table, until you see other Reason field values that are not fully displayed. Then use the ✛ pointer to resize the field.

9. Repeat Step 8, as necessary, until you reach the bottom of the table and have resized all the Reason field values, and then drag the scroll box back up to display the beginning of the table.

The Visit table now contains all the data about patient visits for Chatham Community Health Services. To better understand how to work with this data, Cindi asks you to create simple objects for the other main types of database objects—queries, forms, and reports.

Creating a Simple Query

As noted earlier, a query is a question you ask about the data stored in a database. When you create a query, you tell Access which fields you need and what criteria it should use to select the records that will answer your question. Then Access displays only the information you want, so you don't have to navigate through the entire database for the information. In the Visit table, for example, Cindi might create a query to display only those records for visits that occurred in a specific month. Even though a query can display table information in a different way, the information still exists in the table as it was originally entered.

Cindi wants to see a list of all the visit dates and reasons for visits in the Visit table. She doesn't want the list to include all the fields in the table, such as PatientID and WalkIn. To produce this list for Cindi, you'll use the Simple Query Wizard to create a query based on the Visit table.

To start the Simple Query Wizard:

▶ **1.** On the ribbon, click the **CREATE** tab.

▶ **2.** In the Queries group on the CREATE tab, click the **Query Wizard** button. The New Query dialog box opens.

▶ **3.** Make sure **Simple Query Wizard** is selected, and then click the **OK** button. The first Simple Query Wizard dialog box opens. See Figure 1-21.

Figure 1-21 ▶ **First Simple Query Wizard dialog box**

Because the Visit table is the only object in the Chatham database, it is listed in the Tables/Queries box by default. If the database contained more objects, you could click the Tables/Queries arrow and choose another table or a query as the basis for the new query you are creating. The Available Fields box lists all the fields in the Visit table.

You need to select fields from the Available Fields box to include them in the query. To select fields one at a time, click a field and then click the ▶ button. The selected (highlighted) field moves from the Available Fields box on the left to the Selected Fields box on the right. To select all the fields, click the ▶▶ button. If you change your mind or make a mistake, you can remove a field by clicking it in the Selected Fields box and then clicking the ◀ button. To remove all fields from the Selected Fields box, click the ◀◀ button.

Each Simple Query Wizard dialog box contains buttons on the bottom that allow you to move to the previous dialog box (Back button), move to the next dialog box (Next button), or cancel the creation process (Cancel button). You can also finish creating the object (Finish button) and accept the wizard's defaults for the remaining options.

Cindi wants her list to include data from only the following fields: VisitID, VisitDate, and Reason. You need to select these fields to include them in the query.

TIP

You can also double-click a field to move it from the Available Fields box to the Selected Fields box.

To create the query using the Simple Query Wizard:

1. Click **VisitID** in the Available Fields box to select the field (if necessary), and then click the ⟩ button. The VisitID field moves to the Selected Fields box.

2. Repeat Step 1 for the fields **VisitDate** and **Reason**, and then click the **Next** button. The second, and final, Simple Query Wizard dialog box opens and asks you to choose a name (title) for your query. Access suggests the name "Visit Query" because the query you are creating is based on the Visit table. You'll change the suggested name to "VisitList."

3. Click at the end of the suggested name, use the **Backspace** key to delete the word "Query" and the space, and then type **List**. Now you can view the query results.

4. Click the **Finish** button to complete the query. Access displays the query results in Datasheet view, on a new tab named "VisitList." A query datasheet is similar to a table datasheet, showing fields in columns and records in rows—but only for those fields and records you want to see, as determined by the query specifications you select.

5. Place the pointer on the vertical line to the right of the Reason field name until the pointer changes to a ✛ shape, and then double-click the vertical line to resize the Reason field. See Figure 1-22.

Figure 1-22   **Query results**

only the three selected fields are displayed in the query datasheet

all 86 records are included in the results

VisitID	VisitDate	Reason
1527	11/9/2015	Allergies - environmental
1528	11/9/2015	Diabetes mellitus Type 2 - initial diagnosis
1530	11/10/2015	Seborrheic dermatitis
1535	11/12/2015	Transverse fracture of left ulna
1536	11/17/2015	Gastroenteritis
1538	11/17/2015	Migraine
1539	11/18/2015	Annual wellness visit
1541	11/24/2015	Gastroenteritis - follow up
1542	11/24/2015	Influenza
1544	11/25/2015	Influenza
1548	11/30/2015	Hypertension
1549	11/30/2015	Influenza
1550	12/1/2015	Influenza
1552	12/3/2015	Annual wellness visit
1555	12/7/2015	Annual wellness visit
1557	12/10/2015	Annual wellness visit
1560	12/15/2015	Influenza
1562	12/22/2015	COPD management visit
1563	1/4/2016	Follow-up - cast removal
1564	1/5/2016	Annual wellness visit
1567	1/8/2016	Hypertension monitoring
1569	1/11/2016	COPD management visit
1570	1/11/2016	Nasopharyngitis
1572	1/13/2016	Acute sinusitis
1573	1/13/2016	Cardiac monitoring

Record: 1 of 86   No Filter   Search

Datasheet View

The VisitList query datasheet displays the three selected fields for each record in the Visit table. The fields are shown in the order you selected them in the Simple Query Wizard, from left to right. The records are listed in order by the primary key field, VisitID. Even though the query datasheet displays only the three fields you chose for the query, the Visit table still includes all the fields for all records.

> Notice that the navigation buttons are located at the bottom of the window. You navigate a query datasheet in the same way that you navigate a table datasheet.
>
> ▶ **6.** Click the **Last record** navigation button ⏮. The last record in the query datasheet is now the current record.
>
> ▶ **7.** Click the **Previous record** navigation button ◀. Record 85 in the query datasheet is now the current record.
>
> ▶ **8.** Click the **First record** navigation button ⏮. The first record is now the current record.
>
> ▶ **9.** Click the **Close 'VisitList'** button ⊠ on the object tab. A dialog box opens asking if you want to save the changes to the layout of the query. This dialog box opens because you resized the Reason column.
>
> ▶ **10.** Click the **Yes** button to save the query layout changes and close the query.

The query results are not stored in the database; however, the query design is stored as part of the database with the name you specified. You can re-create the query results at any time by opening the query again. When you open the query at a later date, the results displayed will reflect up-to-date information to include any new records entered in the Visit table.

Next, Cindi asks you to create a form for the Visit table so that Chatham Community Health Services employees can use the form to enter and work with data in the table easily.

Creating a Simple Form

As noted earlier, you use a form to enter, edit, and view records in a database. Although you can perform these same functions with tables and queries, forms can present data in many customized and useful ways.

Cindi wants a form for the Visit table that shows all the fields for one record at a time, with fields listed one below another in a column. This type of form will make it easier for her staff to focus on all the data for a particular visit. You'll use the Form tool to create this form quickly and easily.

> **To create the form using the Form tool:**
>
> ▶ **1.** Make sure the Visit table is still open in Datasheet view. The table or other database object you're using as the basis for the form must either be open or selected in the Navigation Pane when you use the Form tool.
>
>   **Trouble?** If the Visit table is not open, click the Shutter Bar Open/Close Button ⟫ to open the Navigation Pane. Then double-click Visit to open the Visit table in Datasheet view. Click the Shutter Bar Open/Close Button ⟪ to close the pane.
>
> ▶ **2.** Make sure the CREATE tab is displayed.
>
> ▶ **3.** In the Forms group, click the **Form** button. The Form tool creates a simple form showing every field in the Visit table and places it on a tab named "Visit." Access assigns this name because the form is based on the Visit table. See Figure 1-23.

Figure 1-23 Form created by the Form tool

- form graphic identifies the object as a form
- new tab for the form
- field values for the first record displayed
- depending on your computer's settings, your field value boxes might be a different width
- form displayed in Layout view
- record 1 of 86 total records

Trouble? Depending on the size of your monitor and your screen resolution settings, the fields in your form might appear in multiple columns instead of a single column. This difference will not present any problems.

The form displays one record at a time in the Visit table, providing another view of the data that is stored in the table and allowing you to focus on the values for one record. Access displays the field values for the first record in the table and selects the first field value (VisitID) by placing a border around the value. Each field name appears on a separate line and on the same line as its field value, which appears in a box to the right. Depending on your computer's settings, the field value boxes in your form might be wider or narrower than those shown in the figure. As indicated in the status bar, the form is displayed in Layout view. In **Layout view**, you can make design changes to the form while it is displaying data, so that you can see the effects of the changes you make immediately.

To view, enter, and maintain data using a form, you must know how to move from field to field and from record to record. Notice that the form contains navigation buttons, similar to those available in Datasheet view, which you can use to display different records in the form. You'll use these now to navigate the form; then you'll save and close the form.

To navigate, save, and close the form:

1. Click the **Next record** navigation button ▶. The form now displays the values for the second record in the Visit table.

2. Click the **Last record** navigation button ▶| to move to the last record in the table. The form displays the information for VisitID 1700.

3. Click the **Previous record** navigation button ◀ to move to record 85.

▶ **4.** Click the **First record** navigation button |◀ to return to the first record in the Visit table.

Next, you'll save the form with the name "VisitData" in the Chatham database. Then the form will be available for later use.

▶ **5.** On the Quick Access Toolbar, click the **Save** button 🖫. The Save As dialog box opens.

▶ **6.** In the Form Name box, click at the end of the highlighted word "Visit," type **Data**, and then press the **Enter** key. Access saves the form as VisitData in the Chatham database and closes the dialog box. The tab containing the form now displays the name VisitData.

▶ **7.** Click the **Close 'VisitData'** button |✕| on the object tab to close the form.

After attending a staff meeting, Cindi returns with another request. She would like to see the information in the Visit table presented in a more readable and professional format. You'll help Cindi by creating a report.

Creating a Simple Report

As noted earlier, a report is a formatted printout (or screen display) of the contents of one or more tables or queries. You'll use the Report tool to quickly produce a report based on the Visit table for Cindi. The Report tool creates a report based on the selected table or query.

To create the report using the Report tool:

▶ **1.** With the Visit table open in Datasheet view, click the **CREATE** tab on the ribbon.

▶ **2.** In the Reports group, click the **Report** button. The Report tool creates a simple report showing every field in the Visit table and places it on a tab named "Visit." Again, Access assigns this name because the object you created (the report) is based on the Visit table. See Figure 1-24.

Figure 1-24   Report created by the Report tool

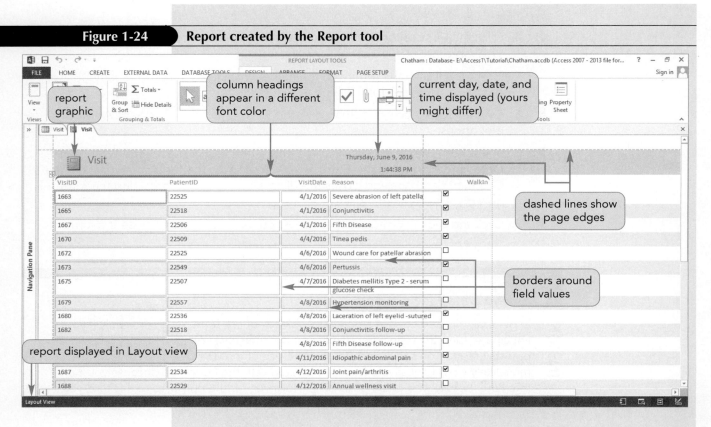

Trouble? The records in your report might appear in a different order from the records shown in Figure 1-24. This difference will not cause any problems.

The report shows each field in a column, with the field values for each record in a row, similar to a table or query datasheet. However, the report offers a more visually appealing format for the data, with the column headings in a different color, borders around each field value, a graphic of a report at the top left, and the current day, date, and time at the top right. Also notice the dashed horizontal and vertical lines on the top and right, respectively; these lines mark the edges of the page and show where text will print on the page.

The report needs some design changes to better display the data. The columns are much wider than necessary for the VisitID and PatientID fields, and the Reason and WalkIn field values and borders are not completely displayed within the page area defined by the dashed lines, which means they would not appear on the same page as the rest of the fields in the printed report. You can resize the columns easily in Layout view.

To resize the VisitID and PatientID columns:

1. Position the pointer on the right border of any field value in the VisitID column until the pointer changes to a ↔ shape.

2. Click and drag the mouse to the left; dark outlines surround the field name and each field value to show the column width as you change it. Drag to the left until the column is slightly wider than the VisitID field name.

3. Release the mouse button. The VisitID column is now narrower, and the other four columns have shifted to the left. The Reason and WalkIn fields, values, and borders are now completely within the page area. See Figure 1-25.

Figure 1-25   **Report after resizing the VisitID column**

field values and borders are now within the area marked by the dashed lines

column is now narrower

VisitID	PatientID	VisitDate	Reason	WalkIn
1663	22525	4/1/2016	Severe abrasion of left patella	☑
1665	22518	4/1/2016	Conjunctivitis	☑
1667	22506	4/1/2016	Fifth Disease	☑

Visit   Thursday, June 9, 2016
                                                    1:55:24 PM

4. Click the first field value for PatientID to establish the field as the current field.

5. Position the pointer on the right border of the first value in the PatientID column until the pointer changes to ↔, click and drag to the left until the column is slightly wider than its field name, and then release the mouse button.

6. Drag the scroll box on the vertical scroll bar all the way down to the bottom of the report to check its entire layout.

   The Report tool displays the number "86" at the bottom left of the report, showing the total number of records in the report and the table on which it is based—the Visit table. The Report tool also displays the page number at the bottom right, but the text "Page 1 of 1" appears cut off through the vertical dashed line. This will cause a problem when you print the report, so you need to move this text to the left.

7. Click anywhere on the words **Page 1 of 1**. An orange outline appears around the text, indicating it is selected. See Figure 1-26.

Figure 1-26   **Report page number selected**

1640	22557	3/9/2016	Hypertension monitoring	☐
1642	22540	3/9/2016	Onychocryptosis	☑
1644	22533	3/11/2016	Annual wellness visit	☐
1645	22531	3/14/2016	UTI	☑
1647	22535	3/18/2016	Hypertension monitoring	☐
1648	22550	3/18/2016	Migrane headache follow-up	☐
1650	22560	3/21/2016	Eczema erythematosum follow-up	☐
1652	22540	3/23/2016	Onychocryptosis follow-up	☐
1653	22551	3/23/2016	Elevated blood lipids-monitoring meds	☐
1659	22531	3/28/2016	UTI follow-up	☐
1662	22502	3/30/2016	Annual wellness visit	☐

text to the right of this dashed line would print on its own page

text is selected and can be moved to the left

86 — shows total number of records in the report

Page 1 of 1

With the text selected, you can use the keyboard arrow keys to move it.

TIP

You can also use the mouse to drag the selected page number, but the arrow key is more precise.

8. Press the ← key repeatedly until the selected box containing the page number is to the left of the vertical dashed line (roughly 35 times). The page number text is now completely within the page area and will print on the same page as the rest of the report.

9. Drag the scroll box back up to redisplay the top of the report.

The report is displayed in Layout view, which doesn't show how many pages there are in the report. To see this, you need to switch to Print Preview.

To view the report in Print Preview:

1. In the Views group on the DESIGN tab, click the **View button arrow**, and then click **Print Preview**. The first page of the report is displayed in Print Preview. See Figure 1-27.

Figure 1-27   **First page of the report in Print Preview**

Print Preview shows exactly how the report will look when printed. Notice that Print Preview provides page navigation buttons at the bottom of the window, similar to the navigation buttons you've used to move through records in a table, query, and form.

2. Click the **Next Page** navigation button ▶. The second page of the report is displayed in Print Preview.

3. Click the **Last Page** navigation button ▶| to move to the last page of the report.

4. Drag the scroll box in the vertical scroll bar (see Figure 1-27) down until the bottom of the report page is displayed. The notation "Page 3 of 3" appears at the bottom of the page, indicating that you are on page 3 out of a total of 3 pages in the report.

Trouble? Depending on the printer you are using, your report might have more or fewer pages, and some of the pages might be blank. If so, don't worry. Different printers format reports in different ways, sometimes affecting the total number of pages and the number of records printed per page.

▶ **5.** Click the **First Page** navigation button ⏮ to return to the first page of the report, and then drag the scroll box in the vertical scroll bar back up so that the top of the report is displayed.

Next you'll save the report as VisitDetails, and then print it.

▶ **6.** On the Quick Access Toolbar, click the **Save** button 💾. The Save As dialog box opens.

▶ **7.** In the Report Name box, click at the end of the highlighted word "Visit," type **Details,** and then press the **Enter** key. Access saves the report as VisitDetails in the Chatham database and closes the dialog box. The tab containing the report now displays the name "VisitDetails."

Printing a Report

After creating a report, you might need to print it to distribute it to others who need to view the report's contents. You can print a report without changing any print settings, or display the Print dialog box and select options for printing.

REFERENCE

Printing a Report

- Open the report in any view, or select the report in the Navigation Pane.
- Click the FILE tab to display Backstage view, click Print, and then click Quick Print to print the report with the default print settings.

or

- Open the report in any view, or select the report in the Navigation Pane.
- Click the FILE tab, click Print, and then click Print (or, if the report is displayed in Print Preview, click the Print button in the Print group on the PRINT PREVIEW tab). The Print dialog box opens, in which you can select the options you want for printing the report.

Cindi asks you to print the entire report with the default settings, so you'll use the Quick Print option in Backstage view.

Note: To complete the following steps, your computer must be connected to a printer. Check with your instructor first to see if you should print the report.

To print the report and then close it:

▶ **1.** On the ribbon, click the **FILE** tab to display Backstage view.

▶ **2.** In the navigation bar, click **Print**, and then click **Quick Print**. The report prints with the default print settings, and you return to the report in Print Preview.

Trouble? If your report did not print, make sure that your computer is connected to a printer, and that the printer is turned on and ready to print. Then repeat Steps 1 and 2.

▶ **3.** Click the **Close 'VisitDetails'** button ✕ on the object tab to close the report.

▶ **4.** Click the **Close 'Visit'** button ✕ on the object tab to close the Visit table.

Trouble? If you are asked to save changes to the layout of the table, click Yes.

You can also use the Print dialog box to print other database objects, such as table and query datasheets. Most often, these objects are used for viewing and entering data, and reports are used for printing the data in a database.

Viewing Objects in the Navigation Pane

The Chatham database now contains four objects—the Visit table, the VisitList query, the VisitData form, and the VisitDetails report. When you work with the database file—such as closing it, opening it, or distributing it to others—the file includes all the objects you created and saved in the database. You can view and work with these objects in the Navigation Pane.

To view the objects in the Chatham database:

1. On the Navigation Pane, click the **Shutter Bar Open/Close Button** 》 to open the pane. See Figure 1-28.

| Figure 1-28 | Chatham database objects displayed in the Navigation Pane |

The Navigation Pane currently displays the default category, **All Access Objects**, which lists all the database objects in the pane. Each object type (Tables, Queries, Forms, and Reports) appears in its own group. Each database object (the Visit table, the VisitList query, the VisitData form, and the VisitDetails report) has a unique icon to its left to indicate the type of object. This makes it easy for you to identify the objects and choose which one you want to open and work with.

The arrow on the All Access Objects bar displays a menu with options for various ways to group and display objects in the Navigation Pane. The Search box enables you to enter text for Access to find; for example, you could search for all objects that contain the word "Visit" in their names. Note that Access searches for objects only in the categories and groups currently displayed in the Navigation Pane.

As you continue to build the Chatham database and add more objects to it in later tutorials, you'll use the options in the Navigation Pane to manage those objects.

Using Microsoft Access Help

The Access program provides a Help system you can use to search for information about specific Access features. You start Help by clicking the Microsoft Access Help button in the top right of the Access window, or by pressing the F1 key. You'll use Help now to learn more about the Navigation Pane.

To search for information about the Navigation Pane in Help:

▶ 1. Click the **Microsoft Access Help** button ? on the title bar. The Access Help window opens, as shown earlier in the Session 1.2 Visual Overview.

▶ 2. Click in the search box, type **Navigation Pane**, and then press the **Enter** key. The Access Help window displays a list of topics related to the Navigation Pane.

▶ 3. Click the topic **Manage database objects in the Navigation Pane**. The Access Help window displays the article you selected. See Figure 1-29.

| Figure 1-29 | Article displayed in the Access Help window |

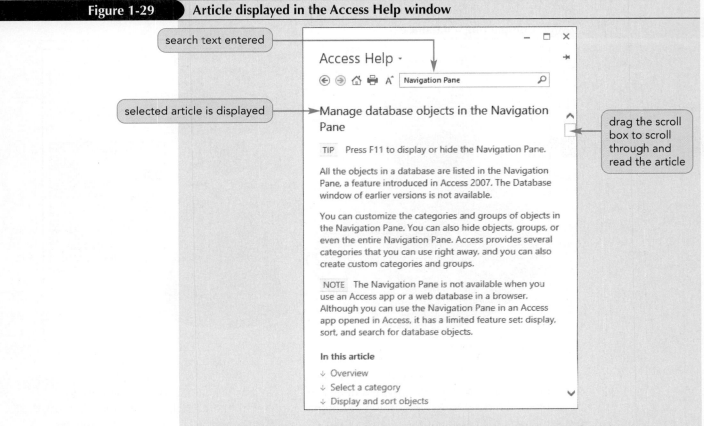

search text entered

selected article is displayed

drag the scroll box to scroll through and read the article

Trouble? If the article on managing database objects is not listed in your Help window, choose another article related to the Navigation Pane to read.

▶ 4. Scroll through the article to read detailed information about working with the Navigation Pane.

▶ 5. When finished, click the **Close** button ✕ on the Access Help window to close it.

The Access Help system is an important reference tool for you to use if you need additional information about databases in general, details about specific Access features, or support with problems you might encounter.

Managing a Database

One of the main tasks involved in working with database software is managing your databases and the data they contain. Some of the activities involved in database management include compacting and repairing a database and backing up and restoring a database. By managing your databases, you can ensure that they operate in the most efficient way, that the data they contain is secure, and that you can work with the data effectively.

Compacting and Repairing a Database

Whenever you open an Access database and work in it, the size of the database increases. Further, when you delete records or when you delete or replace database objects—such as queries, forms, and reports—the storage space that had been occupied by the deleted or replaced records or objects does not automatically become available for other records or objects. To make the space available, and also to increase the speed of data retrieval, you must compact the database. **Compacting** a database rearranges the data and objects in a database to decrease its file size, thereby making more storage space available and enhancing the performance of the database. Figure 1-30 illustrates the compacting process.

Figure 1-30	Compacting a database

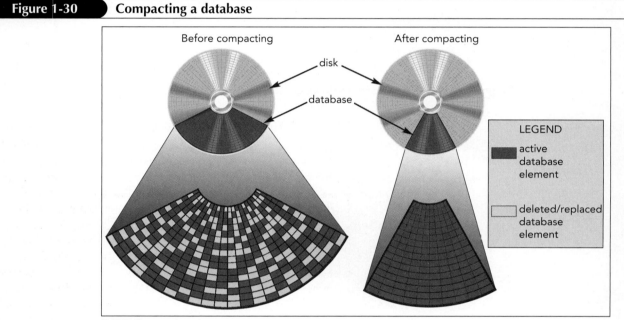

© 2014 Cengage Learning

When you compact a database, Access repairs the database at the same time, if necessary. In some cases, Access detects that a database is damaged when you try to open it and gives you the option to compact and repair it at that time. For example, the data in your database might become damaged, or corrupted, if you exit the Access program suddenly by turning off your computer. If you think your database might be damaged because it is behaving unpredictably, you can use the Compact & Repair Database option to fix it.

REFERENCE

Compacting and Repairing a Database

- Make sure the database file you want to compact and repair is open.
- Click the FILE tab to display the Info screen in Backstage view.
- Click the Compact & Repair Database button.

Access also allows you to set an option to compact and repair a database file automatically every time you close it. The Compact on Close option is available in the Current Database section of the Access Options dialog box, which you open from

Backstage view by clicking the Options command in the navigation bar. By default, the Compact on Close option is turned off.

Next, you'll compact the Chatham database manually using the Compact & Repair Database option. This will make the database smaller and allow you to work with it more efficiently. After compacting the database, you'll close it.

To compact and repair the Chatham database:

▶ **1.** On the ribbon, click the **FILE** tab to display the Info screen in Backstage view.

▶ **2.** Click the **Compact & Repair Database** button. Access closes Backstage view and returns to the HOME tab. Although nothing visible happens on the screen, Access compacts the Chatham database, making it smaller, and repairs it at the same time.

▶ **3.** Click the **FILE** tab to return to the Info screen, and then click **Close** in the navigation bar. Access closes the Chatham database.

Backing Up and Restoring a Database

Backing up a database is the process of making a copy of the database file to protect your database against loss or damage. The Back Up Database command enables you to back up your database file from within the Access program, while you are working on your database. To use this option, click the FILE tab to display the Info screen in Backstage view, click Save As in the navigation bar, click Back Up Database in the Advanced section of the Save Database As pane, and then click the Save As button. In the Save As dialog box that opens, Access provides a default filename for the backup copy that consists of the same filename as the database you are backing up (for example, "Chatham"), and an underscore character, plus the current date. This filenaming system makes it easy for you to keep track of your database backups and when they were created. To restore a backup database file, you simply copy the backup from the location where it is stored to your hard drive, or whatever device you use to work in Access, and start working with the restored database file. (You will not actually back up the Chatham database in this tutorial unless directed by your instructor to do so.)

INSIGHT

Planning and Performing Database Backups

Experienced database users make it a habit to back up a database before they work with it for the first time, keeping the original data intact. They also make frequent backups while continuing to work with a database; these backups are generally on flash drives, recordable CDs or DVDs, external or network hard drives, or cloud-based storage (such as SkyDrive). Also, it is recommended to store the backup copy in a different location from the original. For example, if the original database is stored on a flash drive, you should not store the backup copy on the same flash drive. If you lose the drive or the drive is damaged, you would lose both the original database and its backup copy.

If the original database file and the backup copy have the same name, restoring the backup copy might replace the original. If you want to save the original file, rename it before you restore the backup copy. To ensure that the restored database has the most current data, you should update the restored database with any changes made to the original between the time you created the backup copy and the time the original database became damaged or lost.

By properly planning for and performing backups, you can avoid losing data and prevent the time-consuming effort required to rebuild a lost or damaged database.

In the following tutorials, you'll help Cindi complete and maintain the Chatham database, and you'll use it to meet the specific information needs of the clinic's employees.

PROSKILLS

Decision Making: When to Use Access vs. Excel

Using a spreadsheet application like Microsoft Excel to manage lists or tables of information works well when the data is simple, such as a list of contacts or tasks. As soon as the data becomes complex enough to separate into tables that need to be related, you start to see the limitations of using a spreadsheet application. The strength of a database application such as Access is in its ability to easily relate one table of information to another. Consider a table of contacts that includes home addresses, with a separate row for each person living at the same address. When an address changes, it's too easy to make a mistake and not update the home address for each person who lives there. To ensure you have the most accurate data at all times, it's important to have only one instance of each piece of data. By creating separate tables that are related, and keeping only one instance of each piece of data, you'll ensure the integrity of the data. Trying to accomplish this in Excel is a complex process, whereas Access is specifically designed for this functionality.

Another limitation of using Excel instead of Access to manage data has to do with the volume of data. Although a spreadsheet can hold thousands of records, a database can hold millions. A spreadsheet containing thousands of pieces of information is cumbersome to use. Think of large-scale commercial applications such as enrollment at a college or tracking customers for a large company. It's hard to imagine managing such information in an Excel spreadsheet. Instead, you'd use a database. Finally, with an Access database, multiple users can access the information it contains at the same time. Although an Excel spreadsheet can be shared, there can be problems when users try to open and edit the same spreadsheet at the same time.

When you're trying to decide whether to use Excel or Access, ask yourself the following questions.

1. Do you need to store data in separate tables that are related to each other?
2. Do you have a very large amount of data to store?
3. Will more than one person need to access the data at the same time?

If you answer "yes" to any of these questions, an Access database is most likely the appropriate application to use.

REVIEW

Session 1.2 Quick Check

1. To copy the records from a table in one database to another table in a different database, the two tables must have the same _____.
2. A(n) _____ is a question you ask about the data stored in a database.
3. The quickest way to create a form is to use the _____.
4. Which view enables you to see the total number of pages in a report and navigate through the report pages?
5. In the Navigation Pane, each database object has a unique _____ to its left that identifies the object's type.
6. _____ a database rearranges the data and objects in a database to decrease its file size and enhance the speed and performance of the database.
7. _____ a database is the process of making a copy of the database file to protect the database against loss or damage.

ASSESS

SAM Projects

Put your skills into practice with SAM Projects! SAM Projects for this tutorial can be found online. If you have a SAM account, go to www.cengage.com/sam2013 to download the most recent Project Instructions and Start Files.

PRACTICE

Review Assignments

Data File needed for the Review Assignments: Company.accdb

For Chatham Community Health Services, Cindi asks you to create a new database to contain information about the vendors that the clinic works with to obtain medical supplies and equipment for the clinic, and the vendors who service and maintain the equipment. Complete the following steps:

1. Create a new, blank database named **Vendor** and save it in the folder where you are storing your files, as specified by your instructor.

2. In Datasheet view for the Table1 table, rename the default ID primary key field to **SupplierID**. Change the data type of the SupplierID field to Short Text.

3. Add the following 10 fields to the new table in the order shown; all of them are Short Text fields except InitialContact, which is a Date/Time field: **Company, Category, Address, City, State, Zip, Phone, ContactFirst, ContactLast,** and **InitialContact**. Resize the columns as necessary so that the complete field names are displayed. Save the table as **Supplier**.

4. Enter the records shown in Figure 1-31 in the Supplier table. For the first record, be sure to enter your first name in the ContactFirst field and your last name in the ContactLast field.

   Note: When entering field values that are shown on multiple lines in the figure, do not try to enter the values on multiple lines. The values are shown on multiple lines in the figure for page spacing purposes only.

Figure 1-31 **Supplier table records**

SupplierID	Company	Category	Address	City	State	Zip	Phone	ContactFirst	ContactLast	InitialContact
ARE318	Aresco Surgical, Inc.	Supplies	48 Vienna St	Bridgeport	CT	06601	203-774-3048	*Student First*	*Student Last*	9/2/2015
GRE364	Greinke Labs, Inc.	Supplies	451 Summit Dr	Tiverton	RI	02878	401-208-9843	Evan	Brighton	1/12/2016
DUR368	Durasurg Equipment, Inc.	Equipment	74 Jessie St	Roanoke	VA	24036	540-340-3829	Kristin	Taylor	12/1/2015
STE472	Sterile Labs of CT, Inc.	Service	938 Gormley Ave	North Branford	CT	06517	203-537-5940	Carmine	San Marcos	11/3/2015
GSE420	GSE Medical, Inc.	Equipment	583 Renovo Dr	Claremont	NH	03743	603-202-4951	John	Vereen	9/10/2015

© 2014 Cengage Learning

5. Cindi created a database named Company that contains a Business table with supplier data. The Supplier table you created has the same design as the Business table. Copy all the records from the **Business** table in the **Company** database (located in the Access1 ► Review folder provided with your Data Files) and then paste them at the end of the Supplier table in the Vendor database.

6. Resize all datasheet columns to their best fit, and then save the Supplier table.

7. Close the Supplier table, and then use the Navigation Pane to reopen it. Note that the records are displayed in primary key order by the values in the SupplierID field.

8. Use the Simple Query Wizard to create a query that includes the Company, Category, ContactFirst, ContactLast, and Phone fields (in that order) from the Supplier table. Name the query **SupplierList**, and then close the query.

9. Use the Form tool to create a form for the Supplier table. Save the form as **SupplierInfo**, and then close it.

10. Use the Report tool to create a report based on the Supplier table. In Layout view, resize all fields except the Company field, so that each field is slightly wider than the longest entry (either the field name itself or an entry in the field). Display the report in Print Preview and verify that all the fields fit across two pages in the report. Save the report as **SupplierDetails**, and then close it.

11. Close the Supplier table, and then compact and repair the Vendor database.

12. Close the Vendor database.

Case Problem 1

APPLY

Data File needed for this Case Problem: Program.accdb

GoGopher! Amol Mehta, a recent college graduate living in Boulder, Colorado, spent months earning money by running errands and completing basic chores for family members and acquaintances, while looking for full-time employment. As his list of customers needing such services continued to grow, Amol decided to start his own business called GoGopher! The business, which Amol operates completely online from his home, offers customers a variety of services—from grocery shopping and household chores to yard work and pet care—on a subscription basis. Clients become members of GoGopher! by choosing the plan that best suits their needs. Each plan provides a certain number of tasks per month to members, for a specified period of time. Amol wants to use Access to maintain information about the members who have joined GoGopher! and the types of plans offered. He needs your help in creating this database. Complete the following:

1. Create a new, blank database named **Gopher** and save it in the folder where you are storing your files, as specified by your instructor.

2. In Datasheet view for the Table1 table, rename the default primary key ID field to **PlanID**. Change the data type of the PlanID field to Short Text.

3. Add the following three fields to the new table in the order shown: **PlanDescription** (a Short Text field), **PlanCost** (a Currency field), and **FeeWaived** (a Yes/No field). Save the table as **Plan**.

4. Enter the records shown in Figure 1-32 in the Plan table. Note: When entering the PlanCost field values, you do not have to type the dollar signs, commas, or decimal places; Access will enter them automatically.

Figure 1-32   Plan table records

when entering currency values, you do not have to type the dollar signs, commas, or decimal places

PlanID	PlanDescription	PlanCost	FeeWaived
301	20 tasks per month for 12 months	$6,000.00	Yes
311	10 tasks per month for 3 months	$750.00	No
304	10 tasks per month for 12 months	$3,000.00	Yes
303	15 tasks per month for 12 months	$4,500.00	Yes
312	8 tasks per month for 3 months	$600.00	No

© 2014 Cengage Learning

5. Amol created a database named Program that contains a Service table with plan data. The Plan table you created has the same design as the Service table. Copy all the records from the **Service** table in the **Program** database (located in the Access1 ▶ Case1 folder provided with your Data Files) and then paste them at the end of the Plan table in the Gopher database.

6. Resize all datasheet columns to their best fit, and then save the Plan table.

7. Close the Plan table, and then use the Navigation Pane to reopen it. Note that the records are displayed in primary key order by the values in the PlanID field.

8. Use the Simple Query Wizard to create a query that includes the PlanID, PlanDescription, and PlanCost fields from the Plan table. In the second Simple Query Wizard dialog box, select the Detail option. (This option appears because the query includes a Currency field.) Save the query as **PlanData**, and then close the query.

9. Use the Form tool to create a form for the Plan table. Save the form as **PlanInfo**, and then close it.

10. Use the Report tool to create a report based on the Plan table. In Layout view, resize the PlanID field so it is slightly wider than the longest entry, which is the field name in this case. Also, resize the box containing the total amount that appears below the PlanCost column by clicking the box and then dragging its bottom border down so that the amount is fully displayed. (The Report Tool calculated this total automatically.) Display the report in Print Preview; then verify that all the fields are within the page area and all field values are fully displayed. Save the report as **PlanList**, print the report (only if asked by your instructor to do so), and then close it.

11. Close the Plan table, and then compact and repair the Gopher database.

12. Close the Gopher database.

Case Problem 2

APPLY

Data File needed for this Case Problem: Consulting.accdb

O'Brien Educational Services   After teaching English in a public high school for 15 years, Karen O'Brien decided to channel her experience in education in a new direction and founded O'Brien Educational Services, a small educational consulting company located in South Bend, Indiana. The company offers tutoring services to high school students to help prepare them for standardized tests, such as the SAT and the ACT. The company provides group, private, and semi-private tutoring sessions to best meet the needs of its students. As her business continues to expand, Karen wants to use Access to maintain information about the tutors who work for her, the students who sign up for tutoring, and the contracts they sign. She needs your help in creating this database. Complete the following steps:

1. Create a new, blank database named **OBrien** and save it in the folder where you are storing your files, as specified by your instructor.

2. In Datasheet view for the Table1 table, rename the default primary key ID field to **TutorID**. Change the data type of the TutorID field to Short Text.

3. Add the following five fields to the new table in the order shown; all of them are Short Text fields *except* HireDate, which is a Date/Time field: **FirstName**, **LastName**, **Degree**, **School**, and **HireDate**. Resize the columns, if necessary, so that the complete field names are displayed. Save the table as **Tutor**.

4. Enter the records shown in Figure 1-33 in the Tutor table. For the first record, be sure to enter your first name in the FirstName field and your last name in the LastName field.

Figure 1-33   Tutor table records

TutorID	FirstName	LastName	Degree	School	HireDate
31-1200	*Student First*	*Student Last*	BA	Pierre University	8/2/2015
68-8234	Caitlin	Shea	MS	Towns University	1/5/2016
55-1234	Samuel	Glick	BA	Manoog College	7/23/2016
69-2254	Sachi	Hatanaka	MA	Wyman College	3/23/2015
71-1698	Richard	Keating	Ph.D	Hobert University	5/3/2015

© 2014 Cengage Learning

5. Karen created a database named Consulting that contains an Instructor table with tutor data. The Tutor table you created has the same design as the Instructor table. Copy all the records from the **Instructor** table in the **Consulting** database (located in the Access1 ▶ Case2 folder provided with your Data Files) and then paste them at the end of the Tutor table in the OBrien database.

6. Resize all datasheet columns to their best fit, and then save the Tutor table.

7. Close the Tutor table, and then use the Navigation Pane to reopen it. Note that the records are displayed in primary key order by the values in the TutorID field.

8. Use the Simple Query Wizard to create a query that includes the FirstName, LastName, and HireDate fields from the Tutor table. Save the query as **StartDate**, and then close the query.

9. Use the Form tool to create a form for the Tutor table. Save the form as **TutorInfo**, and then close it.

10. Use the Report tool to create a report based on the Tutor table. In Layout view, resize the TutorID, FirstName, LastName, and Degree fields so they are slightly wider than the longest entry (either the field name itself or an entry in the field). All six fields should fit within the page area after you resize the specified fields. At the bottom of the report, move the text "Page 1 of 1" to the left so it is within the page area. Display the report in Print Preview; then verify that the fields and page number fit within the page area, and that all field values are fully displayed. Save the report as **TutorList**, print the report (only if asked by your instructor to do so), and then close it.

11. Close the Tutor table, and then compact and repair the OBrien database.

12. Close the OBrien database.

Case Problem 3

Data File needed for this Case Problem: Animal.accdb

Rosemary Animal Shelter   Ryan Lang is the director of the Rosemary Animal Shelter in Cobb County, Georgia. The main goals of the shelter, which has several locations in the county, are to rescue dogs and cats and to find people who will adopt them. The shelter was established by Rosemary Hanson, who dedicated her life to rescuing pets and finding good homes for them. Residents of Cobb County generously donate money, food, and equipment in support of the shelter. Some of these patrons also adopt animals from the shelter. Ryan has asked you to create an Access database to manage information about the animals, patrons, and donations. Complete the following steps:

1. Create a new, blank database named **Shelter** and save it in the folder where you are storing your files, as specified by your instructor.

2. In Datasheet view for the Table1 table, rename the default primary key ID field to **PatronID**. Change the data type of the PatronID field to Short Text.

3. Add the following four Short Text fields to the new table in the order shown: **Title**, **FirstName**, **LastName**, and **Phone**. Save the table as **Patron**.

4. Enter the records shown in Figure 1-34 in the Patron table. For the first record, be sure to enter your title in the Title field, your first name in the FirstName field, and your last name in the LastName field.

Figure 1-34   Patron table records

PatronID	Title	FirstName	LastName	Phone
30405	*Student Title*	*Student First*	*Student Last*	770-427-9300
33287	Dr.	Ali	Haddad	770-528-8973
32189	Mrs.	Gini	Smith	770-499-2775
36028	Mr.	Michael	Carlucci	678-283-6334
30753	Ms.	Cynthia	Crosby	678-444-2676

© 2014 Cengage Learning

5. Ryan created a database named Animal that contains a Donor table with data about patrons. The Patron table you created has the same design as the Donor table. Copy all the records from the **Donor** table in the **Animal** database (located in the Access1 ▸ Case3 folder provided with your Data Files) and then paste them at the end of the Patron table in the Shelter database.

6. Resize all datasheet columns to their best fit, and then save the Patron table.

7. Close the Patron table, and then use the Navigation Pane to reopen it. Note that the records are displayed in primary key order by the values in the PatronID field.

⊕ **Explore** 8. Use the Simple Query Wizard to create a query that includes all the fields in the Patron table *except* the Title field. (*Hint*: Use the ⟩⟩ and ⟨ buttons to select the necessary fields.) Save the query using the name **PatronPhoneList**.

⊕ **Explore** 9. The query results are displayed in order by the PatronID field values. You can specify a different order by sorting the query. Display the HOME tab. Then, click the insertion point anywhere in the LastName column to make it the current field. In the Sort & Filter group on the HOME tab, click the Ascending button. The records are now listed in order by the values in the LastName field. Save and close the query.

⊕ **Explore** 10. Use the Form tool to create a form for the Patron table. In the new form, navigate to record 15 (the record with PatronID 33765), and then print the form *for the current record only*. (*Hint*: You must use the Print dialog box in order to print only the current record. Go to Backstage view, click Print in the navigation bar, and then click Print to open the Print dialog box. Click the Selected Record(s) option button and then click the OK button to print the current record.) Save the form as **PatronInfo**, and then close it.

11. Use the Report tool to create a report based on the Patron table. In Layout view, resize each field so it is slightly wider than the longest entry (either the field name itself or an entry in the field). All five fields should fit within the page area after resizing. At the bottom of the report, move the text "Page 1 of 1" to the left so it is within the page area. Display the report in Print Preview, then verify that the fields and page number fit within the page area and that all field values are fully displayed. Save the report as **PatronList**. Print the report (only if asked by your instructor to do so), and then close it.

12. Close the Patron table, and then compact and repair the Shelter database.

13. Close the Shelter database.

Case Problem 4

Data File needed for this Case Problem: Tour.accdb

Stanley EcoTours Janice and Bill Stanley live in Pocatello, Idaho, and are the proud owners and operators of Stanley EcoTours. Their passion is to encourage people to visit natural areas around the world in a responsible manner that does not harm the environment. Their advertising has drawn clients from Idaho, Wyoming, Montana, and Canada. As the interest in ecotourism grows, Janice and Bill's business is also expanding to include more tours in Africa and South America. Because of the growth in business that they anticipate, Janice and Bill realize their current recordkeeping system is inadequate. They would like you to build an Access database to manage information about guests, tours, and reservations. Complete the following:

1. Create a new, blank database named **Stanley** and save it in the folder where you are storing your files, as specified by your instructor.

2. In Datasheet view for the Table1 table, rename the default primary key ID field to **GuestID**. Change the data type of the GuestID field to Short Text.

3. Add the following eight Short Text fields to the new table in the order shown: **GuestFirst**, **GuestLast**, **Address**, **City**, **State/Prov**, **PostalCode**, **Country**, and **Phone**. Save the table as **Guest**.

CHALLENGE

4. Enter the records shown in Figure 1-35 in the Guest table. For the first record, be sure to enter your first name in the GuestFirst field and your last name in the GuestLast field.

Figure 1-35	Guest table records

GuestID	GuestFirst	GuestLast	Address	City	State/Prov	PostalCode	Country	Phone
401	*Student First*	*Student Last*	10 Winter Ave	Boise	ID	83702	USA	208-344-0975
417	Isabelle	Rouy	227 Front Ln	Calgary	AB	T1Y 2N7	Canada	403-226-0065
403	Brian	Anderson	5003 Grant Blvd	Great Falls	MT	59401	USA	406-761-4515
425	Kelly	Skolnik	15 Tobin Dr	Red Deer	AB	T4N 3D5	Canada	403-755-1597
420	Alberto	Lopez	991 Crestview Dr	Butte	MT	59701	USA	406-782-1183

© 2014 Cengage Learning

5. Bill created a database named Tour that contains a Customer table with data about guests. The Guest table you created has the same design as the Customer table. Copy all the records from the **Customer** table in the **Tour** database (located in the Access1 ▶ Case4 folder provided with your Data Files) and then paste them at the end of the Guest table in the Stanley database.

6. Resize all datasheet columns to their best fit, and then save the Guest table.

7. Close the Guest table, and then use the Navigation Pane to reopen it. Note that the records are displayed in primary key order.

8. Use the Simple Query Wizard to create a query that includes the following fields from the Guest table, in the order shown: GuestID, GuestLast, GuestFirst, State/Prov, and Phone. Name the query **GuestData**.

✦ Explore 9. The query results are displayed in order by the GuestID field values. You can specify a different order by sorting the query. Display the HOME tab. Then, click the insertion point anywhere in the State/Prov column to make it the current field. In the Sort & Filter group on the HOME tab, click the Ascending button. The records are now listed in order by the values in the State/Prov field. Save and close the query.

✦ Explore 10. Use the Form tool to create a form for the Guest table. In the new form, navigate to record 10 (the record with GuestID 412), and then print the form *for the current record only*. (*Hint*: You must use the Print dialog box in order to print only the current record. Go to Backstage view, click Print in the navigation bar, and then click Print to open the Print dialog box. Click the Selected Record(s) option button and then click the OK button to print the current record.) Save the form as **GuestInfo**, and then close it.

11. Use the Report tool to create a report based on the Guest table. In Layout view, resize each field so it is slightly wider than the longest entry (either the field name itself or an entry in the field). At the bottom of the report, move the text "Page 1 of 1" to the left so it is within the page area on the report's first page. Display the report in Print Preview and notice that the columns of the report are still spread across two pages, even after resizing the fields. Save the report as **GuestList**.

✦ Explore 12. In the Close Preview group, click the Close Print Preview button to return to the report in Layout view. To make more room on the first page, you'll delete the Address, PostalCode, and Country columns from the report. Click anywhere in the Address column to make it active. Click the ARRANGE tab (one of the REPORT LAYOUT TOOLS contextual tabs), and then click the Select Column button in the Rows & Columns group. Click the HOME tab, and then click the Delete button in the Records group to delete the selected column from the report. Repeat this process to delete the PostalCode and Country columns. The remaining six fields should now all fit on the report's first page.

13. Display the report in Print Preview again, then verify that the fields and page number fit within the page area and that all field values are fully displayed.

14. Save the report, print it (only if asked by your instructor to do so), and then close it.

15. Close the Guest table, and then compact and repair the Stanley database.

16. Close the Stanley database.

Building a Database and Defining Table Relationships

Creating the Billing and Patient Tables

OBJECTIVES

Session 2.1
- Learn the guidelines for designing databases and setting field properties
- Create a table in Design view
- Define fields, set field properties, and specify a table's primary key
- Modify the structure of a table
- Change the order of fields in Design view
- Add new fields in Design view
- Change the Format property for a field in Datasheet view
- Modify field properties in Design view

Session 2.2
- Import data from an Excel worksheet
- Create a table by importing an existing table structure
- Add fields to a table with the Data Type gallery
- Delete and rename fields
- Change the data type for a field in Design view
- Set the Default Value property for a field
- Add data to a table by importing a text file
- Define a relationship between two tables

Case | *Chatham Community Health Services*

The Chatham database currently contains one table, the Visit table. Cindi Rodriguez also wants to track information about the clinic's patients and the invoices sent to them for services provided by Chatham Community Health Services. This information includes such items as each patient's name and address, and the amount and billing date for each invoice.

In this tutorial, you'll create two new tables in the Chatham database—named Billing and Patient—to contain the additional data Cindi wants to track. You will use two different methods for creating the tables, and learn how to modify the fields. After adding records to the tables, you will define the necessary relationships between the tables in the Chatham database to relate the tables, enabling Cindi and her staff to work with the data more efficiently.

STARTING DATA FILES

Access1 → **Tutorial**

Chatham.accdb *(cont.)*
Invoices.xlsx
Kelly.accdb
Patient.txt

Review

Supplies.xlsx
Vendor.accdb *(cont.)*

Case1

Customers.txt
Gopher.accdb *(cont.)*

Case2

Agreements.xlsx
Client.accdb
OBrien.accdb *(cont.)*
Students.txt

Case3

Animals.txt
Donations.xlsx
Shelter.accdb *(cont.)*

Case4

Bookings.txt
Stanley.accdb *(cont.)*
Travel.accdb

Session 2.1 Visual Overview:

Design view allows you to define or modify a table structure or the properties of the fields in a table.

The default name for a new table you create in Design view is Table1. This name appears on the tab for the new table.

The top portion of the Table window in Design view is called the **Table Design grid**. Here, you enter values for the Field Name, Data Type, and Description field properties.

After you assign a data type to a field, the General tab displays additional field properties for that data type. Initially, most field properties are assigned default values.

When defining the fields in a table, you can move from the Table Design grid to the Field Properties pane by pressing the **F6 key**.

TABLE TOOLS   CH

FILE   HOME   CREATE   EXTERNAL DATA   DATABASE TOOLS   DESIGN

View

Primary Key   Builder   Test Validation Rules   Insert Rows   Delete Rows   Modify Lookups   Property Sheet   Indexes   Create Data Macros   Re Dele

Views   Tools   Show/Hide   Field, Record & Ta

Navigation Pane

Table1

Field Name   Data Type

In the Field Name column, you enter the name for each new field in the table. When you first open a new Table window in Design view, Field Name is the current property.

In the Data Type column, you select the appropriate data type for each new field in the table. The data type determines what field values you can enter for a field and what other properties the field will have. The default data type for a new field is Short Text.

Field Prope

General   Lookup

Design view. F6 = Switch panes. F1 = Help.

Table Window in Design View

Chatham : Database- E:\Access1\Tutorial\Chatham.accdb (Access...   ?   —   🗗   ✕

ESIGN   Sign in 👤

E TOOLS

ate Data   Rename/   Relationships   Object
acros ▾   Delete Macro   Dependencies
, Record & Table Events   Relationships

Description (Optional)

> You can use the **Description property** to enter an optional description for a field to explain its purpose or usage. A field's Description property can be up to 255 characters long, and its value appears on the status bar when you view the table datasheet.

> The bottom portion of the Table window in Design view is called the **Field Properties pane**. Here, you select values for all other field properties, most of which are optional.

Field Properties

> The purpose or characteristics of the current property (Field Name, in this case) appear in this section of the Field Properties pane.

A field name can be up to 64 characters long,
including spaces. Press F1 for help on field
names.

> You can display more complete Help information about the current property by pressing the **F1 key**.

Guidelines for Designing Databases

A database management system can be a useful tool, but only if you first carefully design the database so that it meets the needs of its users. In database design, you determine the fields, tables, and relationships needed to satisfy the data and processing requirements. When you design a database, you should follow these guidelines:

- **Identify all the fields needed to produce the required information.** For example, Cindi needs information about patients, visits, and invoices. Figure 2-1 shows the fields that satisfy these information requirements.

Figure 2-1   Cindi's data requirements

VisitID	InvoiceDate
PatientID	Reason
InvoiceAmt	Phone
FirstName	WalkIn
LastName	Email
Address	VisitDate
City	InvoiceNum
State	InvoicePaid
Zip	BirthDate

© 2014 Cengage Learning

- **Organize each piece of data into its smallest useful part.** For example, Cindi could store each patient's complete name in one field called PatientName instead of using two fields called FirstName and LastName, as shown in Figure 2-1. However, doing so would make it more difficult to work with the data. If Cindi wanted to view the records in alphabetical order by last name, she wouldn't be able to do so with field values such as "Ben Li" and "Amanda Fox" stored in a PatientName field. She could do so with field values such as "Li" and "Fox" stored separately in a LastName field.
- **Group related fields into tables.** For example, Cindi grouped the fields related to visits into the Visit table, which you created in Tutorial 1. The fields related to invoices are grouped into the Billing table, and the fields related to patients are grouped into the Patient table. Figure 2-2 shows the fields grouped into all three tables for the Chatham database.

Figure 2-2   Cindi's fields grouped into tables

Visit table	Billing table	Patient table
VisitID	InvoiceNum	PatientID
PatientID	VisitID	LastName
VisitDate	InvoiceDate	FirstName
Reason	InvoiceAmt	BirthDate
WalkIn	InvoicePaid	Phone
		Address
		City
		State
		Zip
		Email

© 2014 Cengage Learning

- **Determine each table's primary key.** Recall that a primary key uniquely identifies each record in a table. For some tables, one of the fields, such as a credit card number, naturally serves the function of a primary key. For other tables, two or more fields might be needed to function as the primary key. In these cases, the primary key is called a **composite key**. For example, a school grade table would use a combination of student number, term, and course code to serve as the primary key. For a third category of tables, no single field or combination of fields can uniquely identify a record in a table. In these cases, you need to add a field whose sole purpose is to serve as the table's primary key. For Cindi's tables, VisitID is the primary key for the Visit table, InvoiceNum is the primary key for the Billing table, and PatientID is the primary key for the Patient table.
- **Include a common field in related tables.** You use the common field to connect one table logically with another table. For example, Cindi's Visit and Patient tables include the PatientID field as a common field. Recall that when you include the primary key from one table as a field in a second table to form a relationship, the field in the second table is called a foreign key; therefore, the PatientID field is a foreign key in the Visit table. With this common field, Cindi can find all visits to the clinic made by a particular patient; she can use the PatientID value for a patient and search the Visit table for all records with that PatientID value. Likewise, she can determine which patient made a particular visit by searching the Patient table to find the one record with the same PatientID value as the corresponding value in the Visit table. Similarly, the VisitID field is a common field, serving as the primary key in the Visit table and a foreign key in the Billing table.
- **Avoid data redundancy.** When you store the same data in more than one place, **data redundancy** occurs. With the exception of common fields to connect tables, you should avoid data redundancy because it wastes storage space and can cause inconsistencies. An inconsistency would exist, for example, if you type a field value one way in one table and a different way in the same table or in a second table. Figure 2-3, which contains portions of potential data stored in the Patient and Visit tables, shows an example of incorrect database design that has data redundancy in the Visit table. In Figure 2-3, the LastName field in the Visit table is redundant, and one value for this field was entered incorrectly, in three different ways.

Figure 2-3   Incorrect database design with data redundancy

Patient table

PatientID	Last Name	FirstName	Address
22542	Diaz	Anna	93 Gates Ln
22544	Sutherland	Max	48 Vine St
22546	Ingram	Julia	834 Kiefer Rd
22560	Lewis	Patrice	15 Prince Rd
22561	Shaw	Daniel	33 Agnes Ct

data redundancy

Visit table

VisitID	PatientID	Last Name	VisitDate	WalkIn
1535	22546	Ingraham	11/12/2015	Yes
1570	22561	Shaw	1/11/2016	Yes
1571	22546	Ingrams	1/15/2016	No
1591	22544	Sutherland	1/26/2016	Yes
1601	22542	Diaz	2/2/2016	No
1620	22546	Engram	3/7/2016	No
1638	22560	Lewis	3/11/2016	Yes

inconsistent data

© 2014 Cengage Learning

• **Determine the properties of each field.** You need to identify the **properties**, or characteristics, of each field so that the DBMS knows how to store, display, and process the field values. These properties include the field's name, data type, maximum number of characters or digits, description, valid values, and other field characteristics. You will learn more about field properties later in this tutorial.

The Billing and Patient tables you need to create will contain the fields shown in Figure 2-2. Before creating these new tables in the Chatham database, you first need to learn some guidelines for setting field properties.

Guidelines for Setting Field Properties

As just noted, the last step of database design is to determine which values to assign to the properties, such as the name and data type, of each field. When you select or enter a value for a property, you **set** the property. Access has rules for naming fields and objects, assigning data types, and setting other field properties.

Naming Fields and Objects

You must name each field, table, and other object in an Access database. Access stores these items in the database, using the names you supply. It's best to choose a field or object name that describes the purpose or contents of the field or object so that later you can easily remember what the name represents. For example, the three tables in the Chatham database are named Visit, Billing, and Patient because these names suggest their contents. Note that a table or query name must be unique within a database. A field name must be unique within a table, but it can be used again in another table.

Assigning Field Data Types

Each field must have a data type, which is either assigned automatically by Access or specifically by the table designer. The data type determines what field values you can enter for the field and what other properties the field will have. For example, the Billing table will include an InvoiceDate field, which will store date values, so you will assign the Date/Time data type to this field. Then Access will allow you to enter and manipulate only dates or times as values in the InvoiceDate field.

Figure 2-4 lists the most commonly used data types in Access, describes the field values allowed for each data type, explains when you should use each data type, and indicates the field size of each data type. You can find more complete information about all available data types in Access Help.

Figure 2-4	**Common data types**

Data Type	Description	Field Size
Short Text	Allows field values containing letters, digits, spaces, and special characters. Use for names, addresses, descriptions, and fields containing digits that are *not used in calculations*.	0 to 255 characters; default is 255
Long Text	Allows field values containing letters, digits, spaces, and special characters. Use for long comments and explanations.	1 to 65,535 characters; exact size is determined by entry
Number	Allows positive and negative numbers as field values. A number can contain digits, a decimal point, commas, a plus sign, and a minus sign. Use for fields that will be used in calculations, except those involving money.	1 to 15 digits
Date/Time	Allows field values containing valid dates and times from January 1, 100 to December 31, 9999. Dates can be entered in month/day/year format, several other date formats, or a variety of time formats, such as 10:35 PM. You can perform calculations on dates and times, and you can sort them. For example, you can determine the number of days between two dates.	8 bytes
Currency	Allows field values similar to those for the Number data type, but is used for storing monetary values. Unlike calculations with Number data type decimal values, calculations performed with the Currency data type are not subject to round-off error.	Accurate to 15 digits on the left side of the decimal point and to 4 digits on the right side
AutoNumber	Consists of integer values created automatically by Access each time you create a new record. You can specify sequential numbering or random numbering, which guarantees a unique field value, so that such a field can serve as a table's primary key.	9 digits
Yes/No	Limits field values to yes and no, on and off, or true and false. Use for fields that indicate the presence or absence of a condition, such as whether an order has been filled or whether an invoice has been paid.	1 character
Hyperlink	Consists of text used as a hyperlink address, which can have up to four parts: the text that appears in a field or control; the path to a file or page; a location within the file or page; and text displayed as a ScreenTip.	Up to 65,535 characters total for the four parts of the hyperlink

© 2014 Cengage Learning

Setting Field Sizes

The **Field Size property** defines a field value's maximum storage size for Short Text, Number, and AutoNumber fields only. The other data types have no Field Size property because their storage size is either a fixed, predetermined amount or is determined automatically by the field value itself, as shown in Figure 2-4. A Short Text field has a default field size of 255 characters; you can also set its field size by entering a number from 0 to 255. For example, the FirstName and LastName fields in the Patient table will be Short Text fields with sizes of 20 characters and 25 characters, respectively. These field sizes will accommodate the values that will be entered in each of these fields.

Decision Making: Specifying the Field Size Property for Number Fields

When you use the Number data type to define a field, you need to decide what the Field Size setting should be for the field. You should set the Field Size property based on the largest value that you expect to store in that field. Access processes smaller data sizes faster, using less memory, so you can optimize your database's performance and its storage space by selecting the correct field size for each field. Field Size property settings for Number fields are as follows:

- **Byte**: Stores whole numbers (numbers with no fractions) from 0 to 255 in one byte
- **Integer**: Stores whole numbers from –32,768 to 32,767 in two bytes
- **Long Integer** (default): Stores whole numbers from –2,147,483,648 to 2,147,483,647 in four bytes
- **Single**: Stores positive and negative numbers to precisely seven decimal places in four bytes
- **Double**: Stores positive and negative numbers to precisely 15 decimal places in eight bytes
- **Replication ID**: Establishes a unique identifier for replication of tables, records, and other objects in databases created using Access 2003 and earlier versions in 16 bytes
- **Decimal**: Stores positive and negative numbers to precisely 28 decimal places in 12 bytes

Choosing an appropriate field size is important to optimize efficiency. For example, it would be wasteful to use the Long Integer field size for a Number field that will store only whole numbers ranging from 0 to 255 because the Long Integer field size uses four bytes of storage space. A better choice would be the Byte field size, which uses one byte of storage space to store the same values. By first gathering and analyzing information about the number values that will be stored in a Number field, you can make the best decision for the field's Field Size property and ensure the most efficient user experience for the database.

Setting the Caption Property for Fields

The **Caption property** for a field specifies how the field name is displayed in database objects, including table and query datasheets, forms, and reports. If you don't set the Caption property, Access displays the field name as the column heading or label for a field. For example, field names such as InvoiceAmt and InvoiceDate in the Billing table can be difficult to read. Setting the Caption property for these fields to "Invoice Amt" and "Invoice Date" would make it easier for users to read the field names and work with the database.

Setting the Caption Property vs. Naming Fields

Although Access allows you to include spaces in field names, this practice is not recommended because the spaces cause problems when you try to perform more complex tasks with the data in your database. Setting the Caption property allows you to follow best practices for naming fields, such as not including spaces in field names, while still providing users with more readable field names in datasheets, forms, and reports.

In Tutorial 1, you created the Chatham database file and, within that file, you created the Visit table working in Datasheet view. According to her plan for the Chatham database, Cindi also wants to track information about the invoices the clinic sends to its patients. Next, you'll create the Billing table for Cindi—this time, working in Design view.

Creating a Table in Design View

Creating a table in Design view involves entering the field names and defining the properties for the fields, specifying a primary key for the table, and then saving the table structure. Cindi documented the design for the new Billing table by listing each field's name and data type; each field's size and description (if applicable); and any other properties to be set for each field. See Figure 2-5.

Figure 2-5	Design for the Billing table

Field Name	Data Type	Field Size	Description	Other
InvoiceNum	Short Text	5	Primary key	Caption = Invoice Num
VisitID	Short Text	4	Foreign key	Caption = Visit ID
InvoiceAmt	Currency			Format = Currency
				Decimal Places = 2
				Caption = Invoice Amt
InvoiceDate	Date/Time			Format = mm/dd/yyyy
				Caption = Invoice Date
InvoicePaid	Yes/No			Caption = Invoice Paid

© 2014 Cengage Learning

You'll use Cindi's design as a guide for creating the Billing table in the Chatham database.

To begin creating the Billing table:

1. Start Access and open the **Chatham** database you created in Tutorial 1.

   Trouble? If the security warning is displayed below the ribbon, click the Enable Content button.

2. If the Navigation Pane is open, click the **Shutter Bar Open/Close Button** « to close it.

3. On the ribbon, click the **CREATE** tab.

4. In the Tables group, click the **Table Design** button. A new table named Table1 opens in Design view. Refer to the Session 2.1 Visual Overview for a complete description of the Table window in Design view.

Defining Fields

When you first create a table in Design view, the insertion point is located in the first row's Field Name box, ready for you to begin defining the first field in the table. You enter values for the Field Name, Data Type, and Description field properties, and then select values for all other field properties in the Field Properties pane. These other properties will appear when you move to the first row's Data Type box.

REFERENCE

Defining a Field in Design View

- In the Field Name box, type the name for the field, and then press the Tab key.
- Accept the default Short Text data type, or click the arrow and select a different data type for the field. Press the Tab key.
- Enter an optional description for the field, if necessary.
- Use the Field Properties pane to type or select other field properties, as appropriate.

The first field you need to define is the InvoiceNum field. This field will be the primary key for the Billing table. Each invoice at Chatham Community Health Services is assigned a specific five-digit number. Although the InvoiceNum field will contain these number values, the numbers will never be used in calculations; therefore, you'll assign the Short Text data type to this field. Any time a field contains number values that will not be used in calculations—such as phone numbers, zip codes, and so on—you should use the Short Text data type instead of the Number data type.

To define the InvoiceNum field:

TIP

You can also press the Enter key to move from one property to the next in the Table Design grid.

1. Type **InvoiceNum** in the first row's Field Name box, and then press the **Tab** key to advance to the Data Type box. The default data type, Short Text, appears highlighted in the Data Type box, which now also contains an arrow, and the field properties for a Short Text field appear in the Field Properties pane. See Figure 2-6.

Figure 2-6	Table window after entering the first field name

Notice that the right side of the Field Properties pane now provides an explanation for the current property, Data Type.

Trouble? If you make a typing error, you can correct it by clicking to position the insertion point, and then using either the Backspace key to delete characters to the left of the insertion point or the Delete key to delete characters to the right of the insertion point. Then type the correct text.

Because the InvoiceNum field values will not be used in calculations, you will accept the default Short Text data type for the field.

2. Press the **Tab** key to accept Short Text as the data type and to advance to the Description (Optional) box.

Next you'll enter the Description property value as "Primary key." The value you enter for the Description property will appear on the status bar when you view the table datasheet. Note that specifying "Primary key" for the Description property does *not* establish the current field as the primary key; you use a button on the ribbon to specify the primary key in Design view, which you will do later in this session.

 3. Type **Primary key** in the Description (Optional) box.

Notice the Field Size property for the field. The default setting of 255 for Short Text fields is displayed. You need to change this number to 5 because all invoice numbers at Chatham Community Health Services contain only five digits.

 4. Double-click the number **255** in the Field Size property box to select it, and then type **5**.

Finally, you need to set the Caption property for the field so that its name appears with a space, as "Invoice Num."

 5. Click the **Caption** property box, and then type **Invoice Num**. The definition of the first field is complete. See Figure 2-7.

Figure 2-7 **InvoiceNum field defined**

Short Text data type is selected

Description property entered

Field Size property set

Caption property set

Field Name	Data Type	
InvoiceNum	Short Text	Primary key

Field Properties

General | Lookup

Field Size	5
Format	
Input Mask	
Caption	Invoice Num
Default Value	
Validation Rule	
Validation Text	
Required	No
Allow Zero Length	Yes
Indexed	Yes (Duplicates OK)
Unicode Compression	Yes
IME Mode	No Control
IME Sentence Mode	None
Text Align	General

Design view. F6 = Switch panes. F1 = Help.

Cindi's Billing table design (Figure 2-5) shows VisitID as the second field. Because Cindi and other staff members need to relate information about invoices to the visit data in the Visit table, the Billing table must include the VisitID field, which is the Visit table's primary key. Recall that when you include the primary key from one table as a field in a second table to connect the two tables, the field is a foreign key in the second table. The field must be defined in the same way in both tables—that is, the field properties, including field size and data type, must match exactly.

Next, you will define VisitID as a Short Text field with a field size of 4. Later in this session, you'll change the Field Size property for the VisitID field in the Visit table to 4 so that the field definition is the same in both tables.

To define the VisitID field:

1. In the Table Design grid, click the second row's Field Name box, type **VisitID** in the box, and then press the **Tab** key to advance to the Data Type box.

2. Press the **Tab** key to accept Short Text as the field's data type. Because the VisitID field is a foreign key to the Visit table, you'll enter "Foreign key" in the Description (Optional) box to help users of the database understand the purpose of this field.

3. Type **Foreign key** in the Description (Optional) box. Next, you'll change the Field Size property to 4.

4. Press the **F6** key to move to the Field Properties pane. The current entry for the Field Size property, 255, is highlighted.

5. Type **4** to set the Field Size property. Finally, you need to set the Caption property for this field.

6. Press the **Tab** key until the insertion point is in the Caption box, and then type **Visit ID** (be sure to include a space between the two words). You have completed the definition of the second field.

TIP

The quickest way to move back to the Table Design grid is to use the mouse.

The third field in the Billing table is the InvoiceAmt field, which will display the dollar amount of each invoice the clinic sends to its patients. Cindi wants the values to appear with two decimal places because invoice amounts include cents. She also wants the values to include dollar signs, so that the values will be formatted as currency when they are printed in bills sent to patients. The Currency data type is the appropriate choice for this field.

To define the InvoiceAmt field:

1. Click the third row's Field Name box, type **InvoiceAmt** in the box, and then press the **Tab** key to advance to the Data Type box.

2. Click the **Data Type** arrow, click **Currency** in the list, and then press the **Tab** key to advance to the Description (Optional) box.

According to Cindi's design (Figure 2-5), you do not need to enter a description for this field. If you've assigned a descriptive field name and the field does not fulfill a special function (such as primary key), you usually do not enter a value for the optional Description property. InvoiceAmt is a field that does not require a value for its Description property.

Cindi wants the InvoiceAmt field values to be displayed with two decimal places. The **Decimal Places property** specifies the number of decimal places that are displayed to the right of the decimal point.

TIP

You can display the arrow and the list simultaneously by clicking the right side of a box.

3. In the Field Properties pane, click the **Decimal Places** box to position the insertion point there. An arrow appears on the right side of the Decimal Places box. When you position the insertion point or select text in many boxes, Access displays an arrow, which you can click to display a list with options.

4. Click the **Decimal Places** arrow, and then click **2** in the list to specify two decimal places for the InvoiceAmt field values.

5. Press the **Tab** key until the insertion point is in the Caption box, and then type **Invoice Amt**. The definition of the third field is now complete. See Figure 2-8.

Figure 2-8   Table window after defining the first three fields

Notice that the Format property is set to "Currency," which formats the values with dollar signs.

The fourth field in the Billing table is the InvoiceDate field. This field will contain the dates on which invoices are generated for the clinic's patients. You'll define the InvoiceDate field using the Date/Time data type. Also, according to Cindi's design (Figure 2-5), the date values should be displayed in the format mm/dd/yyyy, which is a two-digit month, a two-digit day, and a four-digit year.

To define the InvoiceDate field:

1. Click the fourth row's Field Name box, type **InvoiceDate**, and then press the **Tab** key to advance to the Data Type box.

   You can select a value from the Data Type list as you did for the InvoiceAmt field. Alternately, you can type the property value in the box or type just the first character of the property value.

2. Type **d**. The value in the fourth row's Data Type box changes to "date/Time," with the letters "ate/Time" highlighted. See Figure 2-9.

Figure 2-9	Selecting a value for the Data Type property

"d" typed

"ate/Time" highlighted

3. Press the **Tab** key to advance to the Description (Optional) box. Note that Access changes the value for the Data Type property to "Date/Time."

   Cindi wants the values in the InvoiceDate field to be displayed in a format showing the month, the day, and a four-digit year, as in the following example: 03/11/2016. You use the Format property to control the display of a field value.

4. In the Field Properties pane, click the right side of the **Format** box to display the list of predefined formats for Date/Time fields. See Figure 2-10.

Figure 2-10	Displaying available formats for Date/Time fields

Field Properties

General	Lookup

Format		
Input Mask	General Date	11/12/2015 5:34:23 PM
Caption	Long Date	Thursday, November 12, 2015
Default Value	Medium Date	12-Nov-15
Validation Rule	Short Date	11/12/2015
Validation Text	Long Time	5:34:23 PM
Required	Medium Time	5:34 PM
Indexed	Short Time	17:34
IME Mode	No Control	
IME Sentence Mode	None	
Text Align	General	
Show Date Picker	For dates	

formats for Date/Time fields

The display layout for the field. Select a predefined format or enter a custom format. Press F1 for help on formats.

click to display a list of predefined formats

Design view. F6 = Switch panes. F1 = Help.

Trouble? If you see an arrow instead of a list of predefined formats, click the arrow to display the list.

As noted in the right side of the Field Properties pane, you can either choose a predefined format or enter a custom format. Even though the Short Date format seems to match the format Cindi wants, it displays only one digit for months that contain only one digit. For example, it would display the month of March with only the digit "3"—as in 3/11/2016—instead of displaying the month with two digits, as in 03/11/2016.

Because none of the predefined formats matches the exact layout Cindi wants for the InvoiceDate values, you need to create a custom date format. Figure 2-11 shows some of the symbols available for custom date and time formats.

Figure 2-11   **Symbols for some custom date formats**

Symbol	Description
/	date separator
d	day of the month in one or two numeric digits, as needed (1 to 31)
dd	day of the month in two numeric digits (01 to 31)
ddd	first three letters of the weekday (Sun to Sat)
dddd	full name of the weekday (Sunday to Saturday)
w	day of the week (1 to 7)
ww	week of the year (1 to 53)
m	month of the year in one or two numeric digits, as needed (1 to 12)
mm	month of the year in two numeric digits (01 to 12)
mmm	first three letters of the month (Jan to Dec)
mmmm	full name of the month (January to December)
yy	last two digits of the year (01 to 99)
yyyy	full year (0100 to 9999)

© 2014 Cengage Learning

Cindi wants the dates to be displayed with a two-digit month (mm), a two-digit day (dd), and a four-digit year (yyyy). You'll enter this custom format now.

5. Click the **Format** arrow to close the list of predefined formats, and then type **mm/dd/yyyy** in the Format box.

6. Press the **Tab** key until the insertion point is in the Caption box, and then type **Invoice Date**. See Figure 2-12.

Figure 2-12 Specifying the custom date format

current field

custom date format entered

Caption property entered

Design view. F6 = Switch panes. F1 = Help.

The fifth, and final, field to be defined in the Billing table is InvoicePaid. This field will be a Yes/No field to indicate the payment status of each invoice record stored in the Billing table. Recall that the Yes/No data type is used to define fields that store true/false, yes/no, and on/off field values. When you create a Yes/No field in a table, the default Format property is set to Yes/No.

To define the InvoicePaid field:

1. Click the fifth row's Field Name box, type **InvoicePaid**, and then press the **Tab** key to advance to the Data Type box.

2. Type **y**. Access completes the data type as "yes/No."

3. Press the **Tab** key to select the Yes/No data type and move to the Description (Optional) box. In the Field Properties pane, note that the default format of "Yes/No" is selected, so you do not have to change this property.

4. In the Field Properties pane, click the Caption box, and then type **Invoice Paid**.

You've finished defining the fields for the Billing table. Next, you need to specify the primary key for the table.

Specifying the Primary Key

As you learned earlier, the primary key for a table uniquely identifies each record in the table.

REFERENCE

Specifying a Primary Key in Design View

- Display the table in Design view.
- Click in the row for the field you've chosen to be the primary key to make it the active field. If the primary key will consist of two or more fields, click the row selector for the first field, press and hold down the Ctrl key, and then click the row selector for each additional primary key field.
- In the Tools group on the DESIGN tab, click the Primary Key button.

According to Cindi's design, you need to specify InvoiceNum as the primary key for the Billing table. You can do so while the table is in Design view.

To specify InvoiceNum as the primary key:

TIP

This button is a toggle; you can click it to remove the key symbol.

1. Click in the row for the InvoiceNum field to make it the current field.

2. In the Tools group on the DESIGN tab, click the **Primary Key** button. The Primary Key button in the Tools group is now highlighted, and a key symbol appears in the row selector for the first row, indicating that the InvoiceNum field is the table's primary key. See Figure 2-13.

| Figure 2-13 | InvoiceNum field selected as the primary key |

Primary Key button

key symbol indicates the table's primary key

Understanding the Importance of the Primary Key

Although Access does not require a table to have a primary key, including a primary key offers several advantages:

- A primary key uniquely identifies each record in a table.
- Access does not allow duplicate values in the primary key field. For example, if a record already exists in the Visit table with a VisitID value of 1550, Access prevents you from adding another record with this same value in the VisitID field. Preventing duplicate values ensures the uniqueness of the primary key field.
- When a primary key has been specified, Access forces you to enter a value for the primary key field in every record in the table. This is known as **entity integrity**. If you do not enter a value for a field, you have actually given the field a **null value**. You cannot give a null value to the primary key field because entity integrity prevents Access from accepting and processing that record.
- You can enter records in any order, but Access displays them by default in order of the primary key's field values. If you enter records in no specific order, you are ensured that you will later be able to work with them in a more meaningful, primary key sequence.
- Access responds faster to your requests for specific records based on the primary key.

Saving the Table Structure

The last step in creating a table is to name the table and save the table's structure. When you save a table structure, the table is stored in the database file (in this case, the Chatham database file). Once the table is saved, you can enter data into it. According to Cindi's plan, you need to save the table you've defined as "Billing."

To name and save the Billing table:

▶ 1. On the Quick Access Toolbar, click the **Save** button 🔲. The Save As dialog box opens.

▶ 2. Type **Billing** in the Table Name box, and then press the **Enter** key. Access saves the Billing table in the Chatham database. Notice that the tab for the table now displays the name "Billing" instead of "Table1."

Modifying the Structure of an Access Table

Even a well-designed table might need to be modified. Some changes that you can make to a table's structure in Design view include changing the order of fields and adding new fields.

After meeting with her assistant, Kelly Schwarz, and reviewing the structure of the Billing table, Cindi has changes she wants you to make to the table. First, she wants the InvoiceAmt field to be moved so that it appears right before the InvoicePaid field. Then, she wants you to add a new Short Text field named InvoiceItem to the table to include information about what the invoice is for, such as office visits, lab work, and so on. Cindi would like the InvoiceItem field to be inserted between the InvoiceDate and InvoiceAmt fields.

Moving a Field in Design View

To move a field, you use the mouse to drag it to a new location in the Table Design grid. Although you can move a field in Datasheet view by dragging its column heading to a new location, doing so rearranges only the *display* of the table's fields; the table structure is not changed. To move a field permanently, you must move the field in Design view.

Next, you'll move the InvoiceAmt field so that it is before the InvoicePaid field in the Billing table.

To move the InvoiceAmt field:

▶ **1.** Position the pointer on the row selector for the InvoiceAmt field until the pointer changes to a ➡ shape.

▶ **2.** Click the **row selector** to select the entire InvoiceAmt row.

▶ **3.** Place the pointer on the row selector for the InvoiceAmt field until the pointer changes to ⌖, and then click and drag to the row selector for the InvoicePaid field. Notice that as you drag, the pointer changes to ⌖. See Figure 2-14.

| Figure 2-14 | Moving the InvoiceAmt field in the table structure |

▶ **4.** Release the mouse button. The InvoiceAmt field now appears between the InvoiceDate and InvoicePaid fields in the table structure.

Trouble? If the InvoiceAmt field did not move, repeat Steps 1 through 4, making sure you hold down the mouse button during the drag operation.

Adding a Field in Design View

To add a new field between existing fields, you must insert a row. You begin by selecting the row below where you want the new field to be inserted.

REFERENCE

Adding a Field Between Two Existing Fields

- In the Table window in Design view, select the row below where you want the new field to be inserted.
- In the Tools group on the DESIGN tab, click the Insert Rows button.
- Define the new field by entering the field name, data type, optional description, and any property specifications.

Next, you need to add the InvoiceItem field to the Billing table structure between the InvoiceAmt and InvoicePaid fields.

To add the InvoiceItem field to the Billing table:

1. Click the **InvoicePaid** Field Name box. You need to establish this field as the current field so that the row for the new record will be inserted above this field.

2. In the Tools group on the DESIGN tab, click the **Insert Rows** button. Access adds a new, blank row between the InvoiceAmt and InvoicePaid fields. The insertion point is positioned in the Field Name box for the new row, ready for you to type the name for the new field. See Figure 2-15.

Figure 2-15	Table structure after inserting a row

Trouble? If you selected the InvoicePaid field's row selector and then inserted the new row, you need to click the new row's Field Name box to position the insertion point in it.

You'll define the InvoiceItem field in the new row of the Billing table. This field will be a Short Text field with a field size of 40, and you need to set the Caption property to include a space between the words in the field name.

3. Type **InvoiceItem**, press the **Tab** key to move to the Data Type property, and then press the **Tab** key again to accept the default Short Text data type.

4. Press the **F6** key to move to the Field Size box and to select the default field size, and then type **40**.

5. Press the **Tab** key until the insertion point is in the Caption box, and then type **Invoice Item**. The definition of the new field is complete. See Figure 2-16.

Figure 2-16   **InvoiceItem field added to the Billing table**

6. On the Quick Access Toolbar, click the **Save** button 🖫 to save the changes to the Billing table structure.

7. Click the **Close 'Billing'** button ✕ on the object tab to close the Billing table.

Modifying Field Properties

With the Billing table design complete, you can now go back and modify the properties of the fields in the Visit table you created in Tutorial 1, as necessary. You can make some changes to properties in Datasheet view; for others, you'll work in Design view.

Changing the Format Property in Datasheet View

The Formatting group on the FIELDS tab in Datasheet view allows you to modify some formatting for certain field types. When you format a field, you change the way data is displayed, but not the actual values stored in the table.

Next, you'll check the properties of the VisitDate field in the Visit table to see if any changes are needed to improve the display of the date values.

To modify the VisitDate field's Format property:

1. On the Navigation Pane, click the **Shutter Bar Open/Close Button** ≫ to open the pane. Notice that the Billing table is listed above the Visit table in the Tables section. By default, objects are listed in the pane in alphabetical order.

2. Double-click **Visit** to open the Visit table in Datasheet view.

3. On the Navigation Pane, click the **Shutter Bar Open/Close Button** ≪ to close the pane. See Figure 2-17.

Figure 2-17	Visit table datasheet

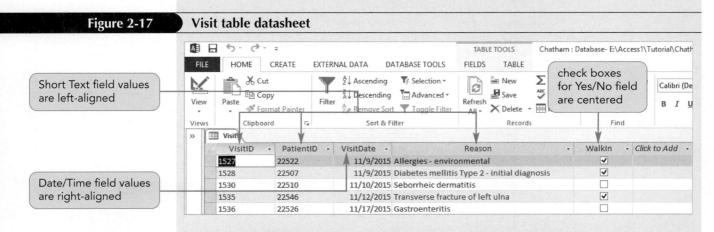

Short Text field values are left-aligned

check boxes for Yes/No field are centered

Date/Time field values are right-aligned

Notice that the values in the three Short Text fields—VisitID, PatientID, and Reason—appear left-aligned within their boxes, and the values in the Date/Time field (VisitDate) appear right-aligned. In Access, values for Short Text fields are left-aligned, and values for Number, Date/Time, and Currency fields are right-aligned. The WalkIn field is a Yes/No field, so its values appear in check boxes that are centered within the column.

4. On the ribbon, click the **FIELDS** tab.

5. Click the first field value in the VisitDate column. The Data Type option shows that this field is a Date/Time field.

   By default, Access assigns the General Date format to Date/Time fields. Note the Format option in the Formatting group; this is the same as the Format property in the Field Properties pane in Design view. Even though the Format box is empty, the VisitDate field has the General Date format applied to it. The General Date format includes settings for date or time values, or a combination of date and time values. However, Cindi wants *only date values* to be displayed in the VisitDate field, so she asks you to specify the Short Date format for the field.

6. In the Formatting group, click the **Format arrow**, and then click **Short Date**. See Figure 2-18.

Figure 2-18   **VisitDate field after modifying the format**

Although no change is apparent in the worksheet—the VisitDate field values already appear with the Short Date setting (for example, 11/9/2015), as part of the default General Date format—the field now has the Short Date format applied to it. This ensures that only date field values, and not time or date/time values, are allowed in the field.

TIP

When working with date values, you can type dates directly or click the date picker shown in Figure 2-18 to select a date from an interactive calendar.

Changing Properties in Design View

Recall that each of the Short Text fields in the Visit table—VisitID, PatientID, and Reason—still has the default field size of 255, which is too large for the data contained in these fields. Also, the VisitID and PatientID fields need descriptions to identify them as the primary and foreign keys, respectively, in the table. Finally, each of these fields needs a caption either to include a space between the words in the field name or to make the name more descriptive. You can make all of these property changes more easily in Design view.

To modify the Field Size, Description, and Caption field properties:

TIP

You can also click the Design View button in the far right of the status bar to switch to Design view.

1. In the Views group on the FIELDS tab, click the **View** button. The table is displayed in Design view with the VisitID field selected. You need to enter a Description property value for this field, the primary key in the table, and change its Field Size property to 4 because each visit number at Chatham Community Health Services consists of four digits.

2. Press the **Tab** key until the insertion point is in the Description (Optional) box, and then type **Primary key**.

3. Press the **F6** key to move to and select the default setting of 255 for the Field Size property, and then type **4**. Next you need to set the Caption property for this field.

4. Press the **Tab** key until the insertion point is in the Caption box, and then type **Visit ID**.

   Next you need to enter a Description property value for the PatientID field, a foreign key in the table, and set its Field Size property to 5 because each PatientID number at Chatham Community Health Services consists of five digits. You also need to set this field's Caption property.

5. Click the **Description (Optional)** box for the PatientID field, and then type **Foreign key**.

6. Press the **F6** key, type **5**, press the **Tab** key until the insertion point is in the Caption box, and then type **Patient ID**.

   Next you'll set the Caption property for the VisitDate field.

7. Click the **VisitDate** Field Name box, click the **Caption** box, and then type **Date of Visit**.

   For the Reason field, you will set the Field Size property to 60. This size can accommodate the longer values in the Reason field. You'll also set this field's Caption property to provide a more descriptive name.

8. Click the **Reason** Field Name box, press the **F6** key, type **60**, press the **Tab** key until the insertion point is in the Caption box, and then type **Reason/Diagnosis**.

   Finally, you'll set the Caption property for the WalkIn field.

9. Click the **WalkIn** Field Name box, click the **Caption** box, and then type **Walk-in?** See Figure 2-19.

Figure 2-19   Visit table after modifying field properties

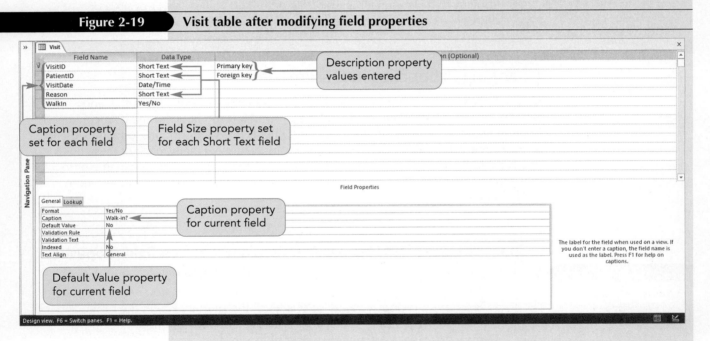

Notice that the WalkIn field's Default Value property is automatically set to "No," which means the check box for this field will be empty for each new record. This is the default for this property for any Yes/No field. You can set the Default Value property for other types of fields to make data entry easier. You'll learn more about setting this property in the next session.

The changes to the Visit table's properties are now complete, so you can save the table and view the results of your changes in Datasheet view.

To save and view the modified Visit table:

1. On the Quick Access Toolbar, click the **Save** button 🔲 to save the modified table. A dialog box opens informing you that some data may be lost because you decreased the field sizes. Because all of the values in the VisitID, PatientID, and Reason fields contain the same number of or fewer characters than the new Field Size properties you set for each field, you can ignore this message.

2. Click the **Yes** button.

3. In the Views group on the DESIGN tab, click the **View** button to display the Visit table in Datasheet view. Notice that each column (field) heading now displays the text you specified in the Caption property for that field. See Figure 2-20.

Figure 2-20   Modified Visit table in Datasheet view

column headings display Caption property values

4. Click the **Close 'Visit'** button ☒ on the object tab to close the Visit table.

5. If you are not continuing to Session 2.2, click the **FILE** tab, and then click **Close** in the navigation bar to close the Chatham database.

You have created the Billing table and made modifications to its design. In the next session, you'll add records to the Billing table and create the Patient table in the Chatham database.

Session 2.1 Quick Check

REVIEW

1. What guidelines should you follow when designing a database?
2. What is the purpose of the Data Type property for a field?
3. The _____ property specifies how a field's name is displayed in database objects, including table and query datasheets, forms, and reports.
4. For which three types of fields can you assign a field size?
5. The default Field Size property setting for a Short Text field is _____.
6. In Design view, which key do you press to move from the Table Design grid to the Field Properties pane?
7. List three reasons why you should specify a primary key for an Access table.

Session 2.2 Visual Overview:

Click the Close button to close the Relationships window.

You click the Show Table button to open the Show Table dialog box. From there, you can choose a table to add to the Relationships window.

The Relationships window illustrates the relationships among a database's tables. Using this window, you can view or change existing relationships, define new relationships between tables, and rearrange the layout of the tables in the window.

The key symbol next to a field name indicates that the field is the table's primary key. For example, PatientID is the primary key for the Patient table.

A one-to-many relationship exists between two tables when one record in the first table matches zero, one, or many records in the second table, and when one record in the second table matches at most one record in the first table. Here, the Patient and Visit tables have a one-to-many relationship because a patient can have many visits, and each visit is associated with only one patient. The two tables are still separate tables, but because they are joined, you can use the data in them as if they were one table.

FILE   HOME   CREATE   EXTERNAL DATA   DATABASE TOOLS   DESIG
RELATIONSHI

Edit Relationships
Clear Layout
Relationship Report
Tools

Show Table
Hide Table
Direct Relationships
All Relationships
Relationships

Close

All Access Obje... «

Search...

Tables
- Billing
- Patient
- Visit

Queries
- VisitList

Forms
- VisitData

Reports
- VisitDetails

Relationships

Patient

1

- PatientID
- LastName
- FirstName
- BirthDate
- Phone
- Address
- City
- State
- Zip
- Email

Ready

Understanding Table Relationships

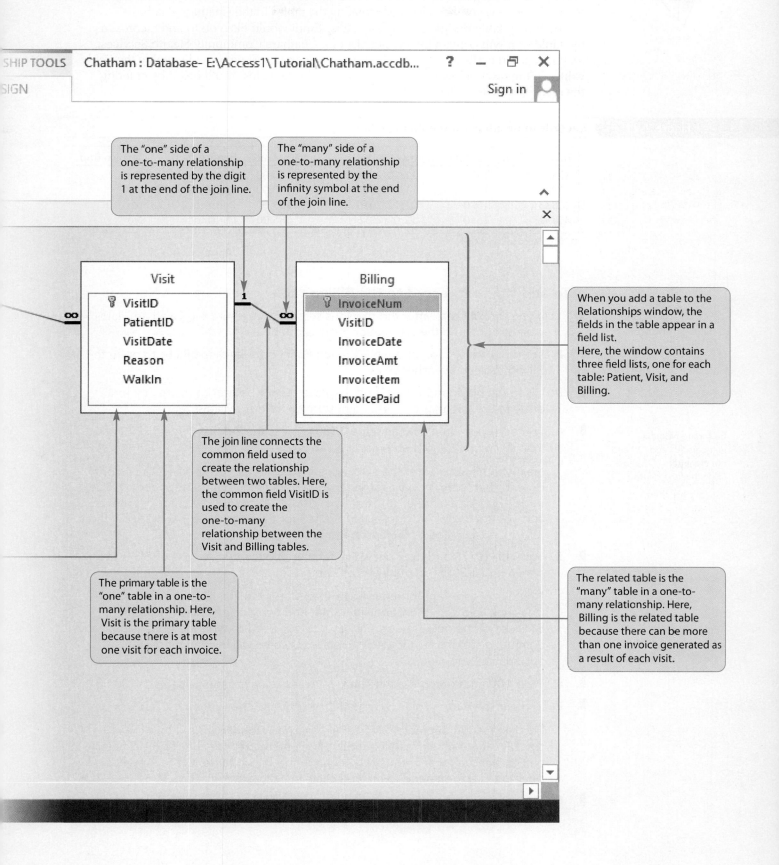

The "one" side of a one-to-many relationship is represented by the digit 1 at the end of the join line.

The "many" side of a one-to-many relationship is represented by the infinity symbol at the end of the join line.

When you add a table to the Relationships window, the fields in the table appear in a field list.
Here, the window contains three field lists, one for each table: Patient, Visit, and Billing.

The join line connects the common field used to create the relationship between two tables. Here, the common field VisitID is used to create the one-to-many relationship between the Visit and Billing tables.

The primary table is the "one" table in a one-to-many relationship. Here, Visit is the primary table because there is at most one visit for each invoice.

The related table is the "many" table in a one-to-many relationship. Here, Billing is the related table because there can be more than one invoice generated as a result of each visit.

Adding Records to a New Table

Before you can begin to define the table relationships illustrated in the Session 2.2 Visual Overview, you need to finish creating the tables in the Chatham database.

The Billing table design is complete. Now, Cindi would like you to add records to the table so it will contain the invoice data for Chatham Community Health Services. As you learned earlier, you add records to a table in Datasheet view by typing the field values in the rows below the column headings for the fields. You'll begin by entering the records shown in Figure 2-21.

Figure 2-21	Records to be added to the Billing table

Invoice Num	Visit ID	Invoice Date	Invoice Amt	Invoice Item	Invoice Paid
35801	1527	11/10/2015	$100.00	Office visit	Yes
35818	1536	11/18/2015	$100.00	Office visit	Yes
35885	1570	01/12/2016	$85.00	Pharmacy	No
35851	1550	12/02/2015	$85.00	Pharmacy	No

© 2014 Cengage Learning

Be sure to type the numbers "0" and "1" and *not* the letters "O" and "I" in the field values.

To add the first record to the Billing table:

1. If you took a break after the previous session, make sure the Chatham database is open and the Navigation Pane is open.

2. In the Tables section of the Navigation Pane, double-click **Billing** to open the Billing table in Datasheet view.

3. Close the Navigation Pane, and then use the ✛ pointer to resize columns, as necessary, so that the field names are completely visible.

4. In the Invoice Num column, type **35801**, press the **Tab** key, type **1527** in the Visit ID column, and then press the **Tab** key.

   Next you need to enter the invoice date. Recall that you specified a custom date format, mm/dd/yyyy, for the InvoiceDate field. You do not need to type each digit; for example, you can type just "3" instead of "03" for the month, and you can type "16" instead of "2016" for the year. Access will display the full value according to the custom date format.

5. Type **11/10/15** and then press the **Tab** key. Notice that Access displays the date "11/10/2015" in the Invoice Date column.

   Next you need to enter the invoice amount for the first record. This is a Currency field with the Currency format and two decimal places specified. Because of the field's properties, you do not need to type the dollar sign, comma, or zeroes for the decimal places; Access will display these items automatically for you.

6. Type **100** and then press the **Tab** key. Access displays the value as "$100.00."

7. In the Invoice Item column, type **Office visit** and then press the **Tab** key.

   The last field in the table, InvoicePaid, is a Yes/No field. Recall that the default value for any Yes/No field is "No"; therefore, the check box is initially empty. For the record you are entering in the Billing table, the invoice has been paid, so you need to insert a checkmark in the check box.

8. Press the **spacebar** to insert a checkmark, and then press the **Tab** key. The values for the first record are entered. See Figure 2-22.

| Figure 2-22 | First record entered in the Billing table |

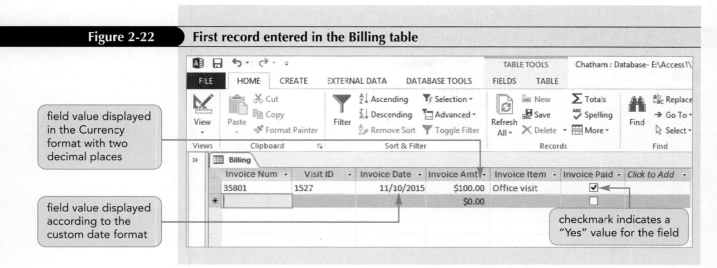

field value displayed in the Currency format with two decimal places

field value displayed according to the custom date format

checkmark indicates a "Yes" value for the field

Now you can add the remaining three records. As you do, you'll learn a keyboard shortcut for inserting the value from the same field in the previous record. A **keyboard shortcut** is a key or combination of keys you press to complete an action more efficiently.

To add the next three records to the Billing table:

1. Refer to Figure 2-21 and enter the values in the second record's Invoice Num, Visit ID, and Invoice Date columns.

    Notice that the value in the second record's Invoice Amt column is $100.00. This value is the exact same value as in the first record. You can quickly insert the value from the same column in the previous record using the **Ctrl + '** (apostrophe) keyboard shortcut. To use this shortcut, you press and hold down the Ctrl key, press the ' key once, and then release both keys. (The plus sign in the keyboard shortcut indicates you're pressing two keys at once; you do not press the + key.)

2. With the insertion point in the Invoice Amt column, press the **Ctrl + '** keys. Access inserts the value "$100.00" in the Invoice Amt column for the second record.

3. Press the **Tab** key to move to the Invoice Item column. Again, the value you need to enter in this column—Office visit—is the same as the value for this column in the previous record. So, you can use the keyboard shortcut again.

4. With the insert on point in the Invoice Item column, press the **Ctrl + '** keys. Access inserts the value "Office visit" in the Invoice Item column for the second record.

5. Press the **Tab** key to move to the Invoice Paid column, press the **spacebar** to insert a checkmark in the check box, and then press the **Tab** key. The second record is entered in the Billing table.

6. Refer to Figure 2-21 to enter the values for the third and fourth records, using the Ctrl + ' keys to enter the values in the fourth record's Invoice Amt and Invoice Item columns. Also, for both records, the invoices have not been paid. Therefore, be sure to press the Tab key to leave the Invoice Paid column values unchecked (signifying "No"). Your table should look like the one in Figure 2-23.

Figure 2-23	Billing table with four records added

To finish entering records in the Billing table, you'll use a method that allows you to import the data.

Importing Data from an Excel Worksheet

Often, the data you want to add to an Access table exists in another file, such as a Word document or an Excel workbook. You can bring the data from other files into Access in different ways. For example, you can copy and paste the data from an open file, or you can **import** the data, which is a process that allows you to copy the data from a source without having to open the source file.

Cindi had been using Excel to track invoice data for Chatham Community Health Services and already created a worksheet, named "Invoices," containing this data. You'll import this Excel worksheet into your Billing table to complete the entry of data in the table. To use the import method, the columns in the Excel worksheet must match the names and data types of the fields in the Access table.

INSIGHT

Caption Property Values and the Import Process

When you import data from an Excel worksheet into an Access table, any Caption property values set for the fields in the table are not considered in the import process. For example, your Access table could have fields such as InvoiceDate and InvoiceAmt with Caption property values of Invoice Date and Invoice Amt, respectively. If the Excel worksheet you are importing has the column headings Invoice Date and Invoice Amt, you might think that the data matches and you can proceed with the import. However, if the underlying field names in the Access table do not match the Excel worksheet column headings exactly, the import process will fail. It's a good idea to double-check to make sure that the actual Access field names—and not just the column headings displayed in a table datasheet (as specified by the Caption property)—match the Excel worksheet column headings. If there are differences, you can change the column headings in the Excel worksheet to match the Access table field names before you import the data, ensuring that the process will work correctly.

The Invoices worksheet contains the following columns: InvoiceNum, VisitID, InvoiceDate, InvoiceAmt, InvoiceItem, and InvoicePaid. These column headings match the field names in the Billing table exactly, so you can import the data. Before you import data into a table, you need to close the table.

To import the Invoices worksheet into the Billing table:

1. Click the **Close 'Billing'** button ⊠ on the object tab to close the Billing table. A dialog box opens asking if you want to save the changes to the table layout. This dialog box opens because you resized the table columns.

2. Click the **Yes** button in the dialog box.

3. On the ribbon, click the **EXTERNAL DATA** tab.

4. In the Import & Link group on the EXTERNAL DATA tab, click the **Excel** button. The Get External Data - Excel Spreadsheet dialog box opens. See Figure 2-24.

Figure 2-24	Get External Data - Excel Spreadsheet dialog box

click to find the Excel workbook containing the data you want to import

you might see a different path here

option for adding records to an existing table

Trouble? If the Export - Excel Spreadsheet dialog box opens instead of the dialog box shown in Figure 2-24, you probably clicked the Excel button in the Export group. If so, click the Cancel button in the dialog box, and then repeat Step 4, being sure to click the Excel button in the Import & Link group.

The dialog box provides options for importing the entire worksheet as a new table in the current database, adding the data from the worksheet to an existing table, or linking the data in the worksheet to the table. You need to add, or append, the worksheet data to the Billing table.

5. Click the **Browse** button. The File Open dialog box opens. The Excel workbook file is named "Invoices" and is located in the Access1 ▸ Tutorial folder provided with your Data Files.

6. Navigate to the **Access1 ▸ Tutorial** folder, where your starting Data Files are stored, and then double-click the **Invoices** Excel file. You return to the dialog box.

7. Click the **Append a copy of the records to the table** option button. The box to the right of this option becomes active and displays the Billing table name, because it is the first table listed in the Navigation Pane.

Trouble? If another table name appears in this box, click the arrow on the box, and then click Billing.

> **8.** Click the **OK** button. The first Import Spreadsheet Wizard dialog box opens. See Figure 2-25.

Figure 2-25   **First Import Spreadsheet Wizard dialog box**

selected check box confirms that the first row contains column headings

data from the worksheet to be imported

The dialog box confirms that the first row of the worksheet you are importing contains column headings. The bottom section of the dialog box displays some of the data contained in the worksheet.

TIP

Carefully check the data to make sure it should be imported into the selected table.

> **9.** Click the **Next** button. The second, and final, Import Spreadsheet Wizard dialog box opens. Notice that the Import to Table box shows that the data from the spreadsheet will be imported into the Billing table.

> **10.** Click the **Finish** button. A dialog box opens asking if you want to save the import steps. If you needed to repeat this same import procedure many times, it would be a good idea to save the steps for the procedure. However, you don't need to save these steps because you'll be importing the data only one time. Once the data is in the Billing table, Cindi will no longer use Excel to track invoice data.

> **11.** Click the **Close** button in the dialog box to close it without saving the steps.

The data from the Invoices worksheet has been added to the Billing table. Next, you'll open the table to view the new records.

To open the Billing table and view the imported data:

> **1.** Open the Navigation Pane, and then double-click **Billing** in the Tables section to open the table in Datasheet view.

> **2.** Resize the Invoice Item column to its best fit, scrolling the worksheet and resizing, as necessary.

3. Press the **Ctrl + Home** keys to scroll to the top of the datasheet. Notice that the table now contains a total of 204 records—four records you entered plus 200 records imported from the Invoices worksheet. The records are displayed in primary key order by the values in the Invoice Num column. See Figure 2-26.

| Figure 2-26 | Billing table after importing data from Excel |

records displayed in order by the values in the Invoice Num column

table contains a total of 204 records

4. Save and close the Billing table, and then close the Navigation Pane.

Two of the tables—Visit and Billing—are now complete. According to Cindi's plan for the Chatham database, you need to create a third table, named "Patient," to track data about the clinic's patients. You'll use a different method to create this table.

Creating a Table by Importing an Existing Table Structure

If another Access database contains a table—or even just the design, or structure, of a table—that you want to include in your database, you can import the table and any records it contains or import only the table structure into your database.

Cindi documented the design for the new Patient table by listing each field's name and data type, as well as any applicable field size, description, and caption property values, as shown in Figure 2-27. Note that each field in the Patient table, except BirthDate, will be a Short Text field, and the PatientID field will be the table's primary key.

Figure 2-27   Design for the Patient table

Field Name	Data Type	Field Size	Description	Caption
PatientID	Short Text	5	Primary key	Patient ID
LastName	Short Text	25		Last Name
FirstName	Short Text	20		First Name
BirthDate	Date/Time			Date of Birth
Phone	Short Text	14		
Address	Short Text	35		
City	Short Text	25		
State	Short Text	2		
Zip	Short Text	10		
Email	Short Text	50		

© 2014 Cengage Learning

Cindi's assistant Kelly already created an Access database containing a Patient table design. She never entered any records into the table because she wasn't sure if the table design was complete or correct. After reviewing the table design, both Kelly and Cindi agree that it contains some of the fields they want to track, but that some changes are needed. So, you can import the table structure in Kelly's database to create the Patient table in the Chatham database, and then modify the imported table to produce the final table structure according to Cindi's design.

To create the Patient table by importing the structure of another table:

1. Make sure the EXTERNAL DATA tab is the active tab on the ribbon.

2. In the Import & Link group, click the **Access** button. The Get External Data - Access Database dialog box opens. This dialog box is similar to the one you used earlier when importing the Excel spreadsheet.

3. Click the **Browse** button. The File Open dialog box opens. The Access database file from which you need to import the table structure is named "Kelly" and is located in the Access1 ▸ Tutorial folder provided with your Data Files.

4. Navigate to the **Access1 ▸ Tutorial** folder, where your starting Data Files are stored, and then double-click the **Kelly** database file. You return to the dialog box.

5. Make sure the **Import tables, queries, forms, reports, macros, and modules into the current database** option button is selected, and then click the **OK** button. The Import Objects dialog box opens. The dialog box contains tabs for importing all the different types of Access database objects—tables, queries, forms, and so on. The Tables tab is the current tab.

6. Click the **Options** button in the dialog box to see all the options for importing tables. See Figure 2-28.

Figure 2-28   Import Objects dialog box

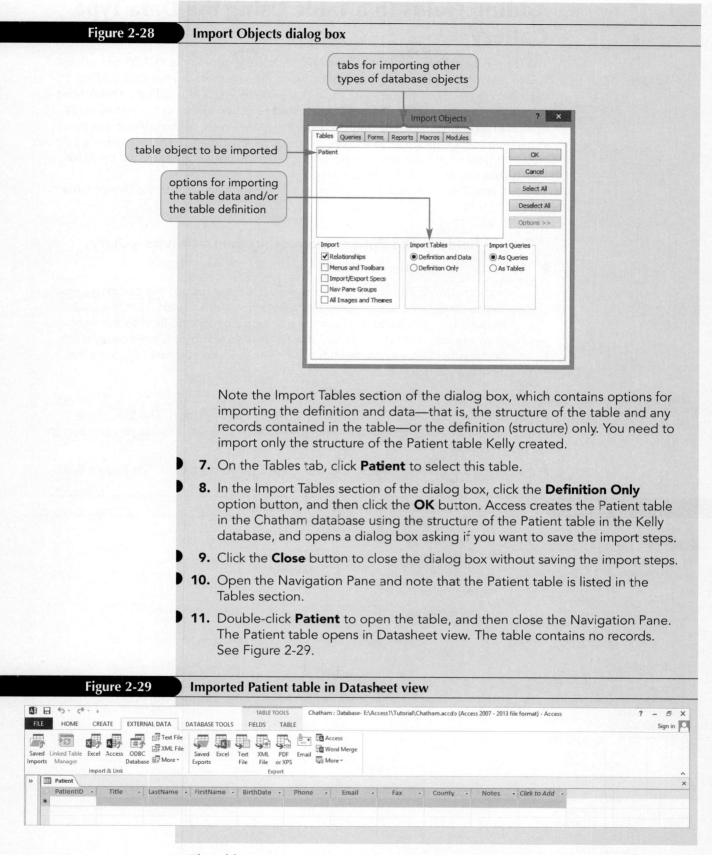

Note the Import Tables section of the dialog box, which contains options for importing the definition and data—that is, the structure of the table and any records contained in the table—or the definition (structure) only. You need to import only the structure of the Patient table Kelly created.

   7. On the Tables tab, click **Patient** to select this table.

   8. In the Import Tables section of the dialog box, click the **Definition Only** option button, and then click the **OK** button. Access creates the Patient table in the Chatham database using the structure of the Patient table in the Kelly database, and opens a dialog box asking if you want to save the import steps.

   9. Click the **Close** button to close the dialog box without saving the import steps.

   10. Open the Navigation Pane and note that the Patient table is listed in the Tables section.

   11. Double-click **Patient** to open the table, and then close the Navigation Pane. The Patient table opens in Datasheet view. The table contains no records. See Figure 2-29.

Figure 2-29   Imported Patient table in Datasheet view

The table structure you imported contains some of the fields Cindi wants, but not all (see Figure 2-27); it also contains some fields Cindi does not want in the Patient table. You can add the missing fields using the Data Type gallery.

Adding Fields to a Table Using the Data Type Gallery

The **Data Type gallery**, available in the Add & Delete group on the FIELDS tab, allows you to add a group of related fields to a table at the same time, rather than adding each field to the table individually. The group of fields you add is called a **Quick Start selection**. For example, the **Address Quick Start selection** adds a collection of fields related to an address, such as Address, City, State, and so on, to the table at one time. When you use a Quick Start selection, the fields added already have properties set. However, you need to review and possibly modify the properties to ensure the fields match your design needs for the database.

Next, you'll use the Data Type gallery to add the missing fields to the Patient table.

To add fields to the Patient table using the Data Type gallery:

1. On the ribbon, click the **FIELDS** tab.

   Note the More Fields button in the Add & Delete group; this button allows you to display the Data Type gallery. Before inserting fields from the Data Type gallery, you need to place the insertion point in the field to the right of where you want to insert the new fields. According to Cindi's design, the Address field should come after the Phone field, so you need to make the next field, Email, the active field.

   Make sure the correct field is active before adding new fields.

2. Click the first row in the **Email** field to make it the active field.

3. In the Add & Delete group, click the **More Fields** button. The Data Type gallery opens and displays options for different types of fields you can add to your table.

4. Scroll the gallery down so the Quick Start section is visible. See Figure 2-30.

Figure 2-30	Patient table with the Data Type gallery displayed

The Quick Start section provides options that will add multiple, related fields to the table at one time. The new fields will be inserted to the left of the current field.

5. In the Quick Start section, click **Address**. Access adds five fields to the table: Address, City, State Province, ZIP Postal, and Country Region. See Figure 2-31.

Figure 2-31 **Patient table after adding fields from the Data Type gallery**

Modifying the Imported Table

Refer back to Cindi's design for the Patient table (Figure 2-27). To finalize the table design, you need to modify the imported table by deleting fields, renaming fields, and changing field data types. You'll begin by deleting fields.

Deleting Fields from a Table Structure

After you've created a table, you might need to delete one or more fields. When you delete a field, you also delete all the values for that field from the table. So, before you delete a field, you should make sure that you want to do so and that you choose the correct field to delete. You can delete fields in either Datasheet view or Design view.

REFERENCE

Deleting a Field from a Table Structure

- In Datasheet view, click anywhere in the column for the field you want to delete.
- In the Add & Delete group on the FIELDS tab, click the Delete button.
or
- In Design view, click the Field Name box for the field you want to delete.
- In the Tools group on the DESIGN tab, click the Delete Rows button.

The Address Quick Start selection added a field named "Country Region" to the Patient table. Cindi doesn't need a field to store country data because all Chatham Community Health Services patients are located in the United States. You'll begin to modify the Patient table structure by deleting the Country Region field.

To delete the Country Region field from the table in Datasheet view:

▶ **1.** Click the first row in the **Country Region** field (if necessary).

▶ **2.** In the Add & Delete group on the FIELDS tab, click the **Delete** button. The Country Region field is removed and the first field, PatientID, is now the active field.

You can also delete fields from a table structure in Design view. You'll switch to Design view to delete the other unnecessary fields.

To delete the fields in Design view:

▶ **1.** In the Views group on the FIELDS tab, click the **View** button. The Patient table opens in Design view. See Figure 2-32.

Figure 2-32	Patient table in Design view

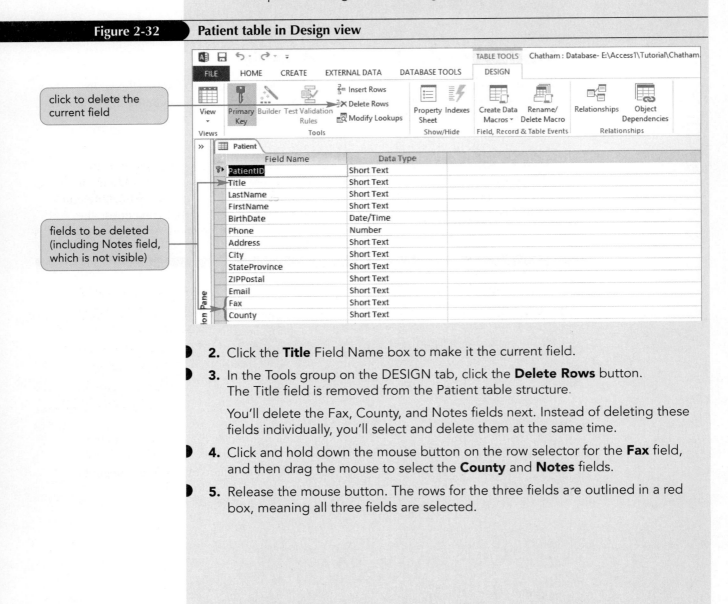

click to delete the current field

fields to be deleted (including Notes field, which is not visible)

▶ **2.** Click the **Title** Field Name box to make it the current field.

▶ **3.** In the Tools group on the DESIGN tab, click the **Delete Rows** button. The Title field is removed from the Patient table structure.

You'll delete the Fax, County, and Notes fields next. Instead of deleting these fields individually, you'll select and delete them at the same time.

▶ **4.** Click and hold down the mouse button on the row selector for the **Fax** field, and then drag the mouse to select the **County** and **Notes** fields.

▶ **5.** Release the mouse button. The rows for the three fields are outlined in a red box, meaning all three fields are selected.

6. In the Tools group, click the **Delete Rows** button. See Figure 2-33.

Figure 2-33   **Patient table after deleting fields**

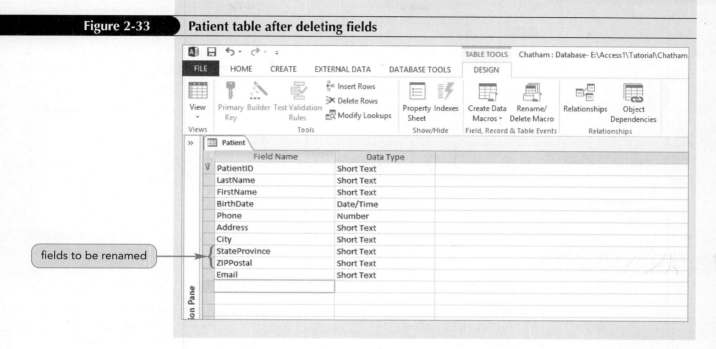

fields to be renamed

Renaming Fields in Design View

To match Cindi's design for the Patient table, you need to rename the StateProvince and ZIPPostal fields. In Tutorial 1, you renamed the default primary key field (ID) in Datasheet view. You can also rename fields in Design view by simply editing the names in the Table Design grid.

To rename the fields in Design view:

1. Click to position the insertion point to the right of the word **StateProvince** in the eighth row's Field Name box, and then press the **Backspace** key eight times to delete the word "Province." The name of the eighth field is now State.

   You can also select an entire field name and then type new text to replace it.

2. In the ninth row's Field Name box, drag to select the text **ZIPPostal**, and then type **Zip**. The text you type replaces the original text. See Figure 2-34.

Figure 2-34   **Patient table after renaming fields**

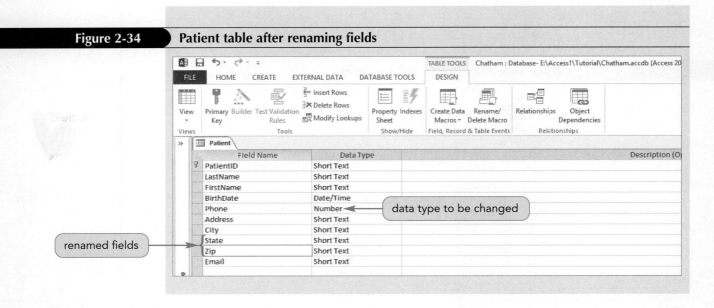

Changing the Data Type for a Field in Design View

According to Cindi's plan, all of the fields in the Patient table, except BirthDate, should be Short Text fields. The table structure you imported specifies the Number data type for the Phone field; you need to change this to Short Text. In Tutorial 1, you used an option in Datasheet view to change a field's data type. You can also change the data type for a field in Design view.

> **To change the data type of the Phone field in Design view:**
>
> ▸ **1.** Click the right side of the **Data Type** box for the Phone field to display the list of data types.
>
> ▸ **2.** Click **Short Text** in the list. The Phone field is now a Short Text field. Note that, by default, the Field Size property is set to 255. According to Cindi's plan, the Phone field should have a Field Size property of 14. You'll make this change next.
>
> ▸ **3.** Press the **F6** key to move to and select the default Field Size property, and then type **14**.

Each of the remaining fields you added using the Address Quick Start selection—Address, City, State, and Zip—also has the default field size of 255. You need to change the Field Size property for these fields to match Cindi's design. You'll also delete any Caption property values for these fields because the field names match how Cindi wants them displayed, so captions are unnecessary.

To change the Field Size and Caption properties for the fields:

▶ **1.** Click the **Address** Field Name box to make it the current field.

▶ **2.** Press the **F6** key to move to and select the default Field Size property, and then type **35**.

Note that the Caption property setting for this field is the same as the field name. This field doesn't need a caption, so you can delete this value.

▶ **3.** Press the **Tab** key until the the word Address is selected in the Caption box, and then press the **Delete** key. The Caption property value is removed.

▶ **4.** Repeat Steps 1 through 3 to change the Field Size property for the City field to **25** and to delete its Caption property value.

▶ **5.** Change the Field Size property for the State field to **2**, and then delete its Caption property value.

▶ **6.** Change the Field Size property for the Zip field to **10**, and then delete its Caption property value.

▶ **7.** On the Quick Access Toolbar, click the **Save** button 🖫 to save your changes to the Patient table.

Finally, Cindi would like you to set the Description property for the Patient ID field and the Caption property for the PatientID, LastName, FirstName, and BirthDate fields. You'll make these changes now.

To enter the Description and Caption property values:

▶ **1.** Click the **Description (Optional)** box for the PatientID field, and then type **Primary key**.

▶ **2.** In the Field Properties pane, click the **Caption** box.

After you leave the Description (Optional) box, the Property Update Options button 📝 appears below this box for the PatientID field. When you change a field's property in Design view, you can use this button to update the corresponding property on forms and reports that include the modified field. For example, if the Chatham database included a form that contained the PatientID field, you could choose to **propagate**, or update, the modified Description property in the form by clicking the Property Update Options button, and then choosing the option to make the update everywhere the field is used. The text on the Property Update Options button varies depending on the task; in this case, if you click the button, the option is "Update Status Bar Text everywhere PatientID is used."

Because the Chatham database does not include any forms or reports that are based on the Patient table, you do not need to update the properties, so you can ignore the button for now. In most cases, however, it is a good idea to perform the update.

▶ **3.** In the Caption box for the PatientID field, type **Patient ID**.

▶ **4.** Click the **LastName** Field Name box to make it the current field.

▶ **5.** Click the **Caption** box, and then type **Last Name**.

▶ **6.** Click the **FirstName** Field Name box to make it the current field, click the **Caption** box, and then type **First Name**.

7. Click the **BirthDate** Field Name box to make it the current field, click the **Caption** box, and then type **Date of Birth**. See Figure 2-35.

Figure 2-35 **Patient table after entering description and captions**

8. On the Quick Access Toolbar, click the **Save** button 🔲 to save your changes to the Patient table.

9. In the Views group on the DESIGN tab, click the **View** button to display the table in Datasheet view.

> **10.** Resize each column to its best fit, and then click in the first row for the **Patient ID** column. See Figure 2-36.

Figure 2-36   **Modified Patient table in Datasheet view**

After viewing the Patient table datasheet, both Cindi and Kelly agree that data entry would be made easier if the State field value of "CT" was automatically filled in for each new record added to the table, because all of the clinic's patients live in Connecticut. You can accomplish this by setting the Default Value property for the field.

Setting the Default Value Property for a Field

The **Default Value property** for a field specifies what value will appear, by default, for the field in each new record you add to a table. Recall the InvoicePaid field in the Billing table; this is a Yes/No field, which automatically includes a Default Value property setting of "No." That's why the check box for the InvoicePaid field is initially empty for a new record in the Billing table.

Because all the patients at Chatham Community Health Services live in Connecticut, you'll specify a default value of "CT" for the State field in the Patient table. With this setting, each new record in the Patient table will have the correct State field value entered automatically.

To set the Default Value property for the State field:

> **1.** In the Views group on the HOME tab, click the **View** button to display the Patient table in Design view.

> **2.** Click the **State** Field Name box to make it the current field.

> **3.** In the Field Properties pane, click the **Default Value** box, type **CT** and then press the Tab key. See Figure 2-37.

Figure 2-37	Specifying the Default Value property for the State field

State field is current

Default Value property entered and enclosed within quotation marks

Note that a text entry in the Default Value property must be enclosed within quotation marks. If you do not type the quotation marks, Access adds them for you. However, for some entries, you would receive an error message indicating invalid syntax if you omitted the quotation marks. In such cases, you have to enter the quotation marks yourself.

4. On the Quick Access Toolbar, click the **Save** button 🖫 to save your changes to the Patient table.

TIP

You can change the value in a record from the default value to another value, if necessary.

5. In the Views group on the DESIGN tab, click the **View** button to display the table in Datasheet view. Note that the State field for the first row now displays the default value "CT" as specified by the Default Value property. Each new record entered in the table will automatically have this State field value entered.

With the Patient table design set, you can now enter records in it. You'll begin by entering two records, and then you'll use a different method to add the remaining records.

Note: *Be sure to enter your last name and first name where indicated.*

To add two records to the Patient table:

▶ **1.** Enter the following values in the columns in the first record; note that you can press Tab to move past the default State field value:

Patient ID = **22500**

Last Name = *[student's last name]*

First Name = *[student's first name]*

Date of Birth = **2/28/1994**

Phone = **860-938-2822**

Address = **501 Perkins Dr**

City = **Hartford**

State = **CT**

Zip = **06120**

Email = **student1@example.edu**

▶ **2.** Enter the following values in the columns in the second record:

Patient ID = **22533**

Last Name = **Rowe**

First Name = **Christina**

Date of Birth = **12/5/1941**

Phone = **860-552-5920**

Address = **27 Tracey Ct**

City = **Windsor**

State = **CT**

Zip = **06095**

Email = **c.rowe@example.com**

▶ **3.** Resize columns to their best fit, as necessary, and then save and close the Patient table.

Before Cindi decided to store data using Access, Kelly managed the clinic's patient data in a different system. She exported that data into a text file and now asks you to import it into the new Patient table. You can import the data contained in this text file to add the remaining records to the Patient table.

Adding Data to a Table by Importing a Text File

There are many ways to import data into an Access database. So far, you've learned how to add data to an Access table by importing an Excel spreadsheet, and you've created a new table by importing the structure of an existing table. You can also import data contained in text files.

To complete the entry of records in the Patient table, you'll import the data contained in Kelly's text file. The file is named "Patient" and is located in the Access1 ▶ Tutorial folder provided with your Data Files.

To import the data contained in the Patient text file:

▶ **1.** On the ribbon, click the **EXTERNAL DATA** tab.

▶ **2.** In the Import & Link group, click the **Text File** button. The Get External Data - Text File dialog box opens. This dialog box is similar to the one you used earlier when importing the Excel spreadsheet and the Access table structure.

▶ **3.** Click the **Browse** button. The File Open dialog box opens.

▶ **4.** Navigate to the Access1 ▶ Tutorial folder, where your starting Data Files are stored, and then double-click the **Patient** file. You return to the dialog box.

▶ **5.** Click the **Append a copy of the records to the table** option button. The box to the right of this option becomes active. Next, you need to select the table to which you want to add the data.

▶ **6.** Click the arrow on the box, and then click **Patient**.

▶ **7.** Click the **OK** button. The first Import Text Wizard dialog box opens. The dialog box indicates that the data to be imported is in a delimited format. A **delimited text file** is one in which fields of data are separated by a character such as a comma or a tab. In this case, the dialog box shows that data is separated by the comma character in the text file.

▶ **8.** Make sure the **Delimited** option button is selected in the dialog box, and then click the **Next** button. The second Import Text Wizard dialog box opens. See Figure 2-38.

Figure 2-38   **Second Import Text Wizard dialog box**

fields in the text file are separated by commas

preview of the data being imported

TIP

Carefully check the data to make sure it should be imported into the selected table.

This dialog box asks you to confirm the delimiter character that separates the fields in the text file you're importing. Access detects that the comma character is used in the Patient text file and selects this option. The bottom area of the dialog box provides a preview of the data you're importing.

▶ **9.** Make sure the **Comma** option button is selected, and then click the **Next** button. The third, and final, Import Text Wizard dialog box opens. Notice that the Import to Table box shows that the data will be imported into the Patient table.

▶ **10.** Click the **Finish** button. A dialog box opens asking if you want to save the import steps. You'll only import the patient data once, so you can close the dialog box without saving the import steps.

▶ **11.** Click the **Close** button in the dialog box to close it without saving the import steps.

Cindi asks you to open the Patient table in Datasheet view so she can see the results of importing the text file.

To view the Patient table datasheet:

▶ **1.** Open the Navigation Pane, and then double-click **Patient** to open the Patient table in Datasheet view. The Patient table contains a total of 51 records.

▶ **2.** Close the Navigation Pane.

▶ **3.** Resize columns to their best fit, scrolling the table datasheet as necessary, so that all field values are displayed. When finished, scroll back to display the first fields in the table, and then click the first row's Patient ID field. See Figure 2-39.

Figure 2-39	Patient table after importing data from the text file

▶ **4.** Save and close the Patient table, and then open the Navigation Pane.

The Chatham database now contains three tables—Patient, Visit, and Billing—and the tables contain all the necessary records. Your final task is to complete the database design by defining the necessary relationships between its tables.

Defining Table Relationships

One of the most powerful features of a relational database management system is its ability to define relationships between tables. You use a common field to relate one table to another. The process of relating tables is often called performing a **join**. When you join tables that have a common field, you can extract data from them as if they were one larger table. For example, you can join the Patient and Visit tables by using the PatientID field in both tables as the common field. Then you can use a query, form, or report to extract selected data from each table, even though the data is contained in two separate tables, as shown in Figure 2-40. The PatientVisits query shown in Figure 2-40 includes the PatientID, LastName, and FirstName fields from the Patient table, and the VisitDate and Reason fields from the Visit table. The joining of records is based on the common field of PatientID. The Patient and Visit tables have a type of relationship called a one-to-many relationship.

Figure 2-40	One-to-many relationship and sample query

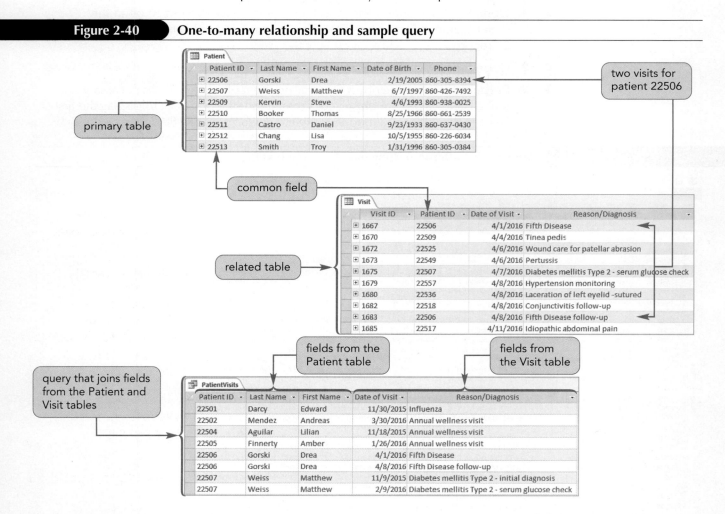

One-to-Many Relationships

As shown earlier in the Session 2.2 Visual Overview, a one-to-many relationship exists between two tables when one record in the first table matches zero, one, or many records in the second table, and when one record in the second table matches at most one record in the first table. For example, as shown in Figure 2-40, patient 22506 has two visits in the Visit table. Other patients have one or more visits. Every visit has a single matching patient.

Access refers to the two tables that form a relationship as the primary table and the related table. The primary table is the "one" table in a one-to-many relationship; in Figure 2-40, the Patient table is the primary table because there is only one patient for each visit. The related table is the "many" table; in Figure 2-40, the Visit table is the related table because a patient can have zero, one, or many visits.

Because related data is stored in two tables, inconsistencies between the tables can occur. Referring to Figure 2-40, consider the following three scenarios:

- Cindi adds a record to the Visit table for a new patient, Jack Perry, using PatientID 22570. She did not first add the new patient's information to the Patient table, so this visit does not have a matching record in the Patient table. The data is inconsistent, and the visit record is considered to be an **orphaned record**.
- In another situation, Cindi changes the PatientID in the Patient table for Drea Gorski from 22506 to 22601. Because there is no longer a patient with the PatientID 22506 in the Patient table, this change creates two orphaned records in the Visit table, and the database is inconsistent.
- In a third scenario, Cindi deletes the record for Drea Gorski, patient 22506, from the Patient table because this patient moved and no longer receives medical services from Chatham Community Health Services. The database is again inconsistent; two records for patient 22506 in the Visit table have no matching record in the Patient table.

You can avoid these types of problems and avoid having inconsistent data in your database by specifying referential integrity between tables when you define their relationships.

Referential Integrity

Referential integrity is a set of rules that Access enforces to maintain consistency between related tables when you update data in a database. Specifically, the referential integrity rules are as follows:

- When you add a record to a related table, a matching record must already exist in the primary table, thereby preventing the possibility of orphaned records.
- If you attempt to change the value of the primary key in the primary table, Access prevents this change if matching records exist in a related table. However, if you choose the **Cascade Update Related Fields option**, Access permits the change in value to the primary key and changes the appropriate foreign key values in the related table, thereby eliminating the possibility of inconsistent data.
- When you attempt to delete a record in the primary table, Access prevents the deletion if matching records exist in a related table. However, if you choose the **Cascade Delete Related Records option**, Access deletes the record in the primary table and also deletes all records in related tables that have matching foreign key values.

INSIGHT

Understanding the Cascade Delete Related Records Option

Although there are advantages to using the Cascade Delete Related Records option for enforcing referential integrity, its use does present risks as well. You should rarely select the Cascade Delete Related Records option because doing so might cause you to inadvertently delete records you did not intend to delete. It is best to use other methods for deleting records that give you more control over the deletion process.

Defining a Relationship Between Two Tables

When two tables have a common field, you can define a relationship between them in the Relationships window (see the Session 2.2 Visual Overview). Next, you need to define a one-to-many relationship between the Patient and Visit tables, with Patient as the primary table and Visit as the related table, and with PatientID as the common field (the primary key in the Patient table and a foreign key in the Visit table). You'll also define a one-to-many relationship between the Visit and Billing tables, with Visit as the primary table and Billing as the related table, and with VisitID as the common field (the primary key in the Visit table and a foreign key in the Billing table).

To define the one-to-many relationship between the Patient and Visit tables:

 1. On the ribbon, click the **DATABASE TOOLS** tab.

 2. In the Relationships group, click the **Relationships** button. The Show Table dialog box opens. See Figure 2-41.

Figure 2-41 **Show Table dialog box**

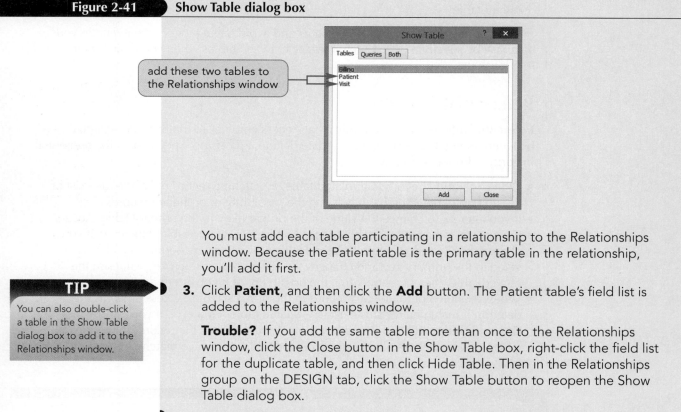

add these two tables to the Relationships window

You must add each table participating in a relationship to the Relationships window. Because the Patient table is the primary table in the relationship, you'll add it first.

 3. Click **Patient**, and then click the **Add** button. The Patient table's field list is added to the Relationships window.

 Trouble? If you add the same table more than once to the Relationships window, click the Close button in the Show Table box, right-click the field list for the duplicate table, and then click Hide Table. Then in the Relationships group on the DESIGN tab, click the Show Table button to reopen the Show Table dialog box.

 4. Click **Visit**, and then click the **Add** button. The Visit table's field list is added to the Relationships window.

 5. Click the **Close** button in the Show Table dialog box to close it.

So that you can view all the fields and complete field names, you'll resize the Patient table field list.

6. Use the 𝕀 pointer to drag the bottom of the Patient table field list to lengthen it until the vertical scroll bar disappears and all the fields are visible.

To form the relationship between the two tables, you drag the common field of PatientID from the primary table to the related table. Then Access opens the Edit Relationships dialog box, in which you select the relationship options for the two tables.

7. Click **PatientID** in the Patient field list, and then drag it to **PatientID** in the Visit field list. When you release the mouse button, the Edit Relationships dialog box opens. See Figure 2-42.

| Figure 2-42 | Edit Relationships dialog box |

The primary table, related table, common field, and relationship type (One-To-Many) appear in the dialog box. Note that Access correctly identifies the "One" side of the relationship and places the primary table Patient in the Table/Query section of the dialog box; similarly, Access correctly identifies the "Many" side of the relationship and places the related table Visit in the Related Table/Query section of the dialog box.

8. Click the **Enforce Referential Integrity** check box.

After you click the Enforce Referential Integrity check box, the two cascade options become available. If you select the Cascade Update Related Fields option, Access will update the appropriate foreign key values in the related table when you change a primary key value in the primary table. You will *not* select the Cascade Delete Related Records option because doing so could cause you to delete records that you do not want to delete; this option is rarely selected.

9. Click the **Cascade Update Related Fields** check box.

10. Click the **Create** button to define the one-to-many relationship between the two tables and to close the dialog box. The completed relationship appears in the Relationships window, with the join line connecting the common field of PatientID in each table. See Figure 2-43.

Figure 2-43   Defined relationship in the Relationships window

Trouble? If a dialog box opens indicating a problem that prevents you from creating the relationship, you most likely made a typing error when entering the two records in the Patient table. If so, click the OK button in the dialog box and then click the Cancel button in the Edit Relationships dialog box. Refer back to the earlier steps instructing you to enter the two records in the Patient table and carefully compare your entries with those shown in the text, especially the PatientID field values. Make any necessary corrections to the data in the Patient table, and then repeat Steps 7 through 10. If you still receive an error message, ask your instructor for assistance.

Now you need to define the one-to-many relationship between the Visit and Billing tables. In this relationship, Visit is the primary ("one") table because there is at most one visit for each invoice. Billing is the related ("many") table because there are zero, one, or many invoices that are generated for each patient visit. For example, some visits require lab work or pharmacy charges, which are invoiced separately.

To define the relationship between the Visit and Billing tables:

1. In the Relationships group on the DESIGN tab, click the **Show Table** button. The Show Table dialog box opens.

2. Make sure the **Billing** table is selected on the Tables tab, click the **Add** button, and then click the **Close** button to close the Show Table dialog box. The Billing table's field list appears in the Relationships window to the right of the Visit table's field list.

3. Use the $\updownarrow$ pointer to drag the bottom of the Billing table field list to lengthen it until the vertical scroll bar disappears.

   Because the Visit table is the primary table in this relationship, you need to drag the VisitID field from the Visit field list to the Billing field list.

4. Click and drag the **VisitID** field in the Visit field list to the **VisitID** field in the Billing field list. When you release the mouse button, the Edit Relationships dialog box opens.

5. Click the **Enforce Referential Integrity** check box, and then click the **Cascade Update Related Fields** check box.

TIP

You can also use the mouse to drag a table from the Navigation Pane to add it to the Relationships window.

6. Click the **Create** button to define the one-to-many relationship between the two tables and to close the dialog box. The completed relationship appears in the Relationships window. See Figure 2-44.

Figure 2-44   **Both relationships defined**

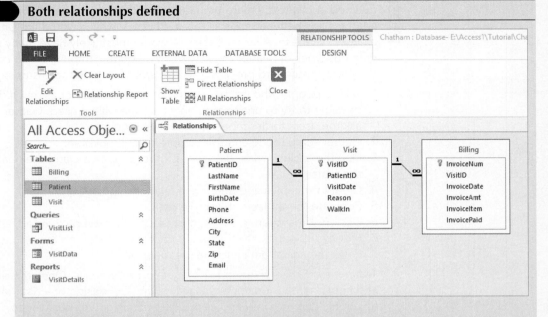

Trouble? If a dialog box opens indicating a problem that prevents you from creating the relationship, you most likely made a typing error when entering the two records in the Visit table. If so, click the OK button in the dialog box and then click the Cancel button in the Edit Relationships dialog box. Refer back to the steps in Tutorial 1 instructing you to enter the records in the Visit table and carefully compare your entries with those shown in the text, especially the VisitID field values. Make any necessary corrections to the data in the Visit table, and then repeat Steps 4 through 6. If you still receive an error message, ask your instructor for assistance.

With both relationships defined, you have connected the data among the three tables in the Chatham database.

7. On the Quick Access Toolbar, click the **Save** button 🔒 to save the layout in the Relationships window.

8. In the Relationships group on the DESIGN tab, click the **Close** button to close the Relationships window.

9. Click the **FILE** tab on the ribbon to display Backstage view.

10. Click the **Compact & Repair Database** button. Access compacts and repairs the Chatham database.

11. Click the **FILE** tab, and then click **Close** to close the Chatham database.

PROSKILLS

Problem Solving: Creating a Larger Database

When you create a small database that contains only a few tables, and the data and the reports you want to generate from it are fairly simple, you could follow the process outlined in this text: create the tables, populate them, and then define the necessary relationships between tables. This method, however, would not be suitable for creating a larger database. A larger database would most likely have many more tables and different types of relationships that can be quite complex. When creating a large database, a standard process to follow would include these steps:

1. Talk to people who will be using the data, and gather as much documentation as possible to try to understand how the data will be used. Gather sample reports, and ask the users to describe the data they require.
2. Gather some representative sample data, if possible.
3. Plan the tables, fields, data types, other properties, and the relationships between the tables.
4. Create the tables and define the relationships between them.
5. Populate the tables with sample data.
6. Design some queries, forms, and reports that will be needed, and then test them.
7. Modify the database structure, if necessary, based on the results of your tests.
8. Enter the actual data into the database tables.

Testing is critical at every stage of creating a database. Once the database is finalized and implemented, it's not actually finished. The design of a database evolves as new functionality is required and as the data that is gathered changes.

REVIEW

Session 2.2 Quick Check

1. What is the keyboard shortcut for inserting the value from the same field in the previous record into the current record?
2. _____ data is a process that allows you to copy the data from a source without having to open the source file.
3. The _____ gallery allows you to add a group of related fields to a table at the same time, rather than adding each field to the table individually.
4. What is the effect of deleting a field from a table structure?
5. A(n) _____ text file is one in which fields of data are separated by a character such as a comma or a tab.
6. The _____ is the "one" table in a one-to-many relationship, and the _____ is the "many" table in the relationship.
7. _____ is a set of rules that Access enforces to maintain consistency between related tables when you update data in a database.

ASSESS

SAM Projects

Put your skills into practice with SAM Projects! SAM Projects for this tutorial can be found online. If you have a SAM account, go to www.cengage.com/sam2013 to download the most recent Project Instructions and Start Files.

PRACTICE

Review Assignments

Data Files needed for the Review Assignments: Vendor.accdb *(cont. from Tutorial 1)* **and Supplies.xlsx**

In addition to tracking information about the vendors Chatham Community Health Services works with, Cindi also wants to track information about their products and services. First, Cindi asks you to modify the necessary properties in the existing Supplier table in the Vendor database; then she wants you to create a new table in the Vendor database to contain product data. Complete the following:

1. Open the **Vendor** database you created in Tutorial 1.
2. Open the **Supplier** table in Design view, and set the field properties as shown in Figure 2-45.

Figure 2-45	Field properties for the Supplier table

Field Name	Data Type	Description	Field Size	Other
SupplierID	Short Text	Primary key	6	Caption = Supplier ID
Company	Short Text		50	
Category	Short Text		15	
Address	Short Text		35	
City	Short Text		25	
State	Short Text		2	
Zip	Short Text		10	
Phone	Short Text		14	Caption = Contact Phone
ContactFirst	Short Text		20	Caption = Contact First Name
ContactLast	Short Text		25	Caption = Contact Last Name
InitialContact	Date/Time			Format = Short Date
				Caption = Initial Contact

© 2014 Cengage Learning

3. Save the Supplier table. Click the Yes button when a message appears indicating some data might be lost. Switch to Datasheet view and resize columns, as necessary, to their best fit. Then save and close the Supplier table.
4. Create a new table in Design view, using the table design shown in Figure 2-46.

Figure 2-46   **Design for the Product table**

Field Name	Data Type	Description	Field Size	Other
ProductID	Short Text	Primary key	5	Caption = Product ID
SupplierID	Short Text	Foreign key	6	Caption = Supplier ID
ProductName	Short Text		75	Caption = Product Name
Price	Currency			Format = Standard
				Decimal Places = 2
TempControl	Yes/No			Caption = Temp Controlled?
Sterile	Yes/No			Caption = Sterile?
Units	Number		Integer	Decimal Places = 0
				Caption = Units/Case
				Default Value = [no entry]

© 2014 Cengage Learning

5. Specify ProductID as the primary key, and then save the table as **Product**.

6. Modify the table structure by adding a new field named **Weight** (data type: **Number**; field size: **Single**; Decimal Places: **2**; Caption: **Weight in Lbs**; Default Value: [no entry]) between the Price and TempControl fields. Then move the **Units** field so that it is positioned between the Price and Weight fields.

7. Enter the records shown in Figure 2-47 in the Product table. Resize all datasheet columns to their best fit. When finished, save and close the Product table.

Figure 2-47   **Records for the Product table**

Product ID	Supplier ID	Product Name	Price	Units/Case	Weight in Lbs	Temp Controlled?	Sterile?
SS582	DUR368	Stethoscopes	65.00	1	1	No	No
AL487	COU392	Alcohol wipes	15.00	1000	12	Yes	Yes

© 2014 Cengage Learning

8. Use the Import Spreadsheet Wizard to add data to the Product table. The data you need to import is contained in the Supplies workbook, which is an Excel file located in the Access1 ▶ Review folder provided with your Data Files.

   a. Specify the Supplies workbook as the source of the data.

   b. Select the option for appending the data.

   c. Select Product as the table.

   d. In the Import Spreadsheet Wizard dialog boxes, make sure Access confirms that the first row contains column headings, and import to the Product table. Do not save the import steps.

9. Open the **Product** table in Datasheet view and resize columns to their best fit, as necessary. Then save and close the Product table.

10. Define a one-to-many relationship between the primary Supplier table and the related Product table. Resize the table field lists so that all field names are visible. Select the referential integrity option and the cascade updates option for the relationship.

11. Save the changes to the Relationships window and close it, compact and repair the Vendor database, and then close the database.

APPLY

Case Problem 1

Data Files needed for this Case Problem: Gopher.accdb *(cont. from Tutorial 1)* and Customers.txt

GoGopher! Amol Mehta wants to use the Gopher database to track information about members who join his online business, which provides a variety of services on a subscription basis, and the plans in which members are enrolled. He asks you to help maintain this database. Complete the following:

1. Open the **Gopher** database you created in Tutorial 1.
2. Open the **Plan** table in Design view, and change the following field properties:
   a. PlanID: Enter **Primary key** for the description, change the field size to **3**, and enter **Plan ID** for the caption.
   b. PlanDescription: Change the field size to **40** and enter **Plan Description** for the caption.
   c. PlanCost: Change the format to **Standard**, specify **0** decimal places, and enter **Plan Cost** for the caption.
   d. FeeWaived: Enter **Fee Waived** for the caption.
3. Save and close the Plan table. Click the Yes button when a message appears indicating some data might be lost.
4. Create a new table in Design view, using the table design shown in Figure 2-48.

Figure 2-48   **Design for the Member table**

Field Name	Data Type	Description	Field Size	Other
MemberID	Short Text	Primary key	4	Caption = Member ID
PlanID	Short Text	Foreign key	3	Caption = Plan ID
FirstName	Short Text		20	Caption = First Name
LastName	Short Text		25	Caption = Last Name
Phone	Short Text		14	
Expiration	Date/Time	Date when membership expires		Format = Short Date
				Caption = Expiration Date

© 2014 Cengage Learning

5. Specify MemberID as the primary key, and then save the table as **Member**.
6. Use the Address Quick Start selection in the Data Type gallery to add five fields between the LastName and Phone fields.
7. Switch to Design view, and then make the following changes to the Member table design:
   a. Address field: Change the name of this field to **Street**, change the field size to **40**, and delete the entry for the caption.
   b. City field: Change the field size to **25** and delete the entry for the caption.
   c. StateProvince field: Change the name of this field to **State**, change the field size to **2**, delete the entry for the caption, and enter **CO** for the default value.
   d. ZIPPostal field: Change the name of this field to **Zip**, change the field size to **10**, and delete the entry for the caption.
   e. Delete the **CountryRegion** field from the Member table structure.
   f. Add a new field named **DateJoined** (data type: **Date/Time**; format: **Short Date**; Caption: **Date Joined**) between the Phone and Expiration fields.
8. Enter the records shown in Figure 2-49 in the Member table. Be sure to enter your first and last names in the appropriate fields for the first new record. Resize all datasheet columns to their best fit. When finished, save and close the Member table.

Figure 2-49 Records for the Member table

Member ID	Plan ID	First Name	Last Name	Street	City	State	Zip	Phone	Date Joined	Expiration Date
1200	311	*Student First*	*Student Last*	45 Lakeview Dr	Boulder	CO	80301	303-559-1238	11/1/2015	2/1/2016
1210	312	Todd	Grant	6 Rosebriar Rd	Erie	CO	80516	303-674-2140	1/20/2016	4/20/2016

© 2014 Cengage Learning

9. Use the Import Text File Wizard to add data to the Member table. The data you need to import is contained in the Customers text file, which is located in the Access1 ► Case1 folder provided with your Data Files.

   a. Specify the Customers text file as the source of the data.

   b. Select the option for appending the data.

   c. Select Member as the table.

   d. In the Import Text File Wizard dialog boxes, choose the options to import delimited data, to use a comma delimiter, and to import the data into the Member table. Do not save the import steps.

10. Open the **Member** table in Datasheet view and resize columns to their best fit, as necessary. Then save and close the Member table.

11. Define a one-to-many relationship between the primary Plan table and the related Member table. Resize the Member table field list so that all field names are visible. Select the referential integrity option and the cascade updates option for this relationship.

12. Save the changes to the Relationships window and close it, compact and repair the Gopher database, and then close the database.

Case Problem 2

Data Files needed for this Case Problem: OBrien.accdb (cont. from Tutorial 1), **Client.accdb, Students.txt, and Agreements.xlsx**

O'Brien Educational Services Karen O'Brien plans to use the OBrien database to maintain information about the students, tutors, and contracts for her educational services company. Karen asks you to help her build the database by updating one table and creating two new tables in the database. Complete the following:

1. Open the **OBrien** database you created in Tutorial 1.

2. Open the **Tutor** table in Design view, and set the field properties as shown in Figure 2-50.

Figure 2-50 Field properties for the Tutor table

Field Name	Data Type	Description	Field Size	Other
TutorID	Short Text	Primary key	7	Caption = Tutor ID
FirstName	Short Text		20	Caption = First Name
LastName	Short Text		25	Caption = Last Name
Degree	Short Text		7	
School	Short Text		50	
HireDate	Date/Time			Format = Short Date
				Caption = Hire Date

© 2014 Cengage Learning

3. Add a new field as the last field in the Tutor table with the field name **Groups**, the **Yes/No** data type, and the caption **Groups Only**.

4. Save the Tutor table. Click the Yes button when a message appears indicating some data might be lost.

5. In the table datasheet, specify that the following tutors conduct group tutoring sessions only: Student First/Student Last (i.e., your name), Amy Hawkins, Lori Burns, Samuel Glick, and Caitlin Shea. Close the Tutor table.

6. Karen created a table named Student in the Client database that is located in the Access1 ▸ Case2 folder provided with your Data Files. Import the structure of the Student table in the Client database into a new table named Student in the OBrien database. Do not save the import steps.

7. Open the **Student** table in Datasheet view, and then add the following two fields to the end of the table: **BirthDate** (Date/Time field) and **Gender** (Short Text field).

8. Use the Phone Quick Start selection in the Data Type gallery to add four fields related to phone numbers between the Zip and BirthDate fields. (*Hint:* Be sure to make the BirthDate field the active field before adding the new fields.)

9. Display the Student table in Design view, delete the BusinessPhone and FaxNumber fields, and then save and close the Student table.

10. Reopen the Student table and modify its design so that it matches the design in Figure 2-51, *including the revised field names and data types.*

    Note: You must type the quotation marks around the Default Property value for the State field.

Figure 2-51   **Field properties for the Student table**

Field Name	Data Type	Description	Field Size	Other
StudentID	Short Text	Primary key	7	Caption = Student ID
LastName	Short Text		25	Caption = Last Name
FirstName	Short Text		20	Caption = First Name
Address	Short Text		35	
City	Short Text		25	
State	Short Text		2	Default Value = "IN"
Zip	Short Text		10	
HomePhone	Short Text		14	
CellPhone	Short Text		14	Caption = Cell Phone
BirthDate	Date/Time			Format = Short Date
				Caption = Date of Birth
Gender	Short Text	F(emale), M(ale)	1	

© 2014 Cengage Learning

you must type the quotation marks for this Default Value property

11. Move the LastName field so it follows the FirstName field.

12. Save your changes to the table design, and then add the records shown in Figure 2-52 to the Student table.

Figure 2-52   **Records for the Student table**

Student ID	First Name	Last Name	Address	City	State	Zip	Home Phone	Cell Phone	Date of Birth	Gender
TUR8005	Lynne	Turner	6 Crowell Ct	South Bend	IN	46614	574-245-2125	574-245-8842	7/24/2002	F
CHA8034	Henry	Chang	1401 Lauren Dr	Oscela	IN	46561	574-607-3045	574-674-2410	10/5/1999	M

© 2014 Cengage Learning

13. Resize the fields to their best fit, and then save and close the Student table.

14. Use the Import Text File Wizard to add data to the Student table. The data you need to import is contained in the Students text file, which is located in the Access1 ▸ Case2 folder provided with your Data Files.

    a. Specify the Students text file as the source of the data.

    b. Select the option for appending the data.

c. Select Student as the table.

d. In the Import Text File Wizard dialog boxes, choose the options to import delimited data, to use a comma delimiter, and to import the data into the Student table. Do not save the import steps.

15. Open the **Student** table in Datasheet view, resize columns in the datasheet to their best fit (as necessary), and then save and close the table.

16. Create a new table in Design view, using the table design shown in Figure 2-53.

Figure 2-53   **Design for the Contract table**

Field Name	Data Type	Description	Field Size	Other
ContractID	Short Text	Primary key	4	Caption = Contract ID
StudentID	Short Text	Foreign key	7	Caption = Student ID
TutorID	Short Text	Foreign key	7	Caption = Tutor ID
SessionType	Short Text		15	Caption = Session Type
Length	Number		Integer	Decimal Places = 0 Caption = Length (Hrs) Default Value = [no entry]
NumSessions	Number		Integer	Decimal Places = 0 Caption = Number of Sessions Default Value = [no entry]
Cost	Currency			Format = Currency Decimal Places = 0 Default Value = [no entry]
Assessment	Yes/No	Pre-assessment exam complete		Caption = Assessment Complete

© 2014 Cengage Learning

17. Specify ContractID as the primary key, and then save the table using the name **Contract**.

18. Add a new field to the Contract table, between the TutorID and SessionType fields, with the field name **ContractDate**, the **Date/Time** data type, the description **Date contract is signed**, the **Short Date** format, and the caption **Contract Date**. Save and close the Contract table.

19. Use the Import Spreadsheet Wizard to add data to the Contract table. The data you need to import is contained in the Agreements workbook, which is an Excel file located in the Access1 ▶ Case2 folder provided with your Data Files.

a. Specify the Agreements workbook as the source of the data.

b. Select the option for appending the data to the table.

c. Select Contract as the table.

d. In the Import Spreadsheet Wizard dialog boxes, choose the Agreements worksheet, make sure Access confirms that the first row contains column headings, and import to the Contract table. Do not save the import steps.

20. Open the **Contract** table and add the records shown in Figure 2-54. (*Hint*: Use the New (blank) record button in the navigation buttons to add a new record.)

Figure 2-54   **Records for the Contract table**

Contract ID	Student ID	Tutor ID	Contract Date	Session Type	Length (Hrs)	Number of Sessions	Cost	Assessment Complete
5168	LUF8037	68-8234	8/30/2016	Group	3	12	$1,440	Yes
5172	GOS8029	71-1698	9/7/2016	Private	2	6	$720	Yes

© 2014 Cengage Learning

21. Resize columns in the datasheet to their best fit (as necessary), and then save and close the Contract table.

22. Define the one-to-many relationships between the database tables as follows: between the primary Student table and the related Contract table, and between the primary Tutor table and the related Contract table. Resize the table field lists so that all field names are visible. Select the referential integrity option and the cascade updates option for each relationship.

23. Save the changes to the Relationships window and close it, compact and repair the OBrien database, and then close the database.

Case Problem 3

CHALLENGE

Data Files needed for this Case Problem: Shelter.accdb *(cont. from Tutorial 1)*, Donations.xlsx, and Animals.txt

Rosemary Animal Shelter Ryan Lang wants to use the Shelter database to maintain information about the patrons, animals, and donations for his not-for-profit agency. Ryan asks you to help him maintain the database by updating one table and creating two new ones. Complete the following:

1. Open the **Shelter** database you created in Tutorial 1.
2. Open the **Patron** table in Design view, and then change the following field properties:
   a. PatronID: Enter **Primary key** for the description, change the field size to **5**, and enter **Patron ID** for the caption.
   b. Title: Change the field size to **4**.
   c. FirstName: Change the field size to **20** and enter **First Name** for the caption.
   d. LastName: Change the field size to **25** and enter **Last Name** for the caption.
   e. Phone: Change the field size to **14.**
3. Save and close the Patron table. Click the Yes button when a message appears indicating some data might be lost.

⊕ **Explore** 4. Use the Import Spreadsheet Wizard to create a table in the Shelter database. As the source of the data, specify the Donations workbook, which is located in the Access1 ▸ Case3 folder provided with your Data Files. Select the option to import the source data into a new table in the database.

⊕ **Explore** 5. Complete the Import Spreadsheet Wizard dialog boxes as follows:
   a. Select Donation as the worksheet you want to import.
   b. Specify that the first row contains column headings.
   c. Accept the field options suggested by the wizard, and do not skip any fields.
   d. Choose DonationID as your own primary key.
   e. Import the data to a table named **Donation**, and do not save the import steps.

6. Open the Donation table in Datasheet view, and then delete the Requires Pickup field.
7. Open the Donation table in Design view, and then modify the table so it matches the design shown in Figure 2-55, including changes to data types, field name, and field position. For the Short Text fields, delete any formats specified in the Format property boxes.

Figure 2-55	Design for the Donation table

Field Name	Data Type	Description	Field Size	Other
DonationID	Short Text	Primary key	4	Caption = Donation ID
PatronID	Short Text	Foreign key	5	Caption = Patron ID
DonationDate	Date/Time			Format = mm/dd/yyyy
				Caption = Donation Date
Description	Short Text		30	
DonationValue	Currency	Dollar amount or estimated value		Format = Currency
				Decimal Places = 2
				Caption = Donation Value
				Default Value = [no entry]

© 2014 Cengage Learning

8. Save your changes to the table design, click Yes for the message about lost data, and then switch to Datasheet view.

9. Resize the columns in the Donation datasheet to their best fit.

✛ **Explore** 10. Ryan decides that the values in the Donation Value column would look better without the two decimal places. Make this field the current field in the datasheet. Then, in the Formatting group on the FIELDS tab, use the Decrease Decimals button to remove the two decimal places and the period from these values. Switch back to Design view, and note that the Decimal Places property for the DonationValue field is now set to 0.

11. Save and close the Donation table.

12. Use Design view to create a table using the table design shown in Figure 2-56.

Figure 2-56 **Design for the Animal table**

Field Name	Data Type	Description	Field Size	Other
AnimalID	Short Text	Primary key	3	Caption = Animal ID
AnimalName	Short Text		15	Caption = Animal Name
Age	Short Text		2	Caption = Age at Arrival
Gender	Short Text		6	
AnimalType	Short Text		5	Caption = Animal Type
Description	Short Text		60	
ArrivalDate	Date/Time			Format = Short Date
				Caption = Arrival Date
AdoptionDate	Date/Time			Format = Short Date
				Caption = Adoption Date
Adopted	Yes/No			
PatronID	Short Text		5	Caption = Patron ID

© 2014 Cengage Learning

13. Specify AnimalID as the primary key, save the table as **Animal**, and then close the table.

14. Use the Import Text File Wizard to add data to the Animal table. The data you need to import is contained in the Animals text file, which is located in the Access1 ▸ Case3 folder provided with your Data Files.

   a. Specify the Animals text file as the source of the data.

   b. Select the option for appending the data.

   c. Select Animal as the table.

   d. In the Import Text File Wizard dialog boxes, choose the options to import delimited data, to use a comma delimiter, and to import the data into the Animal table. Do not save the import steps.

15. Open the Animal table in Datasheet view, and resize all columns to their best fit.

16. Display the Animal table in Design view. Move the PatronID field to make it the second field in the table, and enter the description **Foreign key** for the PatronID field. Then move the Adopted field so it is positioned between the ArrivalDate and AdoptionDate fields. Save the modified Animal table design.

17. Switch to Datasheet view, and then add the records shown in Figure 2-57 to the Animal table. (*Hint*: Use the New (blank) record button in the navigation buttons to add a new record.) Close the table when finished.

Figure 2-57 **Records for the Animal table**

Animal ID	Patron ID	Animal Name	Age at Arrival	Gender	Animal Type	Description	Arrival Date	Adopted	Adoption Date
B45		Gizmo	12	Male	Dog	Hound mix	3/6/2016	No	
R39	38398	Simba	3	Female	Cat	Siamese	4/12/2016	Yes	5/14/2016

© 2014 Cengage Learning

18. Define the one-to-many relationships between the database tables as follows: between the primary Patron table and the related Animal table, and between the primary Patron table and the related Donation table. (*Hint:* Place the Patron table as the middle table in the Relationships window to make it easier to join the tables.) Resize the Animal field list so that all field names are visible. Select the referential integrity option and the cascade updates option for each relationship.

19. Save the changes to the Relationships window and close it, compact and repair the Shelter database, and then close the database.

Case Problem 4

CHALLENGE

Data Files needed for this Case Problem: Stanley.accdb (*cont. from Tutorial 1*), Travel.accdb, and Bookings.txt

Stanley EcoTours   Janice and Bill Stanley use the Stanley database to track the data about the tours they offer to clients of their ecotourism business. They ask you to help them maintain this database. Complete the following:

1. Open the **Stanley** database you created in Tutorial 1.

2. Open the **Guest** table in Design view and change the following field properties:

   a. GuestID: Enter **Primary key** for the description, change the field size to **3**, and enter **Guest ID** for the caption.

   b. GuestFirst: Change the field size to **20** and enter **Guest First Name** for the caption.

   c. GuestLast: Change the field size to **25** and enter **Guest Last Name** for the caption.

   d. Address: Change the field size to **35**.

   e. City: Change the field size to **25**.

   f. State/Prov: Change the field size to **2**.

   g. PostalCode: Change the field size to **10** and enter **Postal Code** for the caption.

   h. Country: Change the field size to **15**.

   i. Phone: Change the field size to **14**.

3. Save the Guest table, click the Yes button when a message appears indicating some data might be lost, resize the Guest First Name and Guest Last Name columns in Datasheet view to their best fit, and then save and close the table.

⊕ **Explore** 4. In addition to importing the structure of an existing Access table, you can also import both the structure *and* the data contained in a table to create a new table. Import the **Trip** table structure and data from the **Travel** database into a new table in the **Stanley** database as follows:

   a. Start the process for importing an Access table structure.

   b. As the source of the data, specify the Travel database, which is located in the Access1 ▶ Case4 folder provided with your Data Files.

   c. Select the option button to import tables, queries, forms, reports, macros, and modules into the current database.

   d. In the Import Objects dialog box, select the Trip table, click the Options button, and then make sure that the correct option is selected to import the table's data and structure (definition).

   e. Do not save your import steps.

⊕ **Explore** 5. Using a shortcut menu in the Navigation Pane, rename the Trip table as **Tour** to give this name to the new table in the Stanley database.

6. Open the **Tour** table in Design view, delete the VIPDiscount field, and then move the PricePerPerson field so that it appears between the Country and SingleSupplement fields.

7. Change the following properties:

  a. TourID: Enter the description **Primary key**, change the field size to **4**, and enter **Tour ID** for the caption.

  b. TourName: Enter **Tour Name** for the caption.

  c. PricePerPerson: Enter **Price Per Person** for the caption.

  d. SingleSupplement: Enter the description **Additional charge for single accommodation**, and enter **Single Supplement** for the caption.

  e. TourType: Change the field size to **15**, and enter **Tour Type** for the caption.

  f. Nights: Enter **Num of Nights** for the caption.

8. Save the modified table, click the Yes button when a message appears indicating some data might be lost, and then display the table in Datasheet view. Resize all datasheet columns to their best fit, and then save and close the table.

9. In Design view, create a table using the table design shown in Figure 2-58.

Figure 2-58 **Design for the Reservation table**

Field Name	Data Type	Description	Field Size	Other
ReservationID	Short Text	Primary key	3	Caption = Reservation ID
GuestID	Short Text	Foreign key	3	Caption = Guest ID
TourID	Short Text	Foreign key	4	Caption = Tour ID
StartDate	Date/Time			Caption = Start Date
People	Number	Number of people in the party	Integer	Decimal Places = 0
				Default Value = [no entry]

© 2014 Cengage Learning

10. Specify ReservationID as the primary key, and then save the table as **Reservation**.

⊕ **Explore** 11. Refer back to Figure 2-11 to review the custom date formats. Change the Format property of the StartDate field to a custom format that displays dates in a format similar to 05/25/16. Save and close the Reservation table.

12. Use the Import Text File Wizard to add data to the Reservation table. The data you need to import is contained in the Bookings text file, which is located in the Access1 ► Case4 folder provided with your Data Files.

  a. Specify the Bookings text file as the source of the data.

  b. Select the option for appending the data.

  c. Select Reservation as the table.

  d. In the Import Text File Wizard dialog boxes, choose the options to import delimited data, to use a comma delimiter, and to import the data into the Reservation table. Do not save the import steps.

13. Resize columns in the **Reservation** table datasheet to their best fit (as necessary), verify that the date values in the StartDate field are displayed correctly according to the custom format, and then save and close the table.

14. Define the one-to-many relationships between the database tables as follows: between the primary Guest table and the related Reservation table, and between the primary Tour table and the related Reservation table. (*Hint:* Place the Reservation table as the middle table in the Relationships window to make it easier to join the tables.) Resize the Guest and Tour field lists so that all field names are visible. Select the referential integrity option and the cascade updates option for each relationship.

15. Save the changes to the Relationships window and close it, compact and repair the Stanley database, and then close the database.

OBJECTIVES

Session 3.1
- Find, modify, and delete records in a table
- Hide and unhide fields in a datasheet
- Work in the Query window in Design view
- Create, run, and save queries
- Update data using a query datasheet
- Create a query based on multiple tables
- Sort data in a query
- Filter data in a query

Session 3.2
- Specify an exact match condition in a query
- Use a comparison operator in a query to match a range of values
- Use the And and Or logical operators in queries
- Change the font size and alternate row color in a datasheet
- Create and format a calculated field in a query
- Perform calculations in a query using aggregate functions and record group calculations
- Change the display of database objects in the Navigation Pane

Maintaining and Querying a Database

Updating and Retrieving Information About Patients, Visits, and Invoices

Case | Chatham Community Health Services

At a recent meeting, Cindi Rodriguez and her staff discussed the importance of maintaining accurate information about the clinic's patients, visits, and invoices, and regularly monitoring the business activities of Chatham Community Health Services. For example, Kelly Schwarz, Cindi's assistant, needs to make sure she has up-to-date contact information, such as phone numbers and email addresses, for all the clinic's patients. The office staff also must monitor billing activity to ensure that invoices are paid on time and in full. Ethan Ward, a staff member who handles marketing and community outreach efforts for the clinic, tracks patient activity to develop new strategies for promoting services provided by the clinic. In addition, Cindi is interested in analyzing other aspects of the business related to patient visits and finances. You can satisfy all these informational needs for Chatham Community Health Services by updating data in the Chatham database and by creating and using queries that retrieve information from the database.

STARTING DATA FILES

Access1 →	Tutorial	Review	Case1
	Chatham.accdb *(cont.)*	Vendor.accdb *(cont.)*	Gopher.accdb *(cont.)*
	Case2	Case3	Case4
	OBrien.accdb *(cont.)*	Shelter.accdb *(cont.)*	Stanley.accdb *(cont.)* Tour.accdb

Session 3.1 Visual Overview:

When you are constructing a query, you can see the results at any time by clicking the View button or the Run button. In response, Access displays the query datasheet, which contains the set of fields and records that results from answering, or **running**, the query.

The top portion of the Query window in Design view contains the field list (or lists) for the table(s) used in the query.

The default query name, Query1, is displayed on the tab for the query. You change the default query name to a more meaningful one when you save the query.

The bottom portion of the Query window in Design view contains the design grid. In the **design grid**, you include the fields and record selection criteria for the information you want to see.

In the Query Type group, the active Select button indicates that you are creating a select query, which is the default type of query. A **select query** is one in which you specify the fields and records you want Access to select.

Each **field list** contains the fields for the table(s) you are querying. The table name appears at the top of the field list, and the fields are listed in the order in which they appear in the table. Notice that the primary key for the table is identified by the key symbol.

You can scroll the field list to see more fields, or you can expand the field list box by dragging its borders to display all the fields and the complete field names. When all the field names are displayed, the scroll bar disappears.

Query Window in Design View

Y TOOLS   Chatham : Database- E:\Access1\Tutorial\Chatham.accdb (Acces...   ?   —   🗗   ✕

:SIGN   Sign in

	Insert Rows	Insert Columns	Σ		Property Sheet
Show Table	Delete Rows	Delete Columns	Totals Parameters		Table Names
	Builder	Return: All ▾			

Query Setup   Show/Hide

> The ribbon displays the QUERY TOOLS DESIGN tab with options for creating and running queries. Note the Query Type group on the DESIGN tab; it provides buttons you can click to create various types of queries.

> In Design view, you specify the data you want to view by constructing a query by example. When you use **query by example (QBE)**, you give Access an example of the information you are requesting. Access then retrieves the information that precisely matches your example.

> Each column in the design grid contains specifications about a field you will use in the query. You can choose a single field for your query by double-clicking its name in the field list to place the field in the next available design grid column.

> The view buttons on the status bar allow you to change to different views; for example, you can click the Datasheet View button to run the query and display the results in Datasheet view.

SQL

Updating a Database

Updating, or **maintaining**, a database is the process of adding, modifying, and deleting records in database tables to keep them current and accurate. After reviewing the data in the Chatham database, Kelly identified some changes that need to be made to the data. She would like you to update the field values in one record in the Patient table, correct an error in one record in the Visit table, and then delete a record in the Visit table.

Modifying Records

To modify the field values in a record, you must first make the record the current record. Then you position the insertion point in the field value to make minor changes, or select the field value to replace it entirely. In Tutorial 1, you used the mouse with the scroll bars and the navigation buttons to navigate the records in a datasheet. You can also use keyboard shortcuts and the F2 key to navigate a datasheet and to select field values. The **F2 key** is a toggle that you use to switch between navigation mode and editing mode:

- In **navigation mode**, Access selects an entire field value. If you type while you are in navigation mode, your typed entry replaces the highlighted field value.
- In **editing mode**, you can insert or delete characters in a field value based on the location of the insertion point.

Figure 3-1 shows some of the navigation mode and editing mode keyboard shortcuts.

Figure 3-1 | **Navigation mode and editing mode keyboard shortcuts**

Press	To Move the Selection in Navigation Mode	To Move the Insertion Point in Editing Mode
←	Left one field value at a time	Left one character at a time
→	Right one field value at a time	Right one character at a time
Home	Left to the first field value in the record	To the left of the first character in the field value
End	Right to the last field value in the record	To the right of the last character in the field value
↑ or ↓	Up or down one record at a time	Up or down one record at a time and switch to navigation mode
Tab or Enter	Right one field value at a time	Right one field value at a time and switch to navigation mode
Ctrl + Home	To the first field value in the first record	To the left of the first character in the field value
Ctrl + End	To the last field value in the last record	To the right of the last character in the field value

© 2014 Cengage Learning

The Patient table record Kelly wants you to change is for Patrice Lewis. This patient recently moved to another location in Windsor and also changed her email address, so you need to update the Patient table record with the new street address and email address.

To open the Patient table in the Chatham database:

▶ **1.** Start Access and open the **Chatham** database you created and worked with in Tutorials 1 and 2.

 Trouble? If the security warning is displayed below the ribbon, click the Enable Content button.

▶ **2.** Open the **Patient** table in Datasheet view.

The Patient table contains many fields. Sometimes, when updating data in a table, it can be helpful to remove the display of some fields on the screen.

Hiding and Unhiding Fields

When you are viewing a table or query datasheet in Datasheet view, you might want to temporarily remove certain fields from the displayed datasheet, making it easier to focus on the data you're interested in viewing. The **Hide Fields** command allows you to remove the display of one or more fields, and the **Unhide Fields** command allows you to redisplay any hidden fields. Hiding fields can be especially useful in a table with many fields.

To make it easier to modify the patient record, you'll first hide a couple of fields in the Patient table.

To hide fields in the Patient table and modify the patient record:

▶ **1.** Right-click the **Date of Birth** field name to display the shortcut menu, and then click **Hide Fields** on the shortcut menu. The Date of Birth column is removed from the datasheet display.

▶ **2.** Right-click the **Phone** field name, and then click **Hide Fields** on the shortcut menu. The Phone column is removed from the datasheet display.

 With the fields hidden, you can now update the patient record. The record you need to modify is near the end of the table and has a PatientID field value of 22560.

▶ **3.** Drag the vertical scroll box down until you see the last records in the table.

▶ **4.** Click the PatientID field value **22560**, for Patrice Lewis. The field value is not selected, indicating you are in editing mode.

▶ **5.** Press the **Tab** key to move to the Last Name field value, Lewis. The field value is selected, indicating you are in navigation mode.

▶ **6.** Press the **Tab** key twice to move to the Address field and select its field value, type **83 Highland St**, press the **Tab** key four times to move to the Email field, type **plewis5@example.org**, and then press the **Tab** key. The changes to the record are complete. See Figure 3-2.

Figure 3-2	Table after changing field values in a record

⊞ 22555	Phillips	Aquon	632 Perkins Dr	Hartford	CT	06120		
⊞ 22556	Grus	Mateo	18 Norman Rd	Hartford	CT	06112	m.grus@example.com	
⊞ 22557	Kirk	Isobel	48 Grafton St	Bloomfield	CT	06002		
⊞ 22558	Ropiak	Jane	637 Filbert St	Hartford	CT	06120	jropiak@example.edu	
⊞ 22559	Morales	Jose	251 Lilac St	West Hartford	CT	06117	j.morales@example.org	
⊞ 22560	Lewis	Patrice	83 Highland St ◀—	Windsor	CT	06095	plewis5@example.org	
⊞ 22561	Shaw	Daniel	33 Agnes Ct	West Hartford	CT	06117	dshaw@example.com	
*					CT			

field values changed

Record: 14 ◀ 51 of 51 ▶ ▶I ▶⁕ No Filter Search

Primary key

Access saves changes to field values when you move to a new field or another record, or when you close the table. You don't have to click the Save button to save changes to field values or records.

Note that the PatientID field value for the last record in the table is selected, indicating you are in navigation mode.

▶ **7.** Press the **Ctrl+Home** keys to move to the first field value in the first record.

With the changes to the record complete, you can unhide the hidden fields.

▶ **8.** Right-click any field name to display the shortcut menu, and then click **Unhide Fields**. The Unhide Columns dialog box opens. See Figure 3-3.

Figure 3-3 Unhide Columns dialog box

All currently displayed fields are checked in this dialog box, and all hidden fields are unchecked. To redisplay them, you simply click their check boxes to select them.

▶ **9.** In the Unhide Columns dialog box, click the **Date of Birth** check box to select it, click the **Phone** check box to select it, and then click the **Close** button to close the dialog box. The two hidden fields are now displayed in the datasheet.

▶ **10.** Close the Patient table. A dialog box opens asking if you want to save changes to the layout of the Patient table. This box appears because you hid fields and redisplayed them.

In this case, you can click either the Yes button or the No button, because no changes were actually made to the table layout or design.

▶ **11.** Click the **No** button to close the dialog box.

Next you need to correct an error in the Visit table for a visit made by Jane Ropiak, Patient ID 22558. A staff member incorrectly entered "COPD management visit" as the reason for the visit, when the patient actually came to the clinic that day suffering from influenza. Ensuring the accuracy of the data in a database is an important maintenance task.

To correct the record in the Visit table:

▶ **1.** Open the **Visit** table in Datasheet view. The record containing the error is for Visit ID 1635.

2. Scroll down the Visit table until you locate Visit ID **1635**, and then click at the end of the **Reason** field value for this record. Because the field value is not selected, you are in editing mode.

3. Press the **Backspace** key until the current entry for the Reason field is deleted, type **Influenza**, and then press the **Enter** key twice. The record now contains the correct value in the Reason field, and Access saves this change automatically in the Visit table.

The next update Kelly asks you to make is to delete a record in the Visit table. One of the clinic's patients, Robert Goldberg, recently notified Kelly that he received an invoice for an annual wellness visit, but that he had cancelled this scheduled appointment to the clinic. Because this patient visit did not take place, the record for this visit needs to be deleted from the Visit table. Rather than scrolling through the table to locate the record to delete, you can have Access find the data for you.

Finding Data in a Table

Access provides options you can use to locate specific field values in a table. Instead of scrolling the Visit table datasheet to find the visit that you need to delete—the record for Visit ID 1688—you can use the Find command to find the record. The **Find command** allows you to search a table or query datasheet, or a form, to locate a specific field value or part of a field value. This feature is particularly useful when searching a table that contains a large number of records.

To search for the record in the Visit table:

TIP

You can click any value in the column containing the field you want to search to make the field current.

1. Make sure the VisitID field value **1638** is still selected. You need to search the VisitID field to find the record containing the value 1688, so the insertion point is already correctly positioned in the field you want to search.

2. Make sure the **HOME** tab is displayed on the ribbon.

3. In the Find group, click the **Find** button. The Find and Replace dialog box opens. See Figure 3-4.

Figure 3-4 ▶ **Find and Replace dialog box**

specifies that the current field will be searched

specifies that Access will search for a match to the entire field value

value selected in the table datasheet

specifies that all records in the table will be searched

The field value 1638 appears in the Find What box because this value is selected in the table datasheet. The Look In box indicates that the current field will be searched for the value. The Match box indicates that the Find command will match the whole field value, which is correct for your search. You also can choose to search for only part of a field value, such as when you need to find all Visit IDs that start with a certain value. The Search box indicates that all the records in the table will be searched for the value you want to find. You also can choose to search up or down from the currently selected record.

Trouble? Some of the settings in your dialog box might be different from those shown in Figure 3-4 depending on the last search performed on the computer you're using. If so, change the settings so that they match those in the figure.

▶ 4. Make sure the value 1638 is selected in the Find What box, type **1688** to replace the selected value, and then click the **Find Next** button. Access scrolls the datasheet to record 81 and selects the field value you specified.

▶ 5. Click the **Cancel** button to close the Find and Replace dialog box.

Deleting Records

To delete a record, you need to select the record in Datasheet view, and then delete it using the Delete button in the Records group on the HOME tab or the Delete Record option on the shortcut menu.

REFERENCE

Deleting a Record

- With the table open in Datasheet view, click the row selector for the record you want to delete.
- In the Records group on the HOME tab, click the Delete button (or right-click the row selector for the record, and then click Delete Record on the shortcut menu).
- In the dialog box asking you to confirm the deletion, click the Yes button.

Now that you have found the record with Visit ID 1688, you can delete it. To delete a record, you must first select the entire row for the record.

To delete the record:

▶ 1. Click the row selector for the record containing the VisitID field value **1688**, which should still be highlighted. The entire row is selected.

▶ 2. In the Records group on the HOME tab, click the **Delete** button. A dialog box opens and indicates that you cannot delete the record because the Billing table contains records that are related to VisitID 1688. Recall that you defined a one-to-many relationship between the Visit and Billing tables and you enforced referential integrity. When you try to delete a record in the primary table (Visit), Access prevents the deletion if matching records exist in the related table (Billing). This protection helps to maintain the integrity of the data in the database.

To delete the record in the Visit table, you first must delete the related records in the Billing table.

▶ 3. Click the **OK** button in the dialog box to close it. Notice the plus sign that appears at the beginning of each record in the Visit table. The **plus sign** indicates that the Visit table is the primary table related to another table—in this case, the Billing table.

▶ 4. Scroll the datasheet down until you see the rest of the records in the table, so that you have room to view the related records for the visit record.

5. Click the **plus sign** next to VisitID 1688. Access displays the one related record from the Billing table for this visit. See Figure 3-5.

Figure 3-5   **Related record from the Billing table in the subdatasheet**

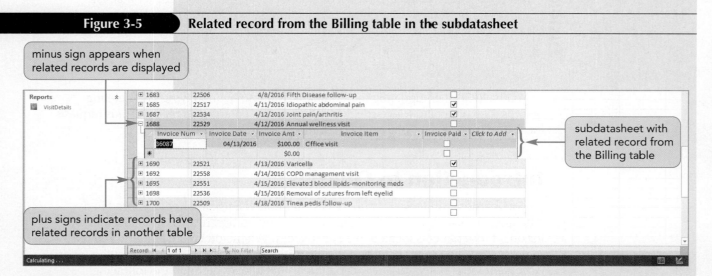

minus sign appears when related records are displayed

subdatasheet with related record from the Billing table

plus signs indicate records have related records in another table

TIP

The plus sign changes to a minus sign for the current record when its related records are displayed.

The related record from the Billing table is displayed in a **subdatasheet**. When you first open a table that is the primary table in a one-to-many relationship, the subdatasheet containing the records from the related table is not displayed. You need to click the plus sign, also called the **expand indicator**, to display the related records in the subdatasheet. When the subdatasheet is open, you can navigate and update it, just as you can using a table datasheet.

You need to delete the record in the Billing table that is related to Visit ID 1688 before you can delete this visit record. The record is for the invoice that was mistakenly sent to the patient, Robert Goldberg, who had cancelled his annual wellness visit at the clinic. You could open the Billing table and find the related record. However, an easier way is to delete the record right in the subdatasheet. The record will be deleted from the Billing table automatically.

6. In the Billing table subdatasheet, click the row selector for invoice number **36087**. The entire row is selected.

7. In the Records group on the HOME tab, click the **Delete** button. Access opens a dialog box asking you to confirm the deletion of one record. Because the deletion of a record is permanent and cannot be undone, Access prompts you to make sure that you want to delete the record.

8. Click the **Yes** button to confirm the deletion and close the dialog box. The record is removed from the Billing table, and the subdatasheet is now empty.

9. Click the **minus sign** next to VisitID 1688 to close the subdatasheet.

Now that you have deleted the related record in the Billing table, you can delete the record for Visit ID 1688. You'll use the shortcut menu to do so.

Be sure to select the correct record before deleting it.

10. Right-click the row selector for the record for Visit ID **1688**. Access selects the record and displays the shortcut menu.

11. Click **Delete Record** on the shortcut menu, and then click the **Yes** button in the dialog box to confirm the deletion. The record is deleted from the Visit table.

12. Close the Visit table.

Process for Deleting Records

When working with more complex databases that are managed by a database administrator, you typically need special permission to delete records from a table. Many companies also follow the practice of archiving records before deleting them so that the information is still available but not part of the active database.

You have finished updating the Chatham database by modifying and deleting records. Next, you'll retrieve specific data from the database to meet various requests for information about Chatham Community Health Services.

Introduction to Queries

As you learned in Tutorial 1, a query is a question you ask about data stored in a database. For example, Cindi might create a query to find records in the Patient table for only those patients located in a specific city. When you create a query, you tell Access which fields you need and what criteria Access should use to select the records. Access provides powerful query capabilities that allow you to do the following:

- Display selected fields and records from a table
- Sort records
- Perform calculations
- Generate data for forms, reports, and other queries
- Update data in the tables in a database
- Find and display data from two or more tables

Most questions about data are generalized queries in which you specify the fields and records you want Access to select. These common requests for information, such as "Which patients are located in Bloomfield?" or "How many invoices have been paid?" are select queries. The answer to a select query is returned in the form of a datasheet. The result of a query is also referred to as a **recordset** because the query produces a set of records that answers your question.

Designing Queries vs. Using a Query Wizard

More specialized, technical queries, such as finding duplicate records in a table, are best formulated using a Query Wizard. A **Query Wizard** prompts you for information by asking a series of questions and then creates the appropriate query based on your answers. In Tutorial 1, you used the Simple Query Wizard to display only some of the fields in the Visit table; Access provides other Query Wizards for more complex queries. For common, informational queries, designing your own query is more efficient than using a Query Wizard.

Ethan wants you to create a query to display the patient ID, last name, first name, city, and email address for each record in the Patient table. He needs this information to complete an email campaign advertising a special blood pressure screening being offered to patients of Chatham Community Health Services. You'll open the Query window in Design view to create the query for Ethan.

To open the Query window in Design view:

▶ **1.** Close the Navigation Pane so that more of the workspace is displayed.

▶ **2.** On the ribbon, click the **CREATE** tab. Access displays the options for creating different database objects.

▶ **3.** In the Queries group, click the **Query Design** button. The Show Table dialog box opens on the Query window in Design view. See Figure 3-6.

Figure 3-6	Show Table dialog box

The Show Table dialog box lists all the tables in the Chatham database. You can choose to base a query on one or more tables, on other queries, or on a combination of tables and queries. The query you are creating will retrieve data from the Patient table, so you need to add this table to the Query window.

▶ **4.** Click **Patient** in the Tables list, click the **Add** button, and then click the **Close** button. Access places the Patient table's field list in the Query window and closes the Show Table dialog box. Refer to the Session 3.1 Visual Overview to familiarize yourself with the Query window in Design view.

Trouble? If you add the wrong table to the Query window, right-click the bar at the top of the field list containing the table name, and then click Remove Table on the shortcut menu. To add the correct table to the Query window, click the Show Table button in the Query Setup group on the DESIGN tab to redisplay the Show Table dialog box, and then repeat Step 4.

Now you'll create and run Ethan's query to display selected fields from the Patient table.

Creating and Running a Query

The default table datasheet displays all the fields in the table in the same order as they appear in the table. In contrast, a query datasheet can display selected fields from a table, and the order of the fields can be different from that of the table, enabling those viewing the query results to see only the information they need and in the order they want.

Ethan wants the PatientID, LastName, FirstName, City, and Email fields from the Patient table to appear in the query results. You'll add each of these fields to the design grid. First you'll resize the Patient table field list to display all of the fields.

To select the fields for the query, and then run the query:

1. Position the pointer on the bottom border of the Patient field list until the pointer changes to a ⫟ shape, and then click and drag the pointer down until the vertical scroll bar in the field list disappears and all fields in the Patient table are displayed in the list.

   Note that it's not necessary to resize the field list in order to create the query, but doing so enables you to see all the fields in the list, making it easier to select fields to include in the query.

2. In the Patient field list, double-click **PatientID** to place the field in the design grid's first column Field box. See Figure 3-7.

Figure 3-7 | **Field added to the design grid**

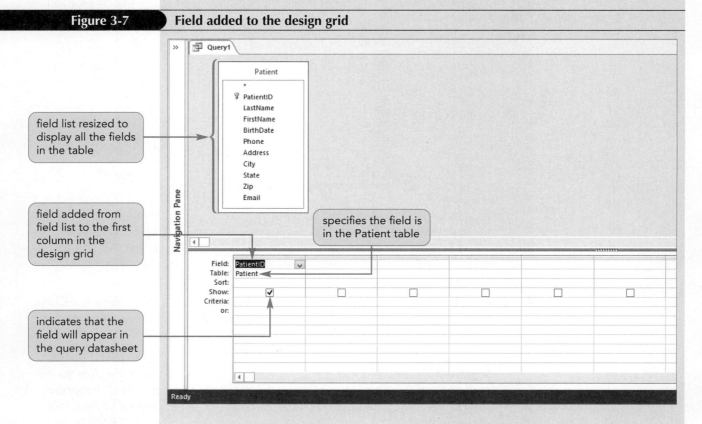

field list resized to display all the fields in the table

field added from field list to the first column in the design grid

specifies the field is in the Patient table

indicates that the field will appear in the query datasheet

In the design grid's first column, the field name PatientID appears in the Field box, the table name Patient appears in the Table box, and the checkmark in the Show check box indicates that the field will be displayed in the datasheet when you run the query. Sometimes you might not want to display a field and its values in the query results. For example, if you are creating a query to list all patients located in Windsor, and you assign the name "WindsorPatients" to the query, you do not need to include the City field value for each record in the query results—the query design only lists patients with the City field value of "Windsor." Even if you choose not to display a field in the query results, you can still use the field as part of the query to select specific records or to specify a particular sequence for the records in the datasheet.

You can also add a field to the design grid using the arrow on the Field box; this arrow appears when you click the right side of an empty Field box.

TIP

You can also use the mouse to drag a field from the field list to a column in the design grid.

3. In the design grid, click the right side of the second column's Field box to display a menu listing all the fields in the Patient table, and then click **LastName**. Access adds this field to the second column in the design grid.

4. Use the method you prefer to add the **FirstName**, **City**, and **Email** fields to the design grid in that order.

   Trouble? If you accidentally add the wrong field to the design grid, you can remove the field from the grid. Select the field's column by clicking the pointer ↓ on the field selector, which is the thin bar above the Field box, for the field you want to delete, and then press the Delete key (or in the Query Setup group on the DESIGN tab, click the Delete Columns button).

   Having selected the five fields for Ethan's query, you can now run the query.

5. In the Results group on the DESIGN tab, click the **Run** button. Access runs the query and displays the results in Datasheet view. See Figure 3-8.

Figure 3-8   **Datasheet displayed after running the query**

The five fields you added to the design grid appear in the datasheet in the same order as they appear in the design grid. The records are displayed in primary key sequence by PatientID. Access selected all 51 records from the Patient table for display in the query datasheet. Ethan asks you to save the query as "PatientEmail" so that he can easily retrieve the same data again.

6. On the Quick Access Toolbar, click the **Save** button 🖫. The Save As dialog box opens.

7. In the Query Name box, type **PatientEmail** and then press the **Enter** key. Access saves the query with the specified name in the Chatham database and displays the name on the tab for the query.

PROSKILLS

Decision Making: Comparing Methods for Adding All Fields to the Design Grid

If the query you are creating includes every field from the specified table, you can use one of the following three methods to transfer all the fields from the field list to the design grid:

- Double-click (or click and drag) each field individually from the field list to the design grid. Use this method if you want the fields in your query to appear in an order that is different from the order in the field list.
- Double-click the asterisk at the top of the field list. Access places the table name followed by a period and an asterisk (as in "Patient.*") in the Field box of the first column in the design grid, which signifies that the order of the fields is the same in the query as it is in the field list. Use this method if you don't need to sort the query or specify conditions based on the fields in the table you added in this way (for example, in a query based on more than one table). The advantage of using this method is that you do not need to change the query if you add or delete fields from the underlying table structure. Such changes are reflected automatically in the query.
- Double-click the field list title bar to highlight all the fields, and then click and drag one of the highlighted fields to the first column in the design grid. Access places each field in a separate column and arranges the fields in the order in which they appear in the field list. Use this method when you need to sort your query or include record selection criteria.

By choosing the most appropriate method to add all the table fields to the query design grid, you can work more efficiently and ensure that the query produces the results you want.

When viewing the query results, Ethan noticed that the record for one of the patients contains information that is not up to date. This patient, Nancy Fraser, had informed the clinic that she was recently married and changed her last name; she also provided a new email address. So Ethan asks you to update the record with the new last name and email address for this patient.

Updating Data Using a Query

A query datasheet is temporary and its contents are based on the criteria in the query design grid; however, you can still update the data in a table using a query datasheet. In this case, Ethan has changes he wants you to make to a record in the Patient table. Instead of making the changes in the table datasheet, you can make them in the PatientEmail query datasheet because the query is based on the Patient table. The underlying Patient table will be updated with the changes you make.

To update data using the PatientEmail query datasheet:

1. Locate the record with PatientID 22523, Nancy Fraser (record 21 in the query datasheet).

2. In the Last Name column for this record, double-click **Fraser** to select the name, and then type **Bennett**.

3. Press the **Tab** key three times to move to the Email column, type **n.bennett@example.com** and then press the **Tab** key.

4. Close the PatientEmail query, and then open the Navigation Pane. Note that the PatientEmail query is listed in the Queries section of the Navigation Pane.

Now you'll check the Patient table to verify that the changes you made in the query datasheet are reflected in the Patient table.

> **5.** Open the **Patient** table in Datasheet view, and then close the Navigation Pane.

> **6.** Locate the record for PatientID 22523 (record 21). Notice that the changes you made in the query datasheet to the Last Name and Email field values were made to the record in the Patient table.

> **7.** Close the Patient table.

INSIGHT

Query Datasheet vs. Table Datasheet

Although a query datasheet looks just like a table datasheet and appears in Datasheet view, the contents of a query datasheet are temporary and are based on the criteria you establish in the design grid. Whenever you run a query, the results displayed reflect the current data in the underlying table. In contrast, a table datasheet shows the permanent data in a table. However, you can update data while viewing a query datasheet, just as you can when working in a table datasheet or form.

Kelly also wants to view specific information in the Chatham database. She would like to review the visit data for patients while also viewing certain contact information for them. So, she needs to see data from both the Patient table and the Visit table at the same time.

Creating a Multitable Query

A multitable query is a query based on more than one table. If you want to create a query that retrieves data from multiple tables, the tables must have a common field. In Tutorial 2, you established a relationship between the Patient (primary) and Visit (related) tables based on the common PatientID field that exists in both tables, so you can now create a query to display data from both tables at the same time. Specifically, Kelly wants to view the values in the City, FirstName, and LastName fields from the Patient table and the VisitDate and Reason fields from the Visit table.

To create the query using the Patient and Visit tables:

> **1.** On the ribbon, click the **CREATE** tab.

> **2.** In the Queries group, click the **Query Design** button. Access opens the Show Table dialog box. You need to add the Patient and Visit tables to the Query window.

> **3.** Click **Patient** in the Tables list, click the **Add** button, click **Visit**, click the **Add** button, and then click the **Close** button. The Patient and Visit field lists appear in the Query window, and the Show Table dialog box closes.

> **4.** Use the ⥕ pointer to resize the Patient and Visit field lists so that all the fields in each list are displayed and the vertical scroll bars disappear.

The one-to-many relationship between the two tables is shown in the Query window in the same way that Access indicates a relationship between two tables in the Relationships window. Note that the join line is thick at both ends; this signifies that you selected the option to enforce referential integrity. If you had not selected this option, the join line would be thin at both ends and neither the "1" nor the infinity symbol would appear, even though the tables have a one-to-many relationship.

You need to place the City, FirstName, and LastName fields (in that order) from the Patient field list into the design grid, and then place the VisitDate and Reason fields from the Visit field list into the design grid. This is the order in which Kelly wants to view the fields in the query results.

▶ **5.** In the Patient field list, double-click **City** to place this field in the design grid's first column Field box.

▶ **6.** Repeat Step 5 to add the **FirstName** and **LastName** fields from the Patient table to the second and third columns of the design grid.

▶ **7.** Repeat Step 5 to add the **VisitDate** and **Reason** fields (in that order) from the Visit table to the fourth and fifth columns of the design grid. The query specifications are complete, so you can now run the query.

▶ **8.** In the Results group on the DESIGN tab, click the **Run** button. Access runs the query and displays the results in Datasheet view. See Figure 3-9.

Figure 3-9	Datasheet for query based on the Patient and Visit tables

fields from the Patient table

fields from the Visit table

City	First Name	Last Name	Date of Visit	Reason/Diagnosis
Hartford	Student First	Student Last	11/17/2015	Migraine
Bloomfield	Edward	Darcy	11/30/2015	Influenza
Windsor	Andreas	Mendez	3/30/2016	Annual wellness visit
Hartford	Lilian	Aguilar	11/18/2015	Annual wellness visit
Hartford	Amber	Finnerty	1/26/2016	Annual wellness visit
Bloomfield	Drea	Gorski	4/1/2016	Fifth Disease
Bloomfield	Drea	Gorski	4/8/2016	Fifth Disease follow-up
Hartford	Matthew	Weiss	11/9/2015	Diabetes mellitis Type 2 - initial diagnosis
Hartford	Matthew	Weiss	2/9/2016	Diabetes mellitis Type 2 - serum glucose check
Hartford	Matthew	Weiss	4/7/2016	Diabetes mellitis Type 2 - serum glucose check
Hartford	Steve	Kervin	4/4/2016	Tinea pedis
Hartford	Steve	Kervin	4/18/2016	Tinea pedis follow-up
Hartford	Thomas	Booker	11/10/2015	Seborrheic dermatitis
Hartford	Thomas	Booker	3/1/2016	Seborrheic dermatitis follow-up
West Hartford	Daniel	Castro	12/3/2015	Annual wellness visit
West Hartford	Daniel	Castro	1/13/2016	Cardiac monitoring
Hartford	Lisa	Chang	1/5/2016	Annual wellness visit
Bloomfield	Troy	Smith	1/13/2016	Broken leg
Bloomfield	Troy	Smith	2/24/2016	Follow-up - cast removal
Hartford	Ian	Parker	12/15/2015	Influenza
Hartford	Ian	Parker	1/14/2016	Hypertension monitoring
Hartford	Susan	King	12/22/2015	COPD management visit
West Hartford	Henry	O'Brien	2/1/2016	Annual wellness visit
West Hartford	Henry	O'Brien	4/11/2016	Idiopathic abdominal pain
Hartford	Sera	Torres	4/1/2016	Conjunctivitis

Only the five selected fields from the Patient and Visit tables appear in the datasheet. The records are displayed in order according to the values in the PatientID field because it is the primary key field in the primary table, even though this field is not included in the query datasheet.

Kelly plans on frequently tracking the data retrieved by the query, so she asks you to save it as "PatientVisits."

▶ **9.** On the Quick Access Toolbar, click the **Save** button 🖫. The Save As dialog box opens.

▶ **10.** In the Query Name box, type **PatientVisits** and then press the **Enter** key. Access saves the query and displays its name on the object tab.

Kelly decides she wants the records displayed in alphabetical order by city. Because the query displays data in order by the field values in the PatientID field, which is the primary key for the Patient table, you need to sort the records by the City field to display the data in the order Kelly wants.

Sorting Data in a Query

Sorting is the process of rearranging records in a specified order or sequence. Sometimes you might need to sort data before displaying or printing it to meet a specific request. For example, Kelly might want to review visit information arranged by the VisitDate field because she needs to know which months are the busiest for Chatham Community Health Services in terms of patient visits. Cindi might want to view billing information arranged by the InvoiceAmt field because she monitors the finances of the clinic.

When you sort data in a query, you do not change the sequence of the records in the underlying tables. Only the records in the query datasheet are rearranged according to your specifications.

To sort records, you must select the **sort field**, which is the field used to determine the order of records in the datasheet. In this case, Kelly wants the data sorted alphabetically by city, so you need to specify City as the sort field. Sort fields can be Short Text, Number, Date/Time, Currency, AutoNumber, or Yes/No fields, but not Long Text, Hyperlink, or Attachment fields. You sort records in either ascending (increasing) or descending (decreasing) order. Figure 3-10 shows the results of each type of sort for these data types.

Figure 3-10	Sorting results for different data types

Data Type	Ascending Sort Results	Descending Sort Results
Short Text	A to Z (alphabetical)	Z to A (reverse alphabetical)
Number	lowest to highest numeric value	highest to lowest numeric value
Date/Time	oldest to most recent date	most recent to oldest date
Currency	lowest to highest numeric value	highest to lowest numeric value
AutoNumber	lowest to highest numeric value	highest to lowest numeric value
Yes/No	yes (checkmark in check box) then no values	no then yes values

© 2014 Cengage Learning

Access provides several methods for sorting data in a table or query datasheet and in a form. One of the easiest ways is to use the AutoFilter feature for a field.

Using an AutoFilter to Sort Data

As you've probably noticed when working in Datasheet view for a table or query, each column heading has an arrow to the right of the field name. This arrow gives you access to the **AutoFilter** feature, which enables you to quickly sort and display field values in various ways. When you click this arrow, a menu opens with options for sorting and displaying field values. The first two options on the menu enable you to sort the values in the current field in ascending or descending order. Unless you save the datasheet or form after you've sorted the records, the rearrangement of records is temporary.

Next, you'll use an AutoFilter to sort the PatientVisits query results by the City field.

To sort the records using an AutoFilter:

▶ 1. Click the **arrow** on the City column heading to display the AutoFilter menu. See Figure 3-11.

| Figure 3-11 | Using AutoFilter to sort records in the datasheet |

Kelly wants the data sorted in ascending (alphabetical) order by the values in the City field, so you need to select the first option in the menu.

▶ 2. Click **Sort A to Z**. The records are rearranged in ascending alphabetical order by city. A small, upward-pointing arrow appears on the right side of the City column heading. This arrow indicates that the values in the field have been sorted in ascending order. If you used the same method to sort the field values in descending order, a small downward-pointing arrow would appear there instead.

After viewing the query results, Kelly decides that she would also like to see the records arranged by the values in the VisitDate field, so that the data is presented in chronological order. She still wants the records to be arranged by the City field values as well. To produce the results Kelly wants, you need to sort using two fields.

Sorting on Multiple Fields in Design View

Sort fields can be unique or nonunique. A sort field is **unique** if the value in the sort field for each record is different. The PatientID field in the Patient table is an example of a unique sort field because each patient record has a different value in this primary key field. A sort field is **nonunique** if more than one record can have the same value for the sort field. For example, the City field in the Patient table is a nonunique sort field because more than one record can have the same City value.

When the sort field is nonunique, records with the same sort field value are grouped together, but they are not sorted in a specific order within the group. To arrange these grouped records in a specific order, you can specify a **secondary sort field**, which is a second field that determines the order of records that are already sorted by the **primary sort field** (the first sort field specified).

Access lets you select up to 10 different sort fields. When you use the buttons on the ribbon to sort by more than one field, the sort fields must be in adjacent columns in the datasheet. (Note that you cannot use an AutoFilter to sort on more than one field. This method works for a single field only.) You can specify only one type of sort—either ascending or descending—for the selected columns in the datasheet. You highlight the adjacent columns, and Access sorts first by the first column and then by each remaining highlighted column in order from left to right.

Kelly wants the records sorted first by the City field values, as they currently are, and then by the VisitDate values. The two fields are in the correct left-to-right order in the query datasheet, but they are not adjacent, so you cannot use the Ascending and Descending buttons on the ribbon to sort them. You could move the City field to the left of the VisitDate field in the query datasheet, but both columns would have to be sorted with the same sort order. This is not what Kelly wants—she wants the City field values sorted in ascending order so that they are in the correct alphabetical order, for ease of reference; and she wants the VisitDate field values to be sorted in descending order, so that she can focus on the most recent patient visits first. To sort the City and VisitDate fields with different sort orders, you must specify the sort fields in Design view.

In the Query window in Design view, Access first uses the sort field that is leftmost in the design grid. Therefore, you must arrange the fields you want to sort from left to right in the design grid, with the primary sort field being the leftmost. In Design view, multiple sort fields do not have to be adjacent to each other, as they do in Datasheet view; however, they must be in the correct left-to-right order.

TIP

The primary sort field is *not* the same as a table's primary key. A table has at most one primary key, which must be unique, whereas any field in a table can serve as a primary sort field.

REFERENCE

Sorting a Query Datasheet

- In the query datasheet, click the arrow on the column heading for the field you want to sort.
- In the menu that opens, click Sort A to Z for an ascending sort, or click Sort Z to A for a descending sort.

or

- In the query datasheet, select the column or adjacent columns on which you want to sort.
- In the Sort & Filter group on the HOME tab, click the Ascending button or the Descending button.

or

- In Design view, position the fields serving as sort fields from left to right.
- Click the right side of the Sort box for each field you want to sort, and then click Ascending or Descending for the sort order.

To achieve the results Kelly wants, you need to modify the query in Design view to specify the sort order for the two fields.

To select the two sort fields in Design view:

TIP

In Design view, the sort fields do not have to be adjacent, and fields that are not sorted can appear between the sort fields.

1. In the Views group on the HOME tab, click the **View** button to open the query in Design view. The fields are currently in the correct left-to-right order in the design grid, so you only need to specify the sort order for the two fields.

   First, you need to specify an ascending sort order for the City field. Even though the records are already sorted by the values in this field, you need to modify the query so that this sort order, and the sort order you will specify for the VisitDate field, are part of the query's design. Any time the query is run, the records will be sorted according to these specifications.

2. Click the right side of the **City Sort** box to display the arrow and the sort options, and then click **Ascending**. You've selected an ascending sort order for the City field, which will be the primary sort field. The City field is a Short Text field, and an ascending sort order will display the field values in alphabetical order.

3. Click the right side of the **VisitDate Sort** box, click **Descending**, and then click in one of the empty text boxes below the VisitDate field to deselect the setting. You've selected a descending sort order for the VisitDate field, which will be the secondary sort field because it appears to the right of the primary sort field (City) in the design grid. The VisitDate field is a Date/Time field, and a descending sort order will display the field values with the most recent dates first. See Figure 3-12.

Figure 3-12 | Selecting two sort fields in Design view

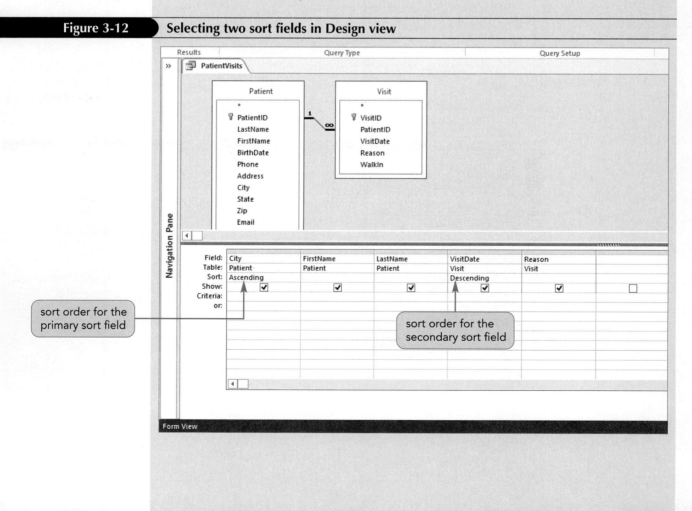

sort order for the primary sort field

sort order for the secondary sort field

You have finished your query changes, so now you can run the query and then save the modified query with the same name.

4. In the Results group on the DESIGN tab, click the **Run** button. Access runs the query and displays the query datasheet. The records appear in ascending order based on the values in the City field. Within groups of records with the same City field value, the records appear in descending order by the values of the VisitDate field. See Figure 3-13.

Figure 3-13   **Datasheet sorted on two fields**

primary sort field
secondary sort field
records grouped by City are shown in descending order by VisitDate

When you save the query, all of your design changes—including the selection of the sort fields—are saved with the query. The next time Kelly runs the query, the records will appear sorted by the primary and secondary sort fields.

5. On the Quick Access Toolbar, click the **Save** button to save the revised PatientVisits query.

Kelly knows that Chatham Community Health Services has seen an increase in the number of patients from Windsor. She would like to focus briefly on the information for patients in that city only. Also, she is interested in knowing how many patients from Windsor have had annual wellness exams. She is concerned that, although more patients are coming to the clinic from this city, not enough of them are scheduling wellness visits. Selecting only the records with a City field value of "Windsor" and a Reason field value beginning with "Annual" is a temporary change that Kelly wants in the datasheet, so you do not need to switch to Design view and change the query. Instead, you can apply a filter.

Filtering Data

A **filter** is a set of restrictions you place on the records in an open datasheet or form to *temporarily* isolate a subset of the records. A filter lets you view different subsets of displayed records so that you can focus on only the data you need. Unless you save a query or form with a filter applied, an applied filter is not available the next time you run the query or open the form.

The simplest technique for filtering records is Filter By Selection. **Filter By Selection** lets you select all or part of a field value in a datasheet or form, and then display only those records that contain the selected value in the field. You can also use the AutoFilter feature to filter records. When you click the arrow on a column heading, the menu that opens provides options for filtering the datasheet based on a field value or the selected part of a field value. Another technique for filtering records is to use **Filter By Form**, which changes your datasheet to display blank fields. Then you can select a value using the arrow that appears when you click any blank field to apply a filter that selects only those records containing that value.

REFERENCE

Using Filter By Selection

- In the datasheet or form, select the part of the field value that will be the basis for the filter; or, if the filter will be based on the entire field value, click anywhere within the field value.
- Make sure the HOME tab is displayed.
- In the Sort & Filter group, click the Selection button.
- Click the type of filter you want to apply.

For Kelly's request, you need to select a City field value of Windsor, and then use Filter By Selection to display only those records with this value. Then you will filter the records further by selecting only those records with a Reason value that begins with "Annual" (for Annual wellness visit).

To display the records using Filter By Selection:

▶ 1. In the query datasheet, locate the first occurrence of a City field containing the value **Windsor**, and then click anywhere within that field value.

▶ 2. In the Sort & Filter group on the HOME tab, click the **Selection** button. A menu opens with options for the type of filter to apply. See Figure 3-14.

Figure 3-14   **Using Filter By Selection**

options for the type of filter to apply

current field is the basis for the filter

The menu provides options for displaying only those records with a City field value that equals the selected value (in this case, Windsor); does not equal the value; contains the value somewhere within the field; or does not contain the value somewhere within the field. You want to display all the records whose City field value equals Windsor.

3. In the Selection menu, click **Equals "Windsor"**. Access displays the filtered results. Only the 24 records that have a City field value of Windsor appear in the datasheet. See Figure 3-15.

Figure 3-15   **Datasheet after applying the filter**

click to display more options for filtering the field

indicate that a filter has been applied to the datasheet

datasheet displays only records with a City value of Windsor

The button labeled "Filtered" to the right of the navigation buttons and the notation "FILTERED" on the status bar both indicate that a filter has been applied to the datasheet. Also, notice that the Toggle Filter button in the Sort & Filter group on the HOME tab is active; you can click this button or the Filtered button next to the navigation buttons to toggle between the filtered and unfiltered displays of the query datasheet. The City column heading also has a filter icon on it; you can click this icon to display additional options for filtering the field.

Next, Kelly wants to view only those records with a Reason field value beginning with the word "Annual" so she can view the records for annual wellness visits. You need to apply an additional filter to the datasheet.

4. In any Reason field value beginning with the word "Annual," select only the word **Annual**.

5. In the Sort & Filter group, click the **Selection** button. The same four filter types are available for this selection as when you filtered the City field.

6. On the Selection menu, click **Begins With "Annual"**. The second filter is applied to the query datasheet, which now shows only the four records for customers located in Windsor who have had annual wellness visits at the clinic.

Now you can redisplay all the query records by clicking the Toggle Filter button, which you use to switch between the filtered and unfiltered displays.

TIP

The ScreenTip for this button is Remove Filter.

7. In the Sort & Filter group, click the **Toggle Filter** button. Access removes the filter and redisplays all 85 records in the query datasheet.

8. Close the PatientVisits query. Access asks if you want to save your changes to the design of the query—in this case, the filtered display, which is still available through the Toggle Filter button. Kelly does not want the query saved with the filter because she doesn't need to view the filtered information on a regular basis.

9. Click the **No** button to close the query without saving the changes.

10. If you are not continuing to Session 3.2, click the **FILE** tab, and then click **Close** in the navigation bar to close the Chatham database.

REVIEW

Session 3.1 Quick Check

1. In Datasheet view, what is the difference between navigation mode and editing mode?

2. What command can you use in Datasheet view to remove the display of one or more fields from the datasheet?

3. What is a select query?

4. Describe the field list and the design grid in the Query window in Design view.

5. How are a table datasheet and a query datasheet similar? How are they different?

6. For a Date/Time field, how do the records appear when sorted in ascending order?

7. When you define multiple sort fields in Design view, describe how the sort fields must be positioned in the design grid.

8. A(n) _____ is a set of restrictions you place on the records in an open datasheet or form to isolate a subset of records temporarily.

Session 3.2 Visual Overview:

When creating queries in Design view, you can enter criteria so that Access will display only selected records in the query results.

Field:	PatientID	LastName	FirstName	BirthDate	City
Table:	Patient	Patient	Patient	Patient	Patient
Sort:					
Show:	✓	✓	✓	✓	✓
Criteria:					"Bloomfield"
or:					

To define a condition for a field, you place the condition in the field's Criteria box in the design grid.

To tell Access which records you want to select, you must specify a condition as part of the query. A **condition** is a criterion, or rule, that determines which records are selected.

Field:	InvoiceNum	InvoiceDate	InvoiceAmt	
Table:	Billing	Billing	Billing	
Sort:				
Show:	✓	✓	✓	☐
Criteria:			>250	
or:				

A condition usually consists of an operator, often a comparison operator, and a value. A **comparison operator** asks Access to compare the value in a field to the condition value and to select all the records for which the condition is true.

Field:	VisitID	PatientID	VisitDate	Reason
Table:	Visit	Visit	Visit	Visit
Sort:				
Show:	✓	✓	✓	✓
Criteria:			Between #12/1/2015# And #12/31/2015#	
or:				

Most comparison operators (such as Between…And…) ask Access to select records that match a range of values for the condition—in this case, all records with dates that fall within the range shown.

Selection Criteria in Queries

The results of a query containing selection criteria include only the records that meet the specified criteria.

BloomfieldPatients

Patient ID	Last Name	First Name	Date of Birth	City
22501	Darcy	Edward	7/15/1986	Bloomfield
22506	Gorski	Drea	2/19/2005	Bloomfield
22513	Smith	Troy	1/31/1996	Bloomfield
22521	Engber	Cathy	4/7/2000	Bloomfield
22522	Li	Siyang	7/25/1986	Bloomfield
22540	Fielder	Pam	12/6/1978	Bloomfield
22557	Kirk	Isobel	11/18/1965	Bloomfield
*				

The results of this query show only patients from Bloomfield because the condition "Bloomfield" in the City field's Criteria box specifies that Access should select records only with City field values of Bloomfield. This type of condition is called an **exact match** because the value in the specified field must match the condition exactly in order for the record to be included in the query results.

LargeInvoiceAmts

Invoice Num	Invoice Date	Invoice Amt
35815	11/16/2015	$300.00
35900	01/20/2016	$300.00
36002	03/15/2016	$450.00
36074	04/12/2016	$450.00
*		$0.00

The results of this query show only those invoices with amounts greater than $250 because the condition >250, which uses the greater than comparison operator, specifies that Access should select records only with InvoiceAmt field values over $250.

DecemberVisits

Visit ID	Patient ID	Date of Visit	Reason/Diagnosis
1550	22549	12/1/2015	Influenza
1552	22511	12/3/2015	Annual wellness visit
1555	22520	12/7/2015	Annual wellness visit
1557	22526	12/10/2015	Annual wellness visit
1560	22514	12/15/2015	Influenza
1562	22516	12/22/2015	COPD management visit
*			

The results of this query show only those patient visits that took place in December 2015 because the condition in the VisitDate's Criteria box specifies that Access should select records only with a visit date between 12/1/2015 and 12/31/2015.

Defining Record Selection Criteria for Queries

Cindi wants to display patient and visit information for all patients who live in Bloomfield. She is considering having the clinic hold a health fair in Bloomfield, with a special emphasis on hypertension, so she is interested in knowing more about the patients from this city. For this request, you could create a query to select the correct fields and all records in the Patient and Visit tables, select a City field value of Bloomfield in the query datasheet, and then click the Selection button and choose the appropriate filter option to display the information for only those patients in Bloomfield. However, a faster way of displaying the data Cindi needs is to create a query that displays the selected fields and only those records in the Patient and Visit tables that satisfy a condition.

Just as you can display selected fields from a database in a query datasheet, you can display selected records. To tell Access which records you want to select, you must specify a condition as part of the query, as illustrated in the Session 3.2 Visual Overview. A condition usually includes one of the comparison operators shown in Figure 3-16.

Figure 3-16   **Access comparison operators**

Operator	Meaning	Example
=	equal to (optional; default operator)	="Hall"
<>	not equal to	<>"Hall"
<	less than	<#1/1/99#
<=	less than or equal to	<=100
>	greater than	>"C400"
>=	greater than or equal to	>=18.75
Between … And …	between two values (inclusive)	Between 50 And 325
In ()	in a list of values	In ("Hall", "Seeger")
Like	matches a pattern that includes wildcards	Like "706*"

© 2014 Cengage Learning

Specifying an Exact Match

For Cindi's request, you need to create a query that will display only those records in the Patient table with the value Bloomfield in the City field. This type of condition is an exact match because the value in the specified field must match the condition exactly in order for the record to be included in the query results. You'll create the query in Design view.

To create the query in Design view:

1. If you took a break after the previous session, make sure that the Chatham database is open and the Navigation Pane is closed.

2. On the ribbon, click the **CREATE** tab.

3. In the Queries group, click the **Query Design** button. The Show Table dialog box opens. You need to add the Patient and Visit tables to the Query window.

4. Click **Patient** in the Tables list, click the **Add** button, click **Visit**, click the **Add** button, and then click the **Close** button.

> **5.** Use the $\updownarrow$ pointer to resize both field lists so that all the fields are displayed and the vertical scroll bars disappear.

> **6.** Add the following fields from the Patient table to the design grid in the order shown: **LastName**, **FirstName**, **Phone**, **Address**, **City**, and **Email**.

> Cindi also wants information from the Visit table included in the query results.

> **7.** Add the following fields from the Visit table to the design grid in the order shown: **VisitID**, **VisitDate**, and **Reason**. See Figure 3-17.

Figure 3-17	Design grid after adding fields from both tables

Field:	LastName	FirstName	Phone	Address	City	Email	VisitID	VisitDate	Reason	∨	
Table:	Patient	Patient	Patient	Patient	Patient	Patient	Visit	Visit	Visit		
Sort:											
Show:	✓	✓	✓	✓	✓	✓	✓	✓	✓	☐	☐
Criteria:											
or:											

enter condition here

Ready

The field lists for the Patient and Visit tables appear in the top portion of the window, and the join line indicating a one-to-many relationship connects the two tables. The fields you selected appear in the design grid.

To display the information Cindi wants, you need to enter the condition for the City field in its Criteria box (see Figure 3-17). Cindi wants to display only those records with a City field value of Bloomfield.

To enter the exact match condition, and then save and run the query:

> **1.** Click the **City Criteria** box, type **Bloomfield**, and then press the **Enter** key. The condition changes to "Bloomfield".

> Access automatically enclosed the condition you typed in quotation marks. You must enclose text values in quotation marks when using them as selection criteria. If you omit the quotation marks, however, Access will include them automatically in most cases. Some words—including "in" and "select"—are special keywords in Access that are reserved for functions and commands. If you want to enter one of these keywords as the condition, you must type the quotation marks around the text or Access will display an error message and will not allow the condition to be entered.

> **2.** On the Quick Access Toolbar, click the **Save** button ⊟ to open the Save As dialog box.

> **3.** In the Query Name box, type **BloomfieldPatients** and then press the **Enter** key. Access saves the query with the specified name and displays the name on the object tab.

> **4.** In the Results group on the DESIGN tab, click the **Run** button. Access runs the query and displays the selected field values for only those records with a City field value of Bloomfield. A total of 14 records is selected and displayed in the datasheet. See Figure 3-18.

Figure 3-18   Datasheet displaying selected fields and records

Last Name	First Name	Phone	Address	City	Email	Visit ID	Date of Visit	Reason/Diagnosis
Darcy	Edward	860-305-3985	723 Oxford Ave	Bloomfield	edarcy@example.org	1549	11/30/2015	Influenza
Gorski	Drea	860-305-8394	83 Everett Ln	Bloomfield		1667	4/1/2016	Fifth Disease
Gorski	Drea	860-305-8394	83 Everett Ln	Bloomfield		1683	4/8/2016	Fifth Disease follow-up
Smith	Troy	860-305-0384	16 Ravine Rd	Bloomfield	t_smith@example.edu	1575	1/13/2016	Broken leg
Smith	Troy	860-305-0384	16 Ravine Rd	Bloomfield	t_smith@example.edu	1626	2/24/2016	Follow-up - cast removal
Engber	Cathy	860-305-3048	58 Deering Pl	Bloomfield		1690	4/13/2016	Varicella
Li	Siyang	860-305-6548	225 Krauss Rd	Bloomfield	li.siyang@example.org	1527	11/9/2015	Allergies - environmental
Li	Siyang	860-305-6548	225 Krauss Rd	Bloomfield	li.siyang@example.org	1634	3/3/2016	Allergies - environmental follow-up
Fielder	Pam	860-305-2689	39 Unger Ave	Bloomfield	pfielder@example.org	1550	12/1/2015	Influenza
Fielder	Pam	860-305-2689	39 Unger Ave	Bloomfield	pfielder@example.org	1673	4/6/2016	Pertussis
Kirk	Isobel	860-305-7384	48 Grafton St	Bloomfield		1613	2/11/2016	Hypertension
Kirk	Isobel	860-305-7384	48 Grafton St	Bloomfield		1628	2/25/2016	Hypertension monitoring
Kirk	Isobel	860-305-7384	48 Grafton St	Bloomfield		1640	3/9/2016	Hypertension monitoring
Kirk	Isobel	860-305-7384	48 Grafton St	Bloomfield		1679	4/8/2016	Hypertension monitoring

only records with a City field value of Bloomfield are selected

14 records are selected

Record: 1 of 14   No Filter   Search

Ready

Cindi realizes that it's not necessary to include the City field values in the query results. The name of the query, BloomfieldPatients, indicates that the query design includes all patients who live in Bloomfield, so the City field values are unnecessary and repetitive. Also, she decides that she would prefer the query datasheet to show the fields from the Visit table first, followed by the Patient table fields. You need to modify the query to produce the results Cindi wants.

Modifying a Query

After you create a query and view the results, you might need to make changes to the query if the results are not what you expected or require. First, Cindi asks you to modify the BloomfieldPatients query so that it does not display the City field values in the query results.

To remove the display of the City field values:

1. In the Views group on the HOME tab, click the **View** button. The BloomfieldPatients query opens in Design view.

   You need to keep the City field as part of the query design because it contains the defined condition for the query. You only need to remove the display of the field's values from the query results.

2. Click the **City Show** check box to remove the checkmark. The query will still find only those records with the value Bloomfield in the City field, but the query results will not display these field values.

Next, you need to change the order of the fields in the query so that the visit information is listed first.

To move the Visit table fields to precede the Patient table fields:

1. Position the pointer on the VisitID field selector until the pointer changes to a ↓ shape, and then click to select the field. See Figure 3-19.

Figure 3-19 Selected VisitID field

- Show check box is cleared
- VisitID field selector
- entire column is selected

2. Position the pointer on the VisitID field selector, and then click and hold down the mouse button; notice that the pointer changes to ↖ and a black vertical line appears to the left of the selected field. This line represents the selected field when you drag the mouse to move it.

3. Drag to the left until the vertical line representing the selected field is positioned to the left of the LastName field. See Figure 3-20.

Figure 3-20 Dragging the field in the design grid

- line representing selected field
- drag pointer to here
- selected field being moved

TIP

Instead of moving a field by dragging, you can also delete the field and then add it back to the design grid in the location you want.

4. Release the mouse button. The VisitID field moves to the left of the LastName field.

You can also select and move multiple fields at once. You need to select and move the VisitDate and Reason fields so that they follow the VisitID field in the query design. To select multiple fields, you click and drag the mouse over the field selectors for the fields you want.

5. Click and hold the pointer ↓ on the VisitDate field selector, drag the pointer to the right to select the Reason field, and then release the mouse button. Both fields are now selected. See Figure 3-21.

Figure 3-21 | **Multiple fields selected to be moved**

6. Position the pointer ⌖ anywhere near the top of the two selected fields, and then click and drag to the left until the vertical line representing the selected fields is positioned to the left of the LastName field.

7. Release the mouse button. The three fields from the Visit table are now the first three fields in the query design.

You have finished making the modifications to the query Cindi requested, so you can now run the query.

8. In the Results group on the DESIGN tab, click the **Run** button. Access displays the results of the modified query. See Figure 3-22.

Figure 3-22 | **Results of the modified query**

fields from the Visit table are now listed first in the query datasheet

City field values are no longer displayed

Note that the City field values are no longer displayed in the query results.

9. Save and close the BloomfieldPatients query.

After viewing the query results, Cindi decides that she would like to see the same fields, but only for those records with a VisitDate field value before 1/1/2016. She is interested to know which patients of Chatham Community Health Services in all cities have not been to the clinic recently, so that her staff can follow up with these patients by sending them reminder notes or emails. To create the query that will produce the results Cindi wants, you need to use a comparison operator to match a range of values—in this case, any VisitDate value less than 1/1/2016.

Using a Comparison Operator to Match a Range of Values

After you create and save a query, you can double-click the query name in the Navigation Pane to run the query again. You can then click the View button to change its design. You can also use an existing query as the basis for creating another query. Because the design of the query you need to create next is similar to the BloomfieldPatients query, you will copy, paste, and rename this query to create the new query. Using this approach keeps the BloomfieldPatients query intact.

To create the new query by copying the BloomfieldPatients query:

1. Open the Navigation Pane. Note that the BloomfieldPatients query is listed in the Queries section.

   You need to use the shortcut menu to copy the BloomfieldPatients query and paste it in the Navigation Pane; then you'll give the copied query a different name.

2. In the Queries section of the Navigation Pane, right-click **BloomfieldPatients** to select it and display the shortcut menu.

3. Click **Copy** on the shortcut menu.

4. Right-click the empty area near the bottom of the Navigation Pane, and then click **Paste** on the shortcut menu. The Paste As dialog box opens with the text "Copy Of BloomfieldPatients" in the Query Name box. Because Cindi wants the new query to show data for patients who have not visited the clinic recently, you'll name the new query "EarlierVisits."

5. In the Query Name box, type **EarlierVisits** and then press the **Enter** key. The new query appears in the Queries section of the Navigation Pane.

6. Double-click the **EarlierVisits** query to open, or run, the query. The design of this query is currently the same as the original BloomfieldPatients query.

7. Close the Navigation Pane.

Next, you need to open the query in Design view and modify its design to produce the results Cindi wants—to display only those records with VisitDate field values that are earlier than, or less than, 1/1/2016.

To modify the design of the new query:

1. In the Views group on the HOME tab, click the **View** button to display the query in Design view.

2. Click the **VisitDate Criteria** box, type **<1/1/2016** and then press the **Tab** key. See Figure 3-23.

Figure 3-23   Criteria entered for the VisitDate field

	VisitID	VisitDate	Reason	LastName	FirstName	Phone	Address	Email	City			
Field:	VisitID	VisitDate	Reason	LastName	FirstName	Phone	Address	Email	City			
Table:	Visit	Visit	Visit	Patient	Patient	Patient	Patient	Patient	Patient			
Sort:												
Show:	✔	✔	✔	✔	✔	✔	✔	✔	☐	☐	☐	☐
Criteria:		<#1/1/2016#							"Bloomfield"			
or:												

new condition entered

original condition needs to be deleted

Note that Access automatically encloses the date criteria with number signs. The condition specifies that a record will be selected only if its VisitDate field value is less than (earlier than) 1/1/2016. Before you run the query, you need to delete the condition for the City field. Recall that the City field is part of the query, but its values are not displayed in the query results. When you modified the query to remove the City field values from the query results, Access moved the field to the end of the design grid. You need to delete the City field's condition, specify that the City field values should be included in the query results, and then move the field back to its original position following the Address field.

▶ **3.** Press the **Tab** key six times until the condition for the City field is highlighted, and then press the **Delete** key. The condition for the City field is removed.

▶ **4.** Click the **Show** check box for the City field to insert a checkmark so that the field values will be displayed in the query results.

▶ **5.** Use the pointer to select the City field, drag the selected field to the left of the Email field, and then click in an empty box to deselect the City field. See Figure 3-24.

| Figure 3-24 | Design grid after moving the City field |

City field moved back to its original location

Show check box is selected

condition removed from City Criteria box

▶ **6.** In the Results group on the DESIGN tab, click the **Run** button. Access runs the query and displays the selected fields for only those records with a VisitDate field value less than 1/1/2016. The query displays a total of 18 records. See Figure 3-25.

Figure 3-25   **Running the modified query**

Visit ID	Date of Visit	Reason/Diagnosis	Last Name	First Name	Phone	Address	City	Email
1527	11/9/2015	Allergies - environmental	Li	Siyang	860-305-6548	225 Krauss Rd	Bloomfield	li.siyang@example.org
1528	11/9/2015	Diabetes mellitis Type 2 - initial diagnosis	Weiss	Matthew	860-426-7492	38 German St	Hartford	matt.weiss@example.org
1530	11/10/2015	Seborrheic dermatitis	Booker	Thomas	860-661-2539	59 Nicola Ave	Hartford	
1535	11/12/2015	Transverse fracture of left ulna	Ingram	Julia	860-661-4937	834 Kiefer Rd	Hartford	
1536	11/17/2015	Gastroenteritis	Swenson	Lucia	860-226-0293	83 Osage Ave	Hartford	
1538	11/17/2015	Migraine	Student Last	Student First	860-938-2822	501 Perkins Dr	Hartford	student1@example.edu
1539	11/18/2015	Annual wellness visit	Aguilar	Lilian	860-374-5724	329 Fairchild Ave	Hartford	laguilar@example.com
1541	11/24/2015	Gastroenteritis - follow up	Swenson	Lucia	860-226-0293	83 Osage Ave	Hartford	
1542	11/24/2015	Influenza	Mehta	Amrita	860-552-0375	28 Aiken Ave	Windsor	a.mehta@example.com
1544	11/25/2015	Influenza	Lewis	Patrice	860-552-5830	83 Highland St	Windsor	plewis5@example.org
1548	11/30/2015	Hypertension	Belanger	Malcolm	860-637-3927	723 Nicola Ave	West Hartford	
1549	11/30/2015	Influenza	Darcy	Edward	860-305-3985	723 Oxford Ave	Bloomfield	edarcy@example.org
1550	12/1/2015	Influenza	Fielder	Pam	860-305-2689	39 Unger Ave	Bloomfield	pfielder@example.org
1552	12/3/2015	Annual wellness visit	Castro	Daniel	860-637-0430	61 Osmond Way	West Hartford	d_castro@example.com
1555	12/7/2015	Annual wellness visit	Hallick	Davis	860-552-4495	84 Churchill Pl	Windsor	dhallick@example.com
1557	12/10/2015	Annual wellness visit	Swenson	Lucia	860-226-0293	83 Osage Ave	Hartford	
1560	12/15/2015	Influenza	Parker	Ian	860-938-1873	12 Adelbert St	Hartford	ian_parker@example.org
1562	12/22/2015	COPD management visit	King	Susan	860-661-9347	48 Fenton St	Hartford	susan.king@example.edu

only records with a VisitDate field value less than 1/1/2016 are selected

Record: 1 of 18   No Filter   Search

18 records are selected

7. Save and close the EarlierVisits query.

Cindi continues to analyze patient visits to Chatham Community Health Services. She is especially concerned about being proactive and reaching out to older patients well in advance of flu season. With this in mind, she would like to see a list of all patients who are age 60 or older and who have visited the clinic suffering from influenza. She wants to track these patients in particular so that her staff can contact them early for flu shots. To produce this list, you need to create a query containing two conditions—one for the patient's date of birth and another for the reason/diagnosis for each patient visit.

Defining Multiple Selection Criteria for Queries

Multiple conditions require you to use **logical operators** to combine two or more conditions. When you want a record selected only if two or more conditions are met, you need to use the **And logical operator**. In this case, Cindi wants to see only those records with a BirthDate field value less than or equal to 12/31/1956 *and* a Reason field value of "Influenza." If you place conditions in separate fields in the *same* Criteria row of the design grid, all conditions in that row must be met in order for a record to be included in the query results. However, if you place conditions in *different* Criteria rows, a record will be selected if at least one of the conditions is met. If none of the conditions are met, Access does not select the record. When you place conditions in different Criteria rows, you are using the **Or logical operator**. Figure 3-26 illustrates the difference between the And and Or logical operators.

| Figure 3-26 | Logical operators And and Or for multiple selection criteria |

© 2014 Cengage Learning

The And Logical Operator

To create the query for Cindi, you need to use the And logical operator to show only the records for patients who were born on or before 12/31/1956 *and* who have visited the clinic because of influenza. You'll create a new query based on both the Patient and Visit tables to produce the necessary results. In the query design, both conditions you specify will appear in the same Criteria row; therefore, the query will select records only if both conditions are met.

To create a new query using the And logical operator:

▶ **1.** On the ribbon, click the **CREATE** tab.

▶ **2.** In the Queries group, click the **Query Design** button.

▶ **3.** Add the **Patient** and **Visit** tables to the Query window, and then close the Show Table dialog box. Resize both field lists to display all the field names.

▶ **4.** Add the following fields from the Patient field list to the design grid in the order shown: **FirstName**, **LastName**, **BirthDate**, **Phone**, and **City**.

▶ **5.** Add the **VisitDate** and **Reason** fields from the Visit table to the design grid.

Now you need to enter the two conditions for the query.

▶ **6.** Click the **BirthDate Criteria** box, and then type **<=12/31/1956**.

▶ **7.** Press the **Tab** key four times to move to the **Reason Criteria** box, type **Influenza**, and then press the **Tab** key. See Figure 3-27.

Figure 3-27   **Query to find older patients who have had influenza**

And logical operator with conditions entered in the same row

Field:	FirstName	LastName	BirthDate	Phone	City	VisitDate	Reason
Table:	Patient	Patient	Patient	Patient	Patient	Visit	Visit
Sort:							
Show:	✓	✓	✓	✓	✓	✓	✓
Criteria:			<=#12/31/1956#				"Influenza"
or:							

Ready

▶ **8.** Run the query. Access displays only those records that meet both conditions: a BirthDate field value less than or equal to 12/31/1956 *and* a Reason field value of Influenza. Two records are selected for two different patients. See Figure 3-28.

Figure 3-28   **Results of query using the And logical operator**

First Name	Last Name	Date of Birth	Phone	City	Date of Visit	Reason/Diagnosis
Ian	Parker	6/3/1953	860-938-1873	Hartford	12/15/2015	Influenza
Jane	Ropiak	2/7/1950	860-938-7830	Hartford	3/3/2016	Influenza

▶ **9.** On the Quick Access Toolbar, click the **Save** button 🖫, and then save the query as **OlderAndFluPatients**.

▶ **10.** Close the query.

Cindi meets with staff member Ethan to discuss the issue of influenza and keeping patients informed about receiving flu shots at the clinic. After viewing the results of the OlderAndFluPatients query, Ethan suggests that the clinic should reach out to all elderly patients regarding flu shots, because this segment of the population is particularly susceptible to the flu. In addition, he thinks they should contact any patient who has visited the clinic suffering from influenza to keep these patients informed about flu shots well in advance of flu season. To help with their planning, Cindi and Ethan have asked you to produce a list of all patients who were born on or before 12/31/1956 or who visited the clinic because of influenza. To create this query, you need to use the Or logical operator.

The Or Logical Operator

To create the query that Cindi and Ethan requested, your query must select a record when either one of two conditions is satisfied or when both conditions are satisfied. That is, a record is selected if the BirthDate field value is less than or equal to 12/31/1956 *or* if the Reason field value is Influenza *or* if both conditions are met. You will enter the condition for the BirthDate field in the Criteria row and the condition for the Reason field in the "or" criteria row, thereby using the Or logical operator.

To display the information Cindi and Ethan want to view, you'll create a new query based on the existing OlderAndFluPatients query, since it already contains the necessary fields. Then you'll specify the conditions using the Or logical operator.

To create a new query using the Or logical operator:

1. Open the Navigation Pane. You'll use the shortcut menu to copy and paste the OlderAndFluPatients query to create the new query.

2. In the Queries section of the Navigation Pane, right-click **OlderAndFluPatients** to select it and display the shortcut menu.

3. Click **Copy** on the shortcut menu.

4. Right-click the empty area near the bottom of the Navigation Pane, and then click **Paste** on the shortcut menu. The Paste As dialog box opens with the text "Copy Of OlderAndFluPatients" in the Query Name box. Because Cindi wants the new query to show data for all older patients or patients who have visited the clinic due to influenza, you'll name the new query "OlderOrFluPatients."

5. In the Query Name box, type **OlderOrFluPatients** and then press the **Enter** key. The new query appears in the Queries section of the Navigation Pane.

6. In the Navigation Pane, right-click the **OlderOrFluPatients** query to select it and display the shortcut menu, and then click **Design View** on the shortcut menu to open the query in Design view.

7. Close the Navigation Pane.

   The query already contains all the fields Cindi and Ethan want to view, as well as the first condition—a BirthDate field value less than or equal to 12/31/1956. Because you want records selected if either the condition for the BirthDate field or the condition for the Reason field is satisfied, you must delete the existing condition for the Reason field in the Criteria row and then enter this same condition in the "or" row of the design grid for the Reason field.

8. In the design grid, click at the end of the **Reason Criteria** box and then press the **Backspace** key until the condition "Influenza" is deleted.

9. Press the ↓ key to move to the "or" row for the Reason field, type **Influenza**, and then press the **Tab** key. See Figure 3-29.

Figure 3-29   **Query window with the Or logical operator**

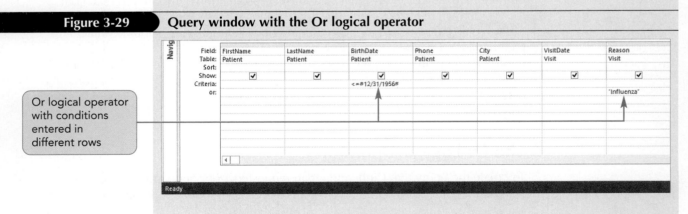

Or logical operator with conditions entered in different rows

Cindi wants the list displayed in descending order by BirthDate to better analyze the data.

10. Click the right side of the **BirthDate Sort** box, and then click **Descending**.

11. Run the query. Access displays only those records that meet either condition: a BirthDate field value less than or equal to 12/31/1956 *or* a Reason field value of Influenza. Access also selects records that meet both conditions. The query displays a total of 38 records. The records in the query datasheet appear in descending order based on the values in the BirthDate field. See Figure 3-30.

Figure 3-30   Results of query using the Or logical operator

datasheet selector

records with a Reason field value of Influenza

records that meet both criteria

records with BirthDate field values less than or equal to 12/31/1956

38 records are selected

Understanding the Results of Using And vs. Or

INSIGHT

When you use the And logical operator to define multiple selection criteria in a query, you *narrow* the results produced by the query because a record must meet more than one condition to be included in the results. For example, the OlderAndFluPatients query you created resulted in only 2 records. When you use the Or logical operator, you *broaden* the results produced by the query because a record must meet only one of the conditions to be included in the results. For example, the OlderOrFluPatients query you created resulted in 38 records. This is an important distinction to keep in mind when you include multiple selection criteria in queries, so that the queries you create will produce the results you want.

Cindi would like to spend some time reviewing the results of the OlderOrFluPatients query. To make this task easier, she asks you to change how the datasheet is displayed.

Changing a Datasheet's Appearance

You can make many formatting changes to a datasheet to improve its appearance or readability. Many of these modifications are familiar types of changes you can also make in Word documents or Excel spreadsheets, such as modifying the font type, size, color, and the alignment of text. You can also apply different colors to the rows and columns in a datasheet to enhance its appearance.

Modifying the Font Size

Depending on the size of the monitor you are using or the screen resolution, you might need to increase or decrease the size of the font in a datasheet to view more or fewer columns of data. Cindi asks you to change the font size in the query datasheet from the default 11 points to 14 points so that she can read the text more easily.

To change the font size in the datasheet:

▶ **1.** In the Text Formatting group on the HOME tab, click the **Font Size** arrow, and then click **14**. The font size for the entire datasheet increases to 14 points.

Next, you need to resize the columns to their best fit, so that all field values are displayed. Instead of resizing each column individually, you'll use the datasheet selector to select all the columns and resize them at the same time.

▶ **2.** Click the **datasheet selector**, which is the box to the left of the First Name column heading (see Figure 3-30). All the columns in the datasheet are highlighted, indicating they are selected.

▶ **3.** Position the pointer ↔ on the vertical line on the right of any column in the datasheet, and then double-click the vertical line. All the columns visible on the screen are resized to their best fit. Scroll down and repeat the resizing, as necessary, to make sure that all field values are fully displayed.

Trouble? If all the columns are not visible on your screen, you need to scroll the datasheet to the right to make sure all field values for all columns are fully displayed. If you need to resize any columns, click a field value first to deselect the columns before resizing an individual column.

▶ **4.** Click any value in the First Name column to make it the current field and to deselect the columns in the datasheet.

Changing the Alternate Row Color in a Datasheet

Access uses themes to format the objects in a database. A **theme** is a predefined set of formats including colors, fonts, and other effects that enhance an object's appearance and usability. When you create a database, Access applies the Office theme to objects as you create them. By default, the Office theme formats every other row in a datasheet with a gray background color to distinguish one row from another, making it easier to view and read the contents of a datasheet. The gray alternate row color provides a subtle difference compared to the rows that have the default white color. You can change the alternate row color in a datasheet to something more noticeable using the Alternate Row Color button in the Text Formatting group on the HOME tab. Cindi suggests that you change the alternate row color in the datasheet to see the effect of using this feature.

To change the alternate row color in the datasheet:

1. In the Text Formatting group on the HOME tab, click the **Alternate Row Color** button arrow to display the gallery of color choices. See Figure 3-31.

Figure 3-31 **Gallery of color choices for alternate row color**

The Theme Colors section provides colors from the default Office theme, so that your datasheet's color scheme matches the one in use for the database. The Standard Colors section provides many standard color choices. You might also see a Recent Colors section, with colors that you have recently used in a datasheet. At the bottom of the gallery, you could also choose the No Color option, which sets each row's background color to white; or the More Colors option, which creates a custom color. You'll use one of the theme colors.

TIP

The name of the color appears in a ScreenTip when you point to a color in the gallery.

2. In the Theme Colors section, click the color box for **Orange, Accent 2, Lighter 60%** (third row, sixth color box). The alternate row color is applied to the query datasheet. See Figure 3-32.

Figure 3-32 **Datasheet formatted with alternate row color**

Every other row in the datasheet uses the selected theme color. Cindi likes how the datasheet looks with this color scheme, so she asks you to save the query.

3. Save and close the OlderOrFluPatients query. The query is saved with both the increased font size and the orange alternate row color.

Next, Cindi turns her attention to some financial aspects of operating the clinic. She wants to use the Chatham database to perform calculations. She is considering imposing a 2% late fee on unpaid invoices and wants to know exactly what the late fee charges would be, should she decide to institute such a policy in the future. To produce the information for Cindi, you need to create a calculated field.

Creating a Calculated Field

In addition to using queries to retrieve, sort, and filter data in a database, you can use a query to perform calculations. To perform a calculation, you define an **expression** containing a combination of database fields, constants, and operators. For numeric expressions, the data types of the database fields must be Number, Currency, or Date/Time; the constants are numbers such as .02 (for the 2% late fee); and the operators can be arithmetic operators (+ − * /) or other specialized operators. In complex expressions, you can enclose calculations in parentheses to indicate which one should be performed first; any calculation within parentheses is completed before calculations outside the parentheses. In expressions without parentheses, Access performs basic calculations using the following order of precedence: multiplication and division before addition and subtraction. When operators have equal precedence, Access calculates them in order from left to right.

To perform a calculation in a query, you add a calculated field to the query. A **calculated field** is a field that displays the results of an expression. A calculated field that you create with an expression appears in a query datasheet or in a form or report; however, it does not exist in a database. When you run a query that contains a calculated field, Access evaluates the expression defined by the calculated field and displays the resulting value in the query datasheet, form, or report.

To enter an expression for a calculated field, you can type it directly in a Field box in the design grid. Alternately, you can open the Zoom box or Expression Builder and use either one to enter the expression. The **Zoom box** is a dialog box that you can use to enter text, expressions, or other values. To use the Zoom box, however, you must know all the parts of the expression you want to create. **Expression Builder** is an Access tool that makes it easy for you to create an expression; it contains a box for entering the expression, an option for displaying and choosing common operators, and one or more lists of expression elements, such as table and field names. Unlike a Field box, which is too narrow to show an entire expression at one time, the Zoom box and Expression Builder are large enough to display longer expressions. In most cases, Expression Builder provides the easiest way to enter expressions because you don't have to know all the parts of the expression; you can choose the necessary elements from the Expression Builder dialog box, which also helps to prevent typing errors.

REFERENCE

Using Expression Builder

- Create and save the query in which you want to include a calculated field.
- Open the query in Design view.
- In the design grid, click the Field box in which you want to create an expression.
- In the Query Setup group on the DESIGN tab, click the Builder button.
- Use the expression elements and common operators to build the expression, or type the expression directly in the expression box.
- Click the OK button.

To produce the information Cindi wants, you need to create a new query based on the Billing and Visit tables and, in the query, create a calculated field that will multiply each InvoiceAmt field value by .02 to calculate the proposed 2% late fee.

To create the new query and the calculated field:

▶ 1. On the ribbon, click the **CREATE** tab.

▶ 2. In the Queries group, click the **Query Design** button. The Show Table dialog box opens.

Cindi wants to see data from both the Visit and Billing tables, so you need to add these two tables to the Query window.

▶ 3. Add the **Visit** and **Billing** tables to the Query window, and then close the Show Table dialog box. The field lists appear in the Query window, and the one-to-many relationship between the Visit (primary) and Billing (related) tables is displayed.

▶ 4. Resize the two field lists so that all field names are visible.

▶ 5. Add the following fields to the design grid in the order given: **VisitID**, **PatientID**, and **VisitDate** from the Visit table; and **InvoiceItem**, **InvoicePaid**, and **InvoiceAmt** from the Billing table.

Cindi is interested in viewing data only for unpaid invoices because a late fee would apply only to them, so you need to enter the necessary condition for the InvoicePaid field. Recall that InvoicePaid is a Yes/No field. The condition you need to enter is the word "No" in the Criteria box for this field, so that Access will retrieve the records for unpaid invoices only.

▶ 6. In the **InvoicePaid Criteria** box, type **No**. As soon as you type the letter "N," a menu appears with options for entering various functions for the criteria. You don't need to enter a function, so you can close this menu.

You must close the menu or you'll enter a function, which will cause an error.

▶ 7. Press the **Esc** key to close the menu.

▶ 8. Press the **Tab** key. The query name you'll use will indicate that the data is for unpaid invoices, so you don't need to include the InvoicePaid values in the query results.

▶ 9. Click the **InvoicePaid Show** check box to remove the checkmark.

▶ 10. Save the query with the name **UnpaidInvoiceLateFee**.

Now you can use Expression Builder to create the calculated field for the InvoiceAmt field.

To create the calculated field:

1. Click the blank Field box to the right of the InvoiceAmt field. This field will contain the expression.

2. In the Query Setup group on the DESIGN tab, click the **Builder** button. The Expression Builder dialog box opens.

The insertion point is positioned in the large box at the top of the dialog box, ready for you to enter the expression. The Expression Categories section of the dialog box lists the fields from the query so you can include them in the expression. The Expression Elements section contains options for including other elements in the expression, including functions, constants, and operators. If the expression you're entering is a simple one, you can type it in the box; if it's more complex, you can use the options in the Expression Elements section to help you build the expression.

The expression for the calculated field will multiply the InvoiceAmt field values by the numeric constant .02 (which represents a 2% late fee).

3. In the Expression Categories section of the dialog box, double-click **InvoiceAmt**. The field name is added to the expression box, within brackets and with a space following it. In an expression, all field names must be enclosed in brackets.

Next you need to enter the multiplication operator, which is the asterisk (*), followed by the constant.

4. Type ***** (an asterisk) and then type **.02**. You have finished entering the expression. See Figure 3-33.

Figure 3-33 **Completed expression for the calculated field**

If you're not sure which operator to use, you can click Operators in the Expression Elements section to display a list of available operators in the center section of the dialog box.

5. Click the **OK** button. Access closes the Expression Builder dialog box and adds the expression to the design grid in the Field box for the calculated field.

   When you create a calculated field, Access uses the default column name "Expr1" for the field. You need to specify a more meaningful column name so it will appear in the query results. You'll enter the name "LateFee," which better describes the field's contents.

6. Click to the left of the text "Expr1:" at the beginning of the expression, and then press the **Delete** key five times to delete the text **Expr1**. *Do not delete the colon*; it is needed to separate the calculated field name from the expression.

7. Type **LateFee**. Next, you'll set this field's Caption property so that the field name will appear as "Late Fee" in the query datasheet.

8. In the Show/Hide group on the DESIGN tab, click the **Property Sheet** button. The Property Sheet for the current field, LateFee, opens on the right side of the window. See Figure 3-34.

Figure 3-34	Property Sheet for the calculated field

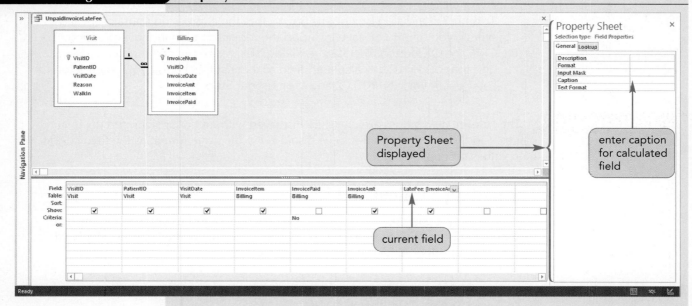

9. Click in the Caption box of the Property Sheet, type **Late Fee** and then close the Property Sheet.

10. Run the query. Access displays the query datasheet, which contains the specified fields and the calculated field with the caption "Late Fee." See Figure 3-35.

Figure 3-35 **Datasheet displaying the calculated field**

specified caption for
the calculated field

calculated field values

Trouble? If a dialog box opens noting that the expression contains invalid syntax, you might not have included the required colon in the expression. Click the OK button to close the dialog box, resize the column in the design grid that contains the calculated field to its best fit, change your expression to LateFee: [InvoiceAmt]*0.02 and then repeat Step 10.

The LateFee field values are currently displayed without dollar signs and decimal places. Cindi wants these values to be displayed in the same format as the InvoiceAmt field values for consistency.

Formatting a Calculated Field

You can specify a particular format for a calculated field, just as you can for any field, by modifying its properties. Next, you'll change the format of the LateFee calculated field so that all values appear in the Currency format.

To format the calculated field:

1. Switch to Design view.

2. In the design grid, click in the **LateFee** calculated field to make it the current field, if necessary.

3. In the Show/Hide group on the DESIGN tab, click the **Property Sheet** button to open the Property Sheet for the calculated field.

   You need to change the Format property to Currency, which displays values with a dollar sign and two decimal places.

4. In the Property Sheet, click the right side of the **Format** box to display the list of formats, and then click **Currency**.

5. Close the Property Sheet for the calculated field, and then run the query. The amounts in the LateFee calculated field are now displayed with dollar signs and two decimal places.

> **6.** Save and close the UnpaidInvoiceLateFee query.

PROSKILLS

Problem Solving: Creating a Calculated Field vs. Using the Calculated Field Data Type

You can also create a calculated field using the Calculated Field data type, which lets you store the result of an expression as a field in a table. However, database experts caution users against storing calculations in a table for several reasons. First, storing calculated data in a table consumes valuable space and increases the size of the database. The preferred approach is to use a calculated field in a query; with this approach, the result of the calculation is not stored in the database—it is produced only when you run the query—and it is always current. Second, the Calculated Field data type provides limited options for creating a calculation, whereas a calculated field in a query provides more functions and options for creating expressions. Third, including a field in a table using the Calculated Field data type limits your options if you need to upgrade the database at some point to a more robust DBMS, such as Oracle or SQL Server, that doesn't support this data type; you would need to redesign your database to eliminate this data type. Finally, most database experts agree that including a field in a table whose value is dependent on other fields in the table violates database design principles. To avoid such problems, it's best to create a query that includes a calculated field to perform the calculation you want, instead of creating a field in a table that uses the Calculated Field data type.

To better analyze costs at Chatham Community Health Services, Cindi wants to view more detailed information about patient invoices. Specifically, she would like to know the minimum, average, and maximum invoice amounts. She asks you to determine these statistics from data in the Billing table.

Using Aggregate Functions

You can calculate statistical information, such as totals and averages, on the records displayed in a table datasheet or selected by a query. To do this, you use the Access aggregate functions. **Aggregate functions** perform arithmetic operations on selected records in a database. Figure 3-36 lists the most frequently used aggregate functions.

Figure 3-36   **Frequently used aggregate functions**

Aggregate Function	Determines	Data Types Supported
Average	Average of the field values for the selected records	AutoNumber, Currency, Date/Time, Number
Count	Number of records selected	AutoNumber, Currency, Date/Time, Long Text, Number, OLE Object, Short Text, Yes/No
Maximum	Highest field value for the selected records	AutoNumber, Currency, Date/Time, Number, Short Text
Minimum	Lowest field value for the selected records	AutoNumber, Currency, Date/Time, Number, Short Text
Sum	Total of the field values for the selected records	AutoNumber, Currency, Date/Time, Number

© 2014 Cengage Learning

Working with Aggregate Functions Using the Total Row

If you want to quickly perform a calculation using an aggregate function in a table or query datasheet, you can use the Totals button in the Records group on the HOME tab. When you click this button, a row labeled "Total" appears at the bottom of the datasheet. You can then choose one of the aggregate functions for a field in the datasheet, and the results of the calculation will be displayed in the Total row for that field.

Cindi wants to know the total amount of all invoices for the clinic. You can quickly display this amount using the Sum function in the Total row in the Billing table datasheet.

To display the total amount of all invoices in the Billing table:

1. Open the Navigation Pane, open the **Billing** table in Datasheet view, and then close the Navigation Pane.

2. Make sure the HOME tab is displayed.

3. In the Records group, click the **Totals** button. Access adds a row with the label "Total" to the bottom of the datasheet.

4. Scroll to the bottom of the datasheet to view the last records in the datasheet and the Total row. You want to display the sum of all the values in the Invoice Amt column.

5. In the Total row, click the **Invoice Amt** column. An arrow appears on the left side of the field.

6. Click the **arrow** to display the menu of aggregate functions. The functions displayed depend on the data type of the current field; in this case, the menu provides functions for a Currency field. See Figure 3-37.

Figure 3-37   **Using aggregate functions in the Total row**

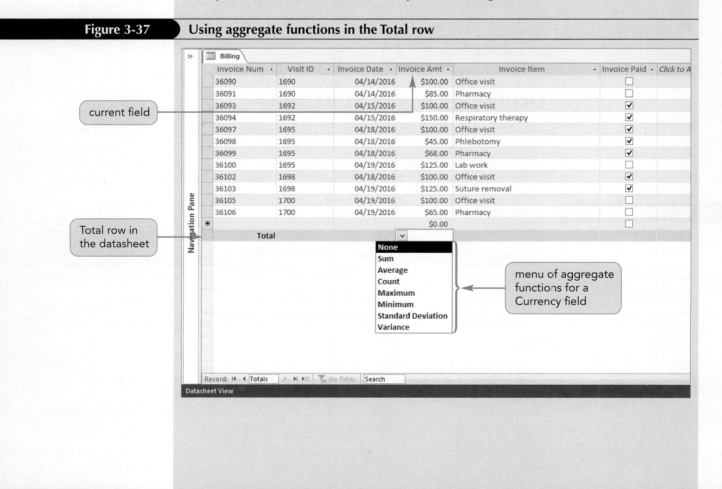

▶ **7.** Click **Sum** in the menu. Access adds all the values in the Invoice Amt column and displays the total $20,603.00 in the Total row for the column.

Cindi doesn't want to change the Billing table to always display this total. You can remove the Total row by clicking the Totals button again; this button works as a toggle to switch between the display of the Total row with the results of any calculations in the row, and the display of the datasheet without this row.

▶ **8.** In the Records group, click the **Totals** button. Access removes the Total row from the datasheet.

▶ **9.** Close the Billing table without saving the changes.

Cindi wants to know the minimum, average, and maximum invoice amounts for Chatham Community Health Services. To produce this information for Cindi, you need to use aggregate functions in a query.

Creating Queries with Aggregate Functions

Aggregate functions operate on the records that meet a query's selection criteria. You specify an aggregate function for a specific field, and the appropriate operation applies to that field's values for the selected records.

To display the minimum, average, and maximum of all the invoice amounts in the Billing table, you will use the Minimum, Average, and Maximum aggregate functions for the InvoiceAmt field.

To calculate the minimum of all invoice amounts:

▶ **1.** Create a new query in Design view, add the **Billing** table to the Query window, and then close the Show Table dialog box. Resize the Billing field list to display all fields.

To perform the three calculations on the InvoiceAmt field, you need to add the field to the design grid three times.

▶ **2.** In the Billing field list, double-click **InvoiceAmt** three times to add three copies of the field to the design grid.

You need to select an aggregate function for each InvoiceAmt field. When you click the Totals button in the Show/Hide group on the DESIGN tab, a row labeled "Total" is added to the design grid. The Total row provides a list of the aggregate functions that you can select.

▶ **3.** In the Show/Hide group on the DESIGN tab, click the **Totals** button. A new row labeled "Total" appears between the Table and Sort rows in the design grid. The default entry for each field in the Total row is the Group By operator, which you will learn about later in this tutorial. See Figure 3-38.

Figure 3-38   Total row inserted in the design grid

Total row

InvoiceAmt field included three times in the design grid

In the Total row, you specify the aggregate function you want to use for a field.

4. Click the right side of the first column's **Total** box, and then click **Min**. This field will calculate the minimum amount of all the InvoiceAmt field values.

When you run the query, Access automatically will assign a datasheet column name of "MinOfInvoiceAmt" for this field. You can change the datasheet column name to a more descriptive or readable name by entering the name you want in the Field box. However, you must also keep the InvoiceAmt field name in the Field box because it identifies the field to use in the calculation. The Field box will contain the datasheet column name you specify followed by the field name (InvoiceAmt) with a colon separating the two names.

Be sure to type the colon following the name or the query will not work correctly.

5. In the first column's Field box, click to the left of InvoiceAmt, and then type **MinimumInvoiceAmt:** (including the colon).

6. Using the ✛ pointer, double-click the column dividing line between the first two columns so that you can see the complete field name, MinimumInvoiceAmt:InvoiceAmt.

Next, you need to set the Caption property for this field so that the field name appears with spaces between words in the query datatsheet.

7. In the Show/Hide group on the DESIGN tab, click the **Property Sheet** button to open the Property Sheet for the current field.

8. In the Caption box, type **Minimum Invoice Amt** and then close the Property Sheet.

You'll follow the same process to complete the query by calculating the average and maximum invoice amounts.

To calculate the average and maximum of all invoice amounts:

1. Click the right side of the second column's **Total** box, and then click **Avg**. This field will calculate the average of all the InvoiceAmt field values.

2. In the second column's Field box, click to the left of InvoiceAmt, and then type **AverageInvoiceAmt:**.

3. Resize the second column to fully display the field name, AverageInvoiceAmt:InvoiceAmt.

4. Open the Property Sheet for the current field, and then set its Caption property to **Average Invoice Amt**. Leave the Property Sheet open.

5. Click the right side of the third column's **Total** box, and then click **Max**. This field will calculate the maximum amount of all the InvoiceAmt field values.

6. In the third column's Field box, click to the left of InvoiceAmt, and then type **MaximumInvoiceAmt:**.

7. Resize the third column to fully display the field name, MaximumInvoiceAmt:InvoiceAmt.

8. In the Property Sheet for the current field, set the Caption property to **Maximum Invoice Amt** and then close the Property Sheet. See Figure 3-39.

Figure 3-39	Query with aggregate functions entered

functions entered and columns resized

	MinimumInvoiceAmt: InvoiceAmt	AverageInvoiceAmt: InvoiceAmt	MaximumInvoiceAmt: InvoiceAmt	
Field:				
Table:	Billing	Billing	Billing	
Total:	Min	Avg	Max	
Sort:				
Show:	☑	☑	☑	☐
Criteria:				
or:				

Ready

Trouble? Carefully compare your field names to those shown in the figure to make sure they match exactly; otherwise the query will not work correctly.

9. Run the query. Access displays one record containing the three aggregate function results. The single row of summary statistics represents calculations based on all the records selected for the query—in this case, all 203 records in the Billing table.

10. Resize all columns to their best fit so that the column names are fully displayed, and then click the field value in the first column to deselect the value and view the results. See Figure 3-40.

Figure 3-40	Result of the query using aggregate functions

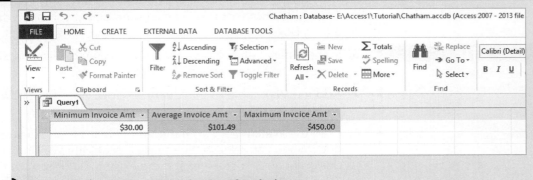

Minimum Invoice Amt	Average Invoice Amt	Maximum Invoice Amt
$30.00	$101.49	$450.00

11. Save the query as **InvoiceAmtStatistics**.

Cindi would like to view the same invoice amount statistics (minimum, average, and maximum) as they relate to both scheduled appointments and walk-in visits to the clinic.

Using Record Group Calculations

In addition to calculating statistical information on all or selected records in selected tables, you can calculate statistics for groups of records. For example, you can determine the number of patients in each city or the average invoice amount by city.

To create a query for Cindi's latest request, you can modify the current query by adding the WalkIn field and assigning the Group By operator to it. The **Group By operator** divides the selected records into groups based on the values in the specified field. Those records with the same value for the field are grouped together, and the datasheet displays one record for each group. Aggregate functions, which appear in the other columns of the design grid, provide statistical information for each group.

You need to modify the current query to add the Group By operator to the WalkIn field from the Visit table. The Group By operator will display the statistical information grouped by the values of the WalkIn field for all the records in the query datasheet. To create the new query, you will save the InvoiceAmtStatistics query with a new name, keeping the original query intact, and then modify the new query.

To create a new query with the Group By operator:

1. Display the InvoiceAmtStatistics query in Design view. Because the query is open, you can use Backstage view to save it with a new name, keeping the original query intact.

2. Click the **FILE** tab to display Backstage view, and then click **Save As** in the navigation bar. The Save As screen opens.

3. In the File Types section on the left, click **Save Object As**. The right side of the screen changes to display options for saving the current database object as a new object.

4. Click the **Save As** button. The Save As dialog box opens, indicating that you are saving a copy of the InvoiceAmtStatistics query.

5. Type **InvoiceAmtStatisticsByWalkIn** to replace the highlighted name, and then press the **Enter** key. The new query is saved with the name you specified and displayed in Design view.

   You need to add the WalkIn field to the query. This field is in the Visit table. To include another table in an existing query, you open the Show Table dialog box.

TIP
You could also open the Navigation Pane and drag the Visit table from the pane to the Query window.

6. In the Query Setup group on the DESIGN tab, click the **Show Table** button to open the Show Table dialog box.

7. Add the **Visit** table to the Query window, close the Show Table dialog box, and then resize the Visit field list.

8. Drag the **WalkIn** field from the Visit field list to the first column in the design grid. When you release the mouse button, the WalkIn field appears in the design grid's first column, and the existing fields shift to the right. Group By, the default option in the Total row, appears for the WalkIn field.

9. Run the query. Access displays 2 records—one for each WalkIn group, Yes and No. Each record contains the WalkIn field value for the group and the three aggregate function values. The summary statistics represent calculations based on the 203 records in the Billing table. See Figure 3-41.

| Figure 3-41 | Aggregate functions grouped by WalkIn |

Cindi notes that the invoice amounts for walk-in visits are higher than those for scheduled appointments.

▶ **10.** Save and close the query.

▶ **11.** Open the Navigation Pane.

You have created and saved many queries in the Chatham database. The Navigation Pane provides options for opening and managing the queries you've created, as well as the other objects in the database, such as tables, forms, and reports.

Working with the Navigation Pane

As noted earlier, the Navigation Pane is the main area for working with the objects in a database. As you continue to create objects in your database, you might want to display and work with them in different ways. The Navigation Pane provides options for grouping database objects in various ways to suit your needs. For example, you might want to view only the queries created for a certain table or all the query objects in the database.

TIP

You can hide the display of a group's objects by clicking the button to the right of the group name; click the button again to expand the group and display its objects.

The Navigation Pane divides database objects into categories, and each category contains groups. The groups contain one or more objects. The default category is **Object Type**, which arranges objects by type—tables, queries, forms, and reports. The default group is **All Access Objects**, which displays all objects in the database. You can also choose to display only one type of object, such as tables.

The default group name, All Access Objects, appears at the top of the Navigation Pane. Currently, each object type—Tables, Queries, Forms, and Reports—is displayed as a heading, and the objects related to each type are listed below the heading. To group objects differently, you can select another category by using the Navigation Pane menu. You'll try this next.

To group objects differently in the Navigation Pane:

▶ **1.** At the top of the Navigation Pane, click the **All Access Objects** button ⊙. A menu is displayed for choosing different categories and groups. See Figure 3-42.

Figure 3-42 | Navigation Pane menu

The top section of the menu provides the options for choosing a different category. The Object Type category has a checkmark next to it, signifying that it is the currently selected category. The lower section of the menu provides options for choosing a different group; these options might change depending on the selected category.

2. In the top section of the menu, click **Tables and Related Views**. The Navigation Pane is now grouped into categories of tables, and each table in the database—Visit, Billing, and Patient—is its own group. All database objects related to a table are listed below the table's name. See Figure 3-43.

Figure 3-43	Database objects grouped by table in the Navigation Pane

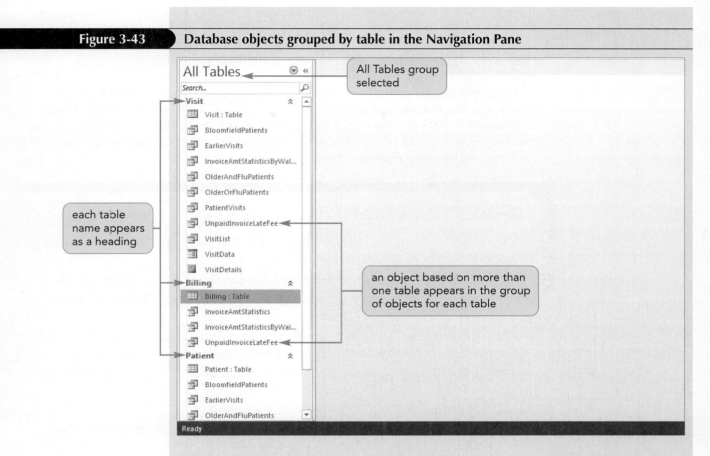

Some objects appear more than once. When an object is based on more than one table, that object appears in the group for each table. For example, the UnpaidInvoiceLateFee query is based on both the Visit and Billing tables, so it is listed in the group for both tables.

You can also choose to display the objects for only one table to better focus on that table.

3. At the top of the Navigation Pane, click the **All Tables** button ⊙ to display the Navigation Pane menu, and then click **Patient**. The Navigation Pane now shows only the objects related to the Patient table—the table itself plus the six queries you created that include fields from the Patient table.

4. At the top of the Navigation Pane, click the **Patient** button ⊙, and then click **Object Type** to return to the default display of the Navigation Pane.

5. Compact and repair the Chatham database, and then close the database.

Trouble? If a dialog box opens and warns that this action will cause Microsoft Access to empty the Clipboard, click the Yes button to continue.

The default All Access Objects category is a predefined category. You can also create custom categories to group objects in the way that best suits how you want to manage your database objects. As you continue to build a database and the list of objects grows, creating a custom category can help you to work more efficiently with the objects in the database.

The queries you've created and saved will help Cindi, Kelly, Ethan, and other staff members to monitor and analyze the business activity of Chatham Community Health Services and its patients. Now any staff member can run the queries at any time, modify them as needed, or use them as the basis for designing new queries to meet additional information requirements.

REVIEW

Session 3.2 Quick Check

1. A(n) _____ is a criterion, or rule, that determines which records are selected for a query datasheet.
2. In the design grid, where do you place the conditions for two different fields when you use the And logical operator, and where do you place them when you use the Or logical operator?
3. To perform a calculation in a query, you define a(n) _____ containing a combination of database fields, constants, and operators.
4. Which Access tool do you use to create an expression for a calculated field in a query?
5. What is an aggregate function?
6. The _____ operator divides selected records into groups based on the values in a field.
7. What is the default category for the display of objects in the Navigation Pane?

ASSESS

SAM Projects

Put your skills into practice with SAM Projects! SAM Projects for this tutorial can be found online. If you have a SAM account, go to www.cengage.com/sam2013 to download the most recent Project Instructions and Start Files.

PRACTICE

Review Assignments

Data File needed for the Review Assignments: Vendor.accdb *(cont. from Tutorial 2)*

Cindi asks you to update some information in the Vendor database and also to retrieve specific information from the database. Complete the following:

1. Open the **Vendor** database you created and worked with in Tutorials 1 and 2, and then click the Enable Content button next to the security warning, if necessary.

2. Open the **Supplier** table in Datasheet view, and then change the following field values for the record with the Supplier ID GRE364: Address to **1550 W Main St**, Contact Phone to **401-625-2745**, Contact First Name to **Andrew**, and Contact Last Name to **Kline**. Close the table.

3. Create a query based on the Supplier table. Include the following fields in the query, in the order shown: Company, Category, ContactFirst, ContactLast, Phone, and InitialContact. Sort the query in ascending order based on the Category field values. Save the query as **ContactList**, and then run the query.

4. Use the ContactList query datasheet to update the Supplier table by changing the Phone field value for Aresco Surgical, Inc. to **203-335-0054**.

5. Change the size of the font in the ContactList query datasheet to 12 points. Resize columns, as necessary, so that all field values and column headings are visible.

6. Change the alternate row color in the ContactList query datasheet to the Theme Color named Green, Accent 6, Lighter 60%, and then save and close the query.

7. Create a query based on the Supplier and Product tables. Select the Company, Category, and State fields from the Supplier table, and the ProductName, Price, Units, and Weight fields from the Product table. Sort the query results in descending order based on price. Select only those records with a State field value of CT, but do not display the State field values in the query results. Save the query as **CTSuppliers**, run the query, and then close it.

8. Create a query that lists all products that cost more than $200 and are sterile. Display the following fields from the Product table in the query results: ProductID, ProductName, Price, Units, and TempControl. (*Hint:* The Sterile field is a Yes/No field that should not appear in the query results.) Save the query as **HighPriceAndSterile**, run the query, and then close it.

9. Create a query that lists information about suppliers who sell equipment or products that require temperature control. Include the Company, Category, ContactFirst, and ContactLast fields from the Supplier table; and the ProductName, Price, TempControl, and Sterile fields from the Product table. Save the query as **EquipmentOrTempControl**, run the query, and then close it.

10. Create a query that lists only those products that cost $1000 or more, along with a 5% discount amount based on the price of the product. Include the Company field from the Supplier table and the following fields from the Product table in the query: ProductID, ProductName, and Price. Save the query as **HighPriceWithDiscount**. Display the discount in a calculated field named **DiscountAmt** that determines a 5% discount based on the Price field values. Set the Caption property **Discount Amt** for the calculated field. Display the query results in descending order by Price. Save and run the query.

11. Modify the format of the DiscountAmt field in the HighPriceWithDiscount query so that it uses the Standard format and two decimal places. Run the query, resize all columns in the datasheet to their best fit, and then save and close the query.

12. Create a query that calculates the lowest, highest, and average prices for all products using the field names **LowestPrice**, **HighestPrice**, and **AveragePrice**, respectively. Set the Caption property for each field to include a space between the two words in the field name. Run the query, resize all columns in the datasheet to their best fit, save the query as **PriceStatistics**, and then close it.

13. In the Navigation Pane, copy the PriceStatistics query, and then rename the copied query as **PriceStatisticsBySupplier**.

14. Modify the PriceStatisticsBySupplier query so that the records are grouped by the Company field in the Supplier table. The Company field should appear first in the query datasheet. Save and run the query, and then close it.

15. Compact and repair the Vendor database, and then close it.

Case Problem 1

Data File needed for this Case Problem: Gopher.accdb (cont. from Tutorial 2)

GoGopher!   Amol Mehta needs to modify a few records in the Gopher database and analyze the data for members enrolled in his company's various plans. To help Amol, you'll update the Gopher database and create queries to answer his questions. Complete the following:

1. Open the **Gopher** database you created and worked with in Tutorials 1 and 2, and then click the Enable Content button next to the security warning, if necessary.

2. In the **Member** table, find the record for MemberID 1251, and then change the Street value to **75 Hemlock Ln** and the Phone to **303-553-1847**.

3. In the **Member** table, find the record for MemberID 1228, and then delete the record. Close the Member table.

4. Create a query that lists members who did not have to pay a fee when they joined. In the query results, display the FirstName, LastName, and DateJoined fields from the Member table, and the PlanCost field from the Plan table. Sort the records in descending order by the date joined. Select records only for members whose fees were waived. (*Hint:* The FeeWaived field is a Yes/No field that should not appear in the query results.) Save the query as **NoFees**, and then run the query.

5. Use the NoFees query datasheet to update the Member table by changing the Last Name value for Kara Murray to **Seaburg**.

6. Use the NoFees query datasheet to display the total Plan Cost for the selected members. Save and close the query.

7. Create a query that lists the MemberID, FirstName, LastName, DateJoined, PlanDescription, and PlanCost fields for members who joined GoGopher! between April 1, 2016 and April 30, 2016. Save the query as **AprilMembers**, run the query, and then close it.

8. Create a query that lists all members who live in Louisville and whose memberships expire on or after 1/1/2017. Display the following fields from the Member table in the query results: MemberID, FirstName, LastName, Phone, and Expiration. (*Hint:* The City field values should not appear in the query results.) Sort the query results in ascending order by last name. Save the query as **LouisvilleAndExpiration**, run the query, and then close it.

9. Copy and paste the LouisvilleAndExpiration query to create a new query named **LouisvilleOrExpiration**. Modify the new query so that it lists all members who live in Louisville or whose memberships expire on or after 1/1/2017. Display the City field values in the query results following the Phone field values, and sort the query results in ascending order by city (this should be the only sort in the query). Save and run the query.

10. Change the size of the font in the LouisvilleOrExpiration query datasheet to 14 points. Resize columns, as necessary, so that all field values and column headings are visible.

11. Change the alternate row color in the LouisvilleOrExpiration query datasheet to the Theme Color named Blue, Accent 1, Lighter 80%, and then save and close the query.

12. Create a query that calculates the lowest, highest, and average cost for all plans using the field names **LowestCost**, **HighestCost**, and **AverageCost**, respectively. Set the Caption property for each field to include a space between the two words in the field name. Run the query, resize all columns in the datasheet to their best fit, save the query as **CostStatistics**, and then close it.

13. Copy and paste the CostStatistics query to create a new query named **CostStatisticsByCity**.

14. Modify the CostStatisticsByCity query to display the same statistics grouped by City, with City appearing as the first field. (*Hint:* Add the Member table to the query.) Run the query, and then save and close it.

15. Compact and repair the Gopher database, and then close it.

Case Problem 2

Data File needed for this Case Problem: OBrien.accdb *(cont. from Tutorial 2)*

O'Brien Educational Services   After reviewing the OBrien database, Karen O'Brien wants to modify some records and then view specific information about the students, tutors, and contracts for her educational services company. She asks you to update and query the OBrien database to perform these tasks. Complete the following:

1. Open the **OBrien** database you created and worked with in Tutorials 1 and 2, and then click the Enable Content button next to the security warning, if necessary.

2. In the **Tutor** table, change the following information for the record with TutorID 79-0678: Degree is **BA** and Hire Date is **9/15/2015**. Close the table.

3. In the **Student** table, find the record with the StudentID MCS8051, and then delete the related record in the subdatasheet for this student. Delete the record for StudentID MCS8051, and then close the Student table.

4. Create a query based on the Student table that includes the LastName, FirstName, and CellPhone fields, in that order. Save the query as **StudentCellList**, and then run the query.

5. In the results of the StudentCellList query, change the cell phone number for Haley Gosnold to **574-252-1973**. Close the query.

6. Create a query based on the Tutor and Contract tables. Display the LastName field from the Tutor table, and the StudentID, ContractDate, SessionType, Length, and Cost fields, in that order, from the Contract table. Sort first in ascending order by the tutor's last name, and then in ascending order by the StudentID. Save the query as **SessionsByTutor**, run the query, and the close it.

7. Copy and paste the SessionsByTutor query to create a new query named **GroupSessions**. Modify the new query so that it displays the same information for records with a Group session type only. Do not display the SessionType field values in the query results. Save and run the query, and then close it.

8. Create and save a query that produces the results shown in Figure 3-44. Close the query when you are finished.

Figure 3-44   **SouthBendPrivate query results**

show only records for students from South Bend who are taking private sessions

sort by Last Name

SouthBendPrivate

Student ID	Last Name	First Name	Contract Date
MAH8053	Mahlau	Albert	7/16/2016
OAT8010	Oates	Kyle	1/26/2016
PAP8024	Pappas	Zach	7/10/2016
SPE8022	Spence	Ross	2/1/2016
TUR8005	Turner	Lynne	9/15/2016
VAR8027	Vargas	Vera	9/20/2016
VAR8027	Vargas	Vera	4/3/2016

format with a font size of 12 and the Gold, Accent 4, Lighter 60% alternate row Theme Color

9. Create and save a query that produces the results shown in Figure 3-45. Close the query when you are finished.

Figure 3-45   **OscelaOrSemi query results**

sort in descending order by Contract Date

show only records for students from Oscela or students taking semi-private sessions

OscelaOrSemi

Student ID	First Name	Last Name	Contract Date	Cost
DRO8048	Emma	Drouin	9/15/2016	$720
NAS8012	Andre	Nastasia	9/12/2016	$800
GUS8002	Michael	Gustafson	9/10/2016	$900
RIV8011	Marco	Rivera	8/10/2016	$1,080
DEN8042	David	DeNardo	8/1/2016	$800
CAR8059	Carol	Carlson	7/15/2016	$1,200
YEN8035	Lila	Yen	6/22/2016	$1,440
MAS8056	Kimberly	Mase	5/8/2016	$960
STI8038	Lily	Stiefel	3/15/2016	$720
BIE8000	Joshua	Biega	3/14/2016	$1,800
HIN8040	Erica	Hinkle	3/1/2016	$960
NAS8012	Andre	Nastasia	2/1/2016	$960
GUS8002	Michael	Gustafson	1/28/2016	$720
MUE8041	Bart	Mueller	1/15/2016	$1,440
YEN8035	Lila	Yen	1/7/2016	$1,280
HEC8018	Eric	Hecht	12/17/2015	$900
WOO8071	Jon	Woodburn	12/15/2015	$1,800
NUN8084	Rodrigo	Nunez	9/30/2015	$800
	Total			$19,280

Navigation Pane

Total row shows the sum of the Cost values

10. Create and save a query to display statistics for the Cost field, as shown in Figure 3-46. Close the query when you are finished.

Figure 3-46   **CostStatistics query results**

set captions to include spaces between words

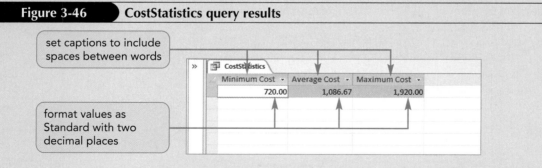

CostStatistics

Minimum Cost	Average Cost	Maximum Cost
720.00	1,086.67	1,920.00

format values as Standard with two decimal places

11. Copy and paste the CostStatistics query to create a new query named **CostStatisticsByCity**.

12. Modify the CostStatisticsByCity query to display the same statistics grouped by City, with City appearing as the first field. (*Hint:* Add the Student table to the query.) Run the query, and then save and close it.

13. Compact and repair the OBrien database, and then close it.

Case Problem 3

Data File needed for this Case Problem: Shelter.accdb *(cont. from Tutorial 2)*

Rosemary Animal Shelter   Ryan Lang needs to modify some records in the Shelter database, and then he wants to find specific information about the animals, patrons, and donations for his not-for-profit agency. Ryan asks you to help him update the database and create queries to find the information he needs. Complete the following:

1. Open the **Shelter** database you created and worked with in Tutorials 1 and 2, and then click the Enable Content button next to the security warning, if necessary.

⊕ **Explore**   2. In the **Patron** table, delete the record with PatronID 36064. (*Hint:* Delete the related record in the Donation subdatasheet first, which you need to display using the Insert Subdatasheet dialog box.) Close the Patron table without saving changes to the table layout.

3. Create a query based on the Animal table that includes the AnimalID, AnimalName, AnimalType, Gender, and ArrivalDate fields, in that order. Save the query as **AnimalsByType**, and then run it.

4. Modify the AnimalsByType query design so that it sorts records in ascending order first by AnimalType and then by Gender. Save and run the query.

5. In the AnimalsByType query datasheet, find the record for the animal with Animal ID D23, and then change the arrival date for this animal to **5/19/2016**. Close the query.

6. Create a query that displays the PatronID, FirstName, and LastName fields from the Patron table, and the Description and DonationValue fields from the Donation table for all donations over $150. Sort the query in ascending order by donation value. Save the query as **LargeDonations**, run the query, and then close it.

7. Copy and paste the LargeDonations query to create a new query named **LargeCashDonations**.

⊕ **Explore**   8. Modify the LargeCashDonations query to display only those records with donations valuing more than $150 in cash. Do not include the Description field values in the query results. Use the query datasheet to calculate the average cash donation. Save and close the query.

9. Create a query that displays the PatronID, FirstName, and LastName fields from the Patron table, and the AnimalName, AnimalType, Age, Gender, and Adopted fields from the Animal table. Specify that the results show records for only those animals that have been adopted. Do not display the Adopted field values in the query results. Save the query as **CatAdoptions**, and then run the query.

10. Filter the results of the CatAdoptions query datasheet to display records for cats only.

⊕ **Explore**   11. Format the datasheet of the CatAdoptions query so that it does not display gridlines, uses an alternate row Standard Color of Purple 2, and displays a font size of 12. (*Hint:* Use the Gridlines button in the Text Formatting group on the HOME tab to select the appropriate gridlines option.) Resize the columns to display the complete field names and values, if necessary. Save and close the query.

CHALLENGE

✛ **Explore** 12. Create a query that displays the PatronID, FirstName, and LastName fields from the Patron table, and the Description, DonationDate, and DonationValue fields from the Donation table. Specify that the query include records for noncash donations only or for donations made in the month of June 2016. Sort the records first in ascending order by the patron's last name, and then in descending order by the donation value. Save the query as **NonCashOrJuneDonations**, run the query, and then close it.

13. Copy and paste the NonCashOrJuneDonations query to create a new query named **DonationsAfterStorageCharge**.

✛ **Explore** 14. Modify the DonationsAfterStorageCharge query so that it displays records for noncash donations made on all dates. Create a calculated field named **NetDonation** that displays the results of subtracting $3.50 from the DonationValue field values to account for the cost of storing each noncash donated item. Set the Caption property **Net Donation** for the calculated field. Display the results in ascending order by donation value. Run the query, and then modify it to format both the DonationValue field and the calculated field as Currency with two decimal places. Run the query again and resize the columns in the datasheet to their best fit, as necessary. Save and close the query.

✛ **Explore** 15. Create a query based on the **Donation** table that displays the sum, average, and count of the DonationValue field for all donations. Then complete the following:

   a. Specify field names of **TotalDonations**, **AverageDonation**, and **NumberofDonations**. Then specify captions to include spaces between words.

   b. Save the query as **DonationStatistics**, and then run it. Resize the query datasheet columns to their best fit.

   c. Modify the field properties so that the values in the Total Donations and Average Donation columns display two decimal places and the Standard format. Run the query again, and then save and close the query.

   d. Copy and paste the DonationStatistics query to create a new query named **DonationStatisticsByDescription**.

   e. Modify the DonationStatisticsByDescription query to display the sum, average, and count of the DonationValue field for all donations grouped by Description, with Description appearing as the first field. Sort the records in descending order by Total Donations. Save, run, and then close the query.

16. Compact and repair the Shelter database, and then close it.

Case Problem 4

Data File needed for this Case Problem: Stanley.accdb *(cont. from Tutorial 2)* and Tour.accdb

Stanley EcoTours   Janice and Bill Stanley need your help to maintain and analyze data about the clients, reservations, and tours for their ecotourism business. Additionally, you'll troubleshoot some problems in another database containing tour information. Complete the following:

1. Open the **Stanley** database you created and worked with in Tutorials 1 and 2, and then click the Enable Content button next to the security warning, if necessary.

2. In the **Guest** table, change the phone number for Paul Barry to **406-497-1068**, and then close the table.

3. Create a query based on the Tour table that includes the TourName, Location, Country, PricePerPerson, and TourType fields, in that order. Sort in ascending order based on the PricePerPerson field values. Save the query as **ToursByPrice**, and then run the query.

4. Use the ToursByPrice query datasheet to display the total Price Per Person for the tours. Save and close the query.

TROUBLESHOOT

5. Create a query that displays the GuestLast, City, and State/Prov fields from the Guest table, and the ReservationID, StartDate, and People fields from the Reservation table. Save the query as **GuestTourDates**, and then run the query. Change the alternate row color in the query datasheet to the Theme Color Green, Accent 6, Lighter 40%. In Datasheet view, use an AutoFilter to sort the query results from oldest to newest Start Date. Save and close the query.

6. Create a query that displays the GuestFirst, GuestLast, City, ReservationID, TourID, and StartDate fields for all guests from Montana (MT). Do not include the State/Prov field in the query results. Sort the query in ascending order by the guest's last name. Save the query as **MontanaGuests** and then run it. Close the query.

7. Create a query that displays data from all three tables in the database, as follows: the GuestLast, City, State/Prov, and Country fields from the Guest table; the StartDate field from the Reservation table; and the TourName, Location, and TourType fields from the Tour table. Specify that the query select only those records for guests from Canada or guests who are taking Jeep tours. Sort the query in ascending order by Location. Save the query as **CanadaOrJeep**, and then run the query. Resize datasheet columns to their best fit, as necessary, and then save and close the query.

8. Copy and paste the CanadaOrJeep query to create a new query named **IdahoAndJuly**.

9. Modify the IdahoAndJuly query to select all guests from Idaho who are taking a tour starting sometime in the month of July 2016. Do not include the State/Prov field values or the Country field values in the query results. Run the query. Resize datasheet columns to their best fit, as necessary, and then save and close the query.

10. Create a query that displays the ReservationID, StartDate, and People fields from the Reservation table, and the TourName, Location, Country, PricePerPerson, and SingleSupplement fields from the Tour table for all reservations with a People field value of 1. Save the query as **SingleReservations**. Add a field to the query named **TotalCost** that displays the results of adding the SingleSupplement field values to the PricePerPerson field values. Set the Caption property **Total Cost** for the calculated field. Display the results in descending order by TotalCost. Do not include the People field values in the query results. Run the query. Modify the query by formatting the TotalCost field to show 0 decimal places. Run the query, resize datasheet columns to their best fit, as necessary, and then save and close the query.

11. Create a query based on the Tour table that determines the minimum, average, and maximum price per person for all tours. Then complete the following:
    a. Specify field names of **LowestPrice**, **AveragePrice**, and **HighestPrice**.
    b. Set the Caption property for each field to include a space between the two words in the field name.
    c. Save the query as **PriceStatistics**, and then run the query.
    d. In Design view, specify the Standard format and two decimal places for each column.
    e. Run the query, resize all the datasheet columns to their best fit, save your changes, and then close the query.
    f. Create a copy of the PriceStatistics query named **PriceStatisticsByTourType**.
    g. Modify the PriceStatisticsByTourType query to display the price statistics grouped by TourType, with TourType appearing as the first field. Save your changes and then run and close the query.

12. Compact and repair the Stanley database, and then close it.

⚙ **Troubleshoot** 13. Open the **Tour** database located in the Access1 ▶ Case4 folder provided with your Data Files, and then click the Enable Content button next to the security warning, if necessary. Run the BookingByDateAndState query in the Tour database. The query is not producing the desired results. Fix the query so that the data from the Booking table is listed first, the data is sorted only by StartDate in ascending order, and the results do not display country values. Save and close the corrected query.

Troubleshoot 14. Run the WYGuestsFewerPeople query, which displays no records in the results. This query is supposed to show data for guests from Wyoming with fewer than four people in their booking. Find and correct the error in the query design, run the query, and then close it.

Troubleshoot 15. Run the CanadaOrSeptStart query. This query should display the records for all guests who are from Canada or whose booking start date is on or after 9/1/2016. Find and correct the errors in the query design, run the query, and then close it. Compact and repair the Tour database, and then close it.

OBJECTIVES

Session 4.1
- Create a form using the Form Wizard
- Apply a theme to a form
- Add a picture to a form
- Change the color of text on a form
- Find and maintain data using a form
- Preview and print selected form records
- Create a form with a main form and a subform

Session 4.2
- Create a report using the Report Wizard
- Apply a theme to a report
- Change the alignment of field values on a report
- Move and resize fields in a report
- Insert a picture in a report
- Change the color of text on a report
- Apply conditional formatting in a report
- Preview and print a report

Creating Forms and Reports

Using Forms and Reports to Display Patient and Visit Data

Case | *Chatham Community Health Services*

Cindi Rodriguez wants to continue enhancing the Chatham database to make it easier for her staff to enter, locate, and maintain data. In particular, she wants the database to include a form based on the Patient table to make it easier for staff members to enter and change data about the clinic's patients. She also wants the database to include a form that shows data from both the Patient and Visit tables at the same time. This form will show the visit information for each patient along with the corresponding patient data, providing a complete picture of Chatham Community Health Services patients and their visits to the clinic.

In addition, Ethan Ward would like the database to include a formatted report of patient and visit data so that he and other staff members will have printed output when completing patient analyses and planning strategies for community outreach efforts. He wants the information to be formatted in a professional manner, to make the report appealing and easy to use.

ACCESS

STARTING DATA FILES

Access1 → **Tutorial**

Chatham.accdb (*cont.*)
Medical.bmp

Review

Supplies.bmp
Vendor.accdb (*cont.*)

Case1

Gopher.accdb (*cont.*)
Tasks.bmp

Case2

OBrien.accdb (*cont.*)
Tests.bmp

Case3

Animals.bmp
Shelter.accdb (*cont.*)

Case4

Hiking.bmp
Stanley.accdb (*cont.*)
Tour.accdb

Session 4.1 Visual Overview:

The form object's name is displayed on the tab for the form.

The form title appears at the top of the form. By default, the form object name is used as the form title, but you can edit the title to display the text you want, as done here—a space was added between the two words for readability.

With the Columnar form layout, the field captions appear in a column on the left side of the form. If captions had not been specified for the fields, the field names would appear here instead.

The navigation buttons allow you to display the first, last, next, or previous record in the form, enter a specific record number and move to that record, and create a new record.

You can add graphic elements, such as a picture, to a form to improve its appearance or add visual appeal.

The Columnar form layout displays the corresponding field values in boxes to the right of the field captions (or field names).

You can use the Search box to find and display a record containing the text you enter.

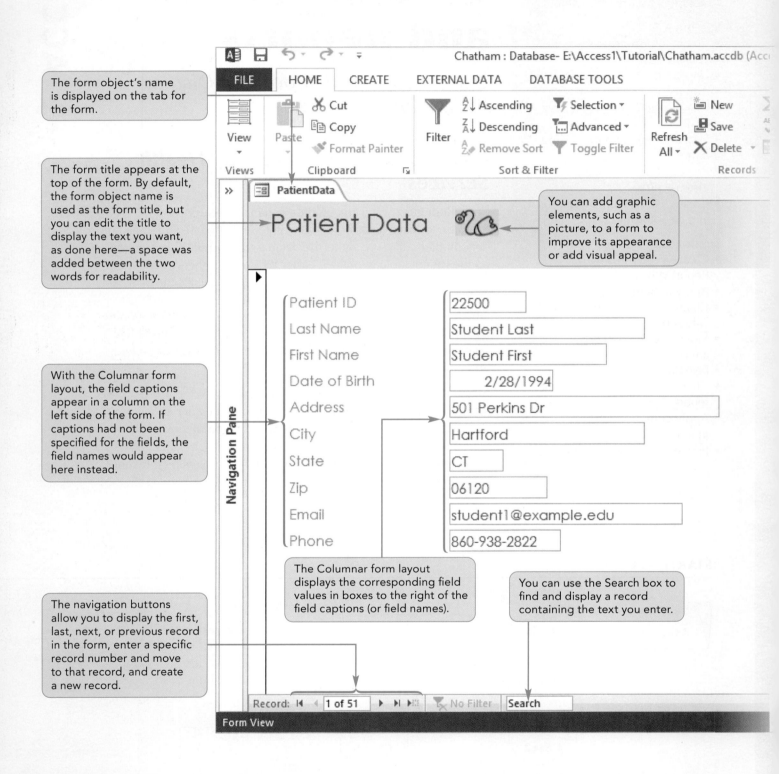

Chatham : Database- E:\Access1\Tutorial\Chatham.accdb (Acc

FILE   HOME   CREATE   EXTERNAL DATA   DATABASE TOOLS

View   Paste   Cut   Copy   Format Painter   Filter   Ascending   Descending   Remove Sort   Selection   Advanced   Toggle Filter   Refresh All   New   Save   Delete

Views   Clipboard   Sort & Filter   Records

PatientData

Patient Data

Patient ID	22500
Last Name	Student Last
First Name	Student First
Date of Birth	2/28/1994
Address	501 Perkins Dr
City	Hartford
State	CT
Zip	06120
Email	student1@example.edu
Phone	860-938-2822

Navigation Pane

Record: 1 of 51   No Filter   Search

Form View

Form Displayed in Form View

...torial\Chatham.accdb (Access 2007 - 2013 file format) - Access   ? — ⊟ ✕

Sign in

New   Σ Totals   ab↲ac
Save   ABC Spelling
Refresh   Find
All ▾   ✕ Delete ▾   More ▾

Records   Find   Text Formatting

You use the Find button to display the Find and Replace dialog box, which lets you search for specific data in the form.

You can apply a theme to a form, as done here with the PatientData form. A theme is a predefined set of formats including colors, fonts, and other effects that enhance a form's appearance and usability.

The PatientData form was created using the **Form Wizard**, which allows you to choose some or all of the fields in the table or query used as the basis for the form, choose fields from other tables and queries, and display the selected fields in any order on the form.

This selected button indicates the form is displayed in **Form view**, which you use to view, enter, and maintain data in the table on which the form is based.

You can click this button to display the form in **Layout view**, which allows you to modify many aspects of a form's layout and design.

Creating a Form Using the Form Wizard

As you learned in Tutorial 1, a form is an object you use to enter, edit, and view records in a database. You can design your own forms or have Access create them for you automatically. In Tutorial 1, you used the Form tool to create the VisitData form in the Chatham database. Recall that the Form tool creates a form automatically, using all the fields in the selected table or query.

Cindi asks you to create a new form that her staff can use to view and maintain data in the Patient table. To create the form for the Patient table, you'll use the Form Wizard, which guides you through the process.

To open the Chatham database and start the Form Wizard:

1. Start Access and open the **Chatham** database you created and worked with in Tutorials 1 through 3.

   Trouble? If the security warning is displayed below the ribbon, click the Enable Content button.

2. Open the Navigation Pane, if necessary. To create a form based on a table or query, you can select the table or query in the Navigation Pane first, or you can select it using the Form Wizard.

3. In the Tables section of the Navigation Pane, click **Patient** to select the Patient table as the basis for the new form.

4. On the ribbon, click the **CREATE** tab. The Forms group on the CREATE tab provides options for creating various types of forms and designing your own forms.

5. In the Forms group, click the **Form Wizard** button. The first Form Wizard dialog box opens. See Figure 4-1.

| Figure 4-1 | First Form Wizard dialog box |

selected table

scrollable list of fields in the selected table

Because you selected the Patient table in the Navigation Pane before starting the Form Wizard, this table is selected in the Tables/Queries box, and the fields for the Patient table are listed in the Available Fields box.

Cindi wants the form to display all the fields in the Patient table, but in a different order. She would like the Phone field to appear at the bottom of the form so that it stands out, making it easier for someone who needs to call patients to use the form and quickly identify the phone number for a patient.

To create the form using the Form Wizard:

▶ **1.** Click the ⟩⟩ button to move all the fields to the Selected Fields box. Next, you need to remove the Phone field, and then add it back as the last selected field so that it will appear at the bottom of the form.

▶ **2.** In the Selected Fields box, click the **Phone** field, and then click the ⟨ button to move the field back to the Available Fields box.

   To add the Phone field to the end of the form, you need to highlight the last field in the list, and then move the Phone field back to the Selected Fields box. A new field is always added after the selected field in the Selected Fields box.

▶ **3.** In the Selected Fields box, click the **Email** field.

▶ **4.** With the Phone field selected in the Available Fields box, click the ⟩ button to move the Phone field to the end of the Selected Fields box.

▶ **5.** Click the **Next** button to display the second Form Wizard dialog box, in which you select a layout for the form. See Figure 4-2.

Figure 4-2	Choosing a layout for the form

The layout choices are Columnar, Tabular, Datasheet, and Justified. A sample of the selected layout appears on the left side of the dialog box.

▶ **6.** Click each of the option buttons and review the corresponding sample layout.

   The Tabular and Datasheet layouts display the fields from multiple records at one time, whereas the Columnar and Justified layouts display the fields from one record at a time. Cindi thinks the Columnar layout is the appropriate arrangement for displaying and updating data in the table, so that anyone using the form can focus on just one patient record at a time.

▶ **7.** Click the **Columnar** option button (if necessary), and then click the **Next** button.

Access displays the third and final Form Wizard dialog box and shows the Patient table's name as the default form name. "Patient" is also the default title that will appear on the tab for the form.

You'll use "PatientData" as the form name and, because you don't need to change the form's design at this point, you'll display the form.

▶ **8.** Click to position the insertion point to the right of Patient in the text box, type **Data**, and then click the **Finish** button.

▶ **9.** Close the Navigation Pane to display only the Form window. The completed form is displayed in Form view. See Figure 4-3.

| Figure 4-3 | PatientData form in Form view |

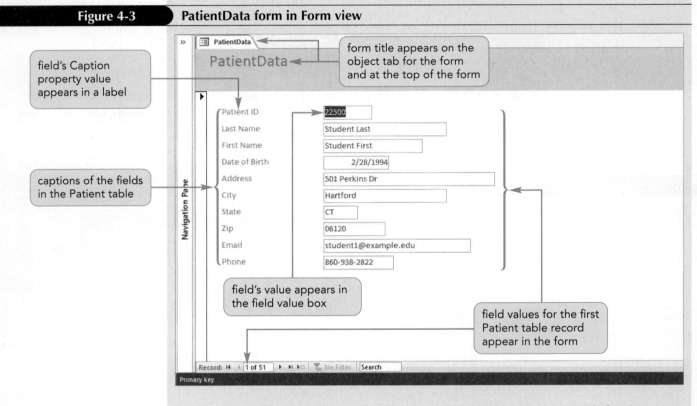

Notice that the title you specified for the form appears on the tab for the object and as a title on the form itself. The Columnar layout you selected places the field captions in labels on the left and the corresponding field values in boxes on the right, which vary in width depending on the size of the field. The form currently displays the field values for the first record in the Patient table.

After viewing the form, Cindi decides that she doesn't like its appearance. The font used in the labels on the left is somewhat light in color and small, making the labels a bit difficult to read. Also, she thinks inserting a graphic on the form would add visual interest, and modifying other form elements—such as the color of the title text—would improve the look of the form. You can make all of these changes working with the form in Layout view.

Modifying a Form's Design in Layout View

TIP

Some form design changes require you to switch to Design view, which gives you a more detailed view of the form's structure.

After you create a form, you might need to modify its design in Layout view to improve its appearance or to make the form easier to use. In Layout view, you see the form as it appears in Form view, but you can still modify the form's design; in Form view, you cannot make any design changes. Because you can see the form and its data while you are modifying the form, Layout view makes it easy for you to see the results of any design changes you make. You can continue to make changes, undo modifications, and rework the design in Layout view to achieve the look you want for the form.

The first modification you'll make to the PatientData form is to change its appearance by applying a theme.

Applying a Theme to a Form

By default, a form you create is formatted with the Office theme, which determines the color and font used on the form. Access, like other Microsoft Office programs, provides many built-in themes, including the Office theme, making it easy for you to create objects with a unified look. You can also create a customized theme if none of the built-in themes suit your needs. To change a form's appearance, you can easily apply a new theme to it.

REFERENCE

Applying a Theme to a Form

- Display the form in Layout view.
- In the Themes group on the DESIGN tab, click the Themes button.
- In the displayed gallery, click the theme you want to apply to all objects; or, right-click the theme to display the shortcut menu, and then choose to apply the theme to the current object only or to all matching objects.

Cindi would like to see if the PatientData form's appearance can be improved with a different theme. To apply a theme, you first need to switch to Layout view.

To apply a theme to the PatientData form:

1. Make sure the HOME tab is displayed.

2. In the Views group, click the **View** button. The form is displayed in Layout view. See Figure 4-4.

Figure 4-4 **Form displayed in Layout view**

Trouble? If the Field List or Property Sheet opens on the right side of your window, close it before continuing.

You can use Layout view to modify an existing form. In Layout view, an orange outline identifies the currently selected object on the form. In this case, the field value for the PatientID field, 22500, is selected. You need to apply a theme to the PatientData form.

3. In the Themes group on the DESIGN tab, click the **Themes** button. A gallery opens showing the available themes for the form. See Figure 4-5.

Figure 4-5	Themes gallery displayed

TIP

Themes other than the Office theme are listed in alphabetical order in the gallery.

The Office theme, which is shown in the "In this Database" section and is also the first theme listed in the section containing other themes, is the default theme currently applied in the database. Each theme provides a design scheme for the colors and fonts used in the database objects. You can point to each theme in the gallery to see its name in a ScreenTip. Also, when you point to a theme, the Live Preview feature shows the effect of applying the theme to the open object.

4. In the gallery, point to each of the themes to see how they would format the PatientData form. Notice the changes in color and font type of the text, for example.

   Trouble? If you click a theme by mistake, repeat Step 3 to redisplay the gallery, and then continue to Step 5.

   Cindi likes the Slice theme because of its bright blue color in the title area at the top and its larger font size, which makes the text in the form easier to read. She asks you to apply this theme to the form.

5. Right-click the **Slice** theme. A shortcut menu opens with options for applying the theme. See Figure 4-6.

Figure 4-6 **Shortcut menu for applying the theme**

The menu provides options for applying the theme to all matching objects—for example, all the forms in the database—or to the current object only. You can also choose to make the theme the default theme in the database, which means any new objects you create will be formatted with the selected theme. Because Cindi is not sure if all forms in the Chatham database will look better with the Slice theme, she asks you to apply it only to the PatientData form.

Choose this option to avoid applying the theme to other forms in the database.

6. On the shortcut menu, click **Apply Theme to This Object Only**.

The gallery closes, and Access formats the form's colors and fonts with the Slice theme.

Trouble? If you choose the wrong option by mistake, you might have applied the selected theme to other forms and/or reports in the database. Repeat Steps 3 through 6 to apply the Slice theme to the PatientData form. You can also follow the same process to reapply the default Office theme to the other forms and reports in the Chatham database, as directed by your instructor.

INSIGHT

Working with Themes

Themes provide a quick and easy way for you to format the objects in a database with a consistent look, which is a good design principle to follow. In general, all objects of a type in a database—for example, all forms—should have a consistent design. However, keep in mind that when you select a theme in the Themes gallery and choose the option to apply the theme to all matching objects or to make the theme the default for the database, Access might apply it to *all* the existing forms and reports in the database as well as to new forms and reports you create. Although this ensures a consistent design, this approach can cause problems. For example, if you have already created a form or report and its design is suitable, applying a theme that includes a larger font size could cause the text in labels and field value boxes to be cut off or to extend into other objects on the form or report. The colors applied by the theme could also interfere with elements on existing forms and reports. To handle these unintended results, you would have to spend time checking the existing forms and reports and fixing any problems introduced by applying the theme. A better approach is to select the option "Apply Theme to This Object Only," available on the shortcut menu for a theme in the Themes gallery, for each existing form and report. If the newly applied theme causes problems for any individual form or report, you can then reapply the original theme to return the object to its original design.

Next, Cindi asks you to add a picture to the form for visual interest. The picture, which is included on various flyers and other patient correspondence for Chatham Community Health Services, is a small graphic of a stethoscope. You'll add this picture to the form.

Adding a Picture to a Form

A picture is one of many controls you can add and modify on a form. A **control** is an item on a form, report, or other database object that you can manipulate to modify the object's appearance. The controls you can add and modify in Layout view for a form are available in the Controls group and the Header/Footer group on the DESIGN tab. The picture you need to add is contained in a file named Medical.bmp, which is located in the Access1 ▸ Tutorial folder provided with your Data Files.

To add the picture to the form:

▶ 1. Make sure the form is still displayed in Layout view and that the DESIGN tab is active.

▶ 2. In the Header/Footer group, click the **Logo** button. The Insert Picture dialog box opens.

▶ 3. Navigate to the **Access1 ▸ Tutorial** folder provided with your Data Files, click the **Medical** file, and then click the **OK** button. The picture appears as a selected object on top of the form's title. See Figure 4-7.

Figure 4-7 **Form with picture added**

picture appears on the form title and is selected

move picture to here

control layout containing the picture

A solid orange outline surrounds the picture, indicating it is selected. The picture is placed in a **control layout**, which is a set of controls grouped together in a form or report so that you can manipulate the set as a single control. The dotted bright blue outline indicates the control layout (see Figure 4-7). The easiest way to move the picture off the form title is to first remove it from the control layout. Doing so allows you to move the picture independently.

4. Right-click the selected picture to display the shortcut menu, point to **Layout**, and then click **Remove Layout**. The picture is removed from the control layout. Now you can move the picture to the right of the form title.

5. Position the pointer 🔆 on the picture, and then click and drag the picture to the right to move it to the right of the form title.

TIP

You can resize a selected image by dragging one of its corners.

6. When the pointer is roughly one-half inch to the right of the form's title, release the mouse button. The picture is positioned to the right of the form title.

7. Click in a blank area on the main form (to the right of the field values) to deselect the picture. See Figure 4-8.

Trouble? Don't be concerned if your picture is not in the exact location as the one shown in Figure 4-8. Just make sure the picture is not blocking any part of the form title and that it appears to the right of the form title and within the blue shaded area at the top of the form. Also, if your picture is too large or too small, you can resize it by first selecting it and then dragging a corner of the orange outline in the appropriate direction to increase or decrease the picture size.

Figure 4-8   **Form with theme applied and picture repositioned**

picture moved to the right of the form title

Slice theme colors and fonts applied to the form elements

Next, Cindi asks you to change the color of the form title to a darker color so that it will coordinate better with the picture next to the title and stand out more on the form.

Changing the Color of the Form Title

The Font group on the FORMAT tab provides many options you can use to change the appearance of text on a form. For example, you can bold, italicize, and underline text; change the font, font color, and font size; and change the alignment of text. Before you change the color of the "PatientData" title on the form, you'll change the title to two words so it is easier to read.

To change the form title's text and color:

1. Click the **PatientData** form title. An orange box surrounds the title, indicating it is selected.

2. Click between the letters "t" and "D" to position the insertion point, and then press the **spacebar**. The title on the form is now "Patient Data" but the added space caused the words to appear on two lines. You can fix this by resizing the box containing the title.

TIP

Changing the form's title does not affect the form object name; it is still PatientData, as shown on the object tab.

3. Position the pointer on the right vertical line of the box containing the form title until the pointer changes to ↔, and then click and drag to the right until the word "Data" appears on the same line as the word "Patient."

   Trouble? You might need to repeat Step 3 more than once in order for the text to appear correctly. Also, you might have to move the picture further to the right to make room for the title.

4. Click in the main form area again to deselect the title and check the results, and then click **Patient Data** to reselect the title. The orange outline appears around the words of the title.

5. On the ribbon, click the **FORMAT** tab.

6. In the Font group, click the **Font Color button arrow** [A▾] to display the gallery of available colors. The gallery provides theme colors and standard colors, as well as an option for creating a custom color. The theme colors available depend on the theme applied to the form—in this case, the colors are related to the Slice theme. The current color of the title text—Black, Text 1, Lighter 50%—is outlined in the gallery, indicating it is selected.

7. In the Theme Colors palette, point to the second color box in the fourth row of boxes. The ScreenTip indicates this is the Black, Text 1, Lighter 25% color.

8. Click the **Black, Text 1, Lighter 25%** color box.

9. Click in a blank area of the main form to deselect the title text. The darker black color is applied to the form title text, coordinating it with the picture on the form. See Figure 4-9.

Figure 4-9   **Form title with new color applied**

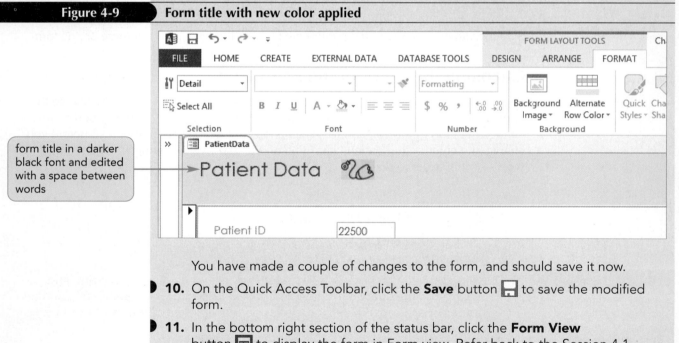

form title in a darker black font and edited with a space between words

You have made a couple of changes to the form, and should save it now.

10. On the Quick Access Toolbar, click the **Save** button 🖫 to save the modified form.

11. In the bottom right section of the status bar, click the **Form View** button 🖽 to display the form in Form view. Refer back to the Session 4.1 Visual Overview; your form should match the PatientData form shown there.

Cindi is pleased with the modified appearance of the form. Later, she plans to revise the existing VisitData form and make the same changes to it, so that it matches the appearance of the PatientData form.

Written Communication: Understanding the Importance of Form Design

Similar to any document, a form must convey written information clearly and effectively. When you create a form, it's important to consider how the form will be used, so that its design will accommodate the needs of people using the form to view, enter, and maintain data. For example, if a form in a database mimics a paper form that users will enter data from, the form in the database should have the same fields in the same order as those on the paper form. This will enable users to easily tab from one field to the next in the database form to enter the necessary information from the paper form. Also, it's important to include a meaningful title on the form to identify its purpose and to enhance the appearance of the form. A form that is visually appealing makes working with the database more user-friendly and can improve the readability of the form, thereby helping to prevent errors in data entry. Also, be sure to use a consistent design for the forms in your database whenever possible. Users will expect to see similar elements—titles, pictures, fonts, and so on—in each form contained in a database. A mix of form styles and elements among the forms in a database could lead to problems when working with the forms. Finally, make sure the text on your form does not contain any spelling or grammatical errors. By producing a well-designed and well-written form, you can help to ensure that users will be able to work with the form in a productive and efficient manner.

Navigating a Form

Cindi wants to use the PatientData form to view some data in the Patient table. As you saw earlier, you use Layout view to modify the appearance of a form. To view, navigate, and change data using a form, you need to display the form in Form view. As you learned in Tutorial 1, you navigate a form in the same way that you navigate a table datasheet. Also, the navigation mode and editing mode keyboard shortcuts you used with datasheets in Tutorial 3 are the same when navigating a form.

The PatientData form is already displayed in Form view, so you can use it to navigate through the fields and records of the Patient table.

To navigate the PatientData form:

1. If necessary, click in the Patient ID field value box to make it current.

2. Press the **Tab** key twice to move to the First Name field value box, and then press the **End** key to move to the Phone field value box.

3. Press the **Home** key to move back to the Patient ID field value box. The first record in the Patient table still appears in the form.

4. Press the **Ctrl+End** keys to move to the Phone field value box for record 51, which is the last record in the table. The record number for the current record appears in the Current Record box between the navigation buttons at the bottom of the form.

5. Click the **Previous record** navigation button ◀ to move to the Phone field value box in record 50.

6. Press the ↑ key twice to move to the Zip field value box in record 50.

7. Click to position the insertion point between the numbers "8" and "3" in the Address field value to switch to editing mode, press the **Home** key to move the insertion point to the beginning of the field value, and then press the **End** key to move the insertion point to the end of the field value.

> **8.** Click the **First record** navigation button ◄ to move to the Address field value box in the first record. The entire field value is highlighted because you switched from editing mode to navigation mode.

> **9.** Click the **Next record** navigation button ► to move to the Address field value box in record 2, the next record.

Next, Cindi asks you to find the record for a patient named Sam. The paper form containing all the original contact information for this patient was damaged. Other than the patient's first name, Cindi knows only the street the patient lives on. Now she wants to use the form to view the complete data for this patient so she can contact the patient and make any necessary corrections.

Finding Data Using a Form

As you learned in Tutorial 3, the Find command lets you search for data in a datasheet so you can display only those records you want to view. You can also use the Find command to search for data in a form. You choose a field to serve as the basis for the search by making that field the current field, and then you enter the value you want Access to match in the Find and Replace dialog box.

REFERENCE

Finding Data in a Form or Datasheet

- Open the form or datasheet, and then make the field you want to search the current field.
- In the Find group on the HOME tab, click the Find button to open the Find and Replace dialog box.
- In the Find What box, type the field value you want to find.
- Complete the remaining options, as necessary, to specify the type of search to conduct.
- Click the Find Next button to begin the search.
- Click the Find Next button to continue searching for the next match.
- Click the Cancel button to stop the search operation.

You need to find the record for the patient Cindi wants to contact. In addition to the patient's first name (Sam), Cindi knows the name of the street on which this patient lives—Bunnell Place—so you'll search for the record using the Address field.

To find the record using the PatientData form:

> **1.** Make sure the **Address** field value is still selected for the current record. This is the field you need to search.

> You can search for a record that contains part of the address anywhere in the Address field value. Performing a partial search such as this is often easier than matching the entire field value and is useful when you don't know or can't remember the entire field value.

> **2.** In the Find group on the HOME tab, click the **Find** button. The Find and Replace dialog box opens. The Look In box shows that the current field (in this case, Address) will be searched. You'll search for records that contain the word "bunnell" in the address.

3. In the Find What box, type **bunnell**. Note that you do not have to enter the word as "Bunnell" with a capital letter "B" because the Match Case option is not selected in the Find and Replace dialog box. Access will find any record containing the word "bunnell" with any combination of uppercase and lowercase letters.

4. Click the **Match** arrow to display the list of matching options, and then click **Any Part of Field**. Access will find any record that contains the word "bunnell" in any part of the Address field. See Figure 4-10.

Figure 4-10 **Completed Find and Replace dialog box**

search value entered

specifies that Access will search the current field

specifies that Access will search for the value in any part of the current field

5. Click the **Find Next** button. The PatientData form now displays record 37, which is the record for Sam Boucher (PatientID 22543). The word "Bunnell" is selected in the Address field value box because you searched for this word. Cindi calls the patient and confirms that all the information is correct.

The search value you enter can be an exact value or it can include wildcard characters. A **wildcard character** is a placeholder you use when you know only part of a value or when you want to start or end with a specific character or match a certain pattern. Figure 4-11 shows the wildcard characters you can use when finding data.

Figure 4-11 **Wildcard characters**

Wildcard Character	Purpose	Example
*	Match any number of characters. It can be used as the first and/or last character in the character string.	th* finds the, that, this, therefore, and so on
?	Match any single alphabetic character.	a?t finds act, aft, ant, apt, and art
[]	Match any single character within the brackets.	a[fr]t finds aft and art but not act, ant, or apt
!	Match any character not within brackets.	a[!fr]t finds act, ant, and apt but not aft or art
-	Match any one of a range of characters. The range must be in ascending order (a to z, not z to a).	a[d-p]t finds aft, ant, and apt but not act or art
#	Match any single numeric character.	#72 finds 072, 172, 272, 372, and so on

© 2014 Cengage Learning

Next, to see how a wildcard works, you'll view the records for any patients with phone numbers that contain the exchange 226 as part of the phone number. The exchange consists of the three digits that follow the area code in the phone number. You could search for any record containing the digits 226 in any part of the Phone field, but this search would also find records with the digits 226 in any part of the phone number. To find only those records with the digits 226 as the exchange, you'll use the * wildcard character.

To find the records using the * wildcard character:

▶ **1.** Make sure the Find and Replace dialog box is still open.

▶ **2.** Click anywhere in the PatientData form to make it active, and then press the **Tab** key until you reach the Phone field value box. This is the field you want to search.

▶ **3.** Click the title bar of the Find and Replace dialog box to make it active, and then drag the Find and Replace dialog box to the right so you can see the Phone field on the form, if necessary. The Look In box setting is still Current field, which is now the Phone field; this is the field that will be searched.

▶ **4.** Double-click **bunnell** in the Find What box to select the entire value, and then type **860-226***.

▶ **5.** Click the **Match** arrow, and then click **Whole Field**. Because you're using a wildcard character in the search value, you want Access to search the whole field.

   With the settings you've entered, Access will find records in which any field value in the Phone field begins with the area code 860 followed by a hyphen and the exchange 226.

▶ **6.** Click the **Find Next** button. Access displays record 46, which is the first record found for a customer with the exchange 226. Notice that the search process started from the point of the previously displayed record in the form, which was record 37.

▶ **7.** Click the **Find Next** button. Access displays record 5, which is the next record found for a customer with the exchange 226. Notice that the search process cycles back through the beginning of the records in the underlying table.

▶ **8.** Click the **Find Next** button. Access displays record 11, the third record found.

▶ **9.** Click the **Find Next** button. Access displays record 23, the fourth record found.

▶ **10.** Click the **Find Next** button. Access displays record 34.

▶ **11.** Click the **Find Next** button. Access displays record 37 for Sam Boucher; this is the patient record that was active when you started the search process.

▶ **12.** Click the **Find Next** button. Access displays a dialog box informing you that the search is finished.

▶ **13.** Click the **OK** button to close the dialog box.

▶ **14.** Click the **Cancel** button to close the Find and Replace dialog box.

Cindi has identified some patient updates she wants you to make. You'll use the PatientData form to update the data in the Patient table.

Maintaining Table Data Using a Form

Maintaining data using a form is often easier than using a datasheet because you can focus on all the changes for a single record at one time. In Form view, you can edit the field values for a record, delete a record from the underlying table, or add a new record to the table. You already know how to navigate a form and find specific records. Now you'll use the PatientData form to make the changes Cindi wants to the Patient table.

First, you'll update the record for Felipe Ramos. This patient recently moved from Hartford to West Hartford and provided an email address, so you need to update the necessary fields for this patient. In addition to using the Find and Replace dialog box to locate a specific record, you can use the Search box to the right of the navigation buttons. You'll use the Search box to search for the patient's last name, Ramos, and display the patient record in the form.

To change the record using the PatientData form:

1. To the right of the navigation buttons, click the **Search** box and then type **Ramos**. As soon as you start to type, Access begins searching through all fields in the records to match your entry. Record 33 (Felipe Ramos) is now current.

   You need to update this record with the new information for this patient.

TIP

Note that the pencil symbol appears in the upper-left corner of the form, indicating that the form is in editing mode.

2. Select the current entry in the Address field value box, and then type **145 Jackson Dr** to replace it.

3. Click at the beginning of the City field value box, type **West** and then press the **spacebar**. The City field value is now West Hartford.

4. Press the **Tab** key twice to move to and select the Zip field value, and then type **06117**.

5. Press the **Tab** key to move to the Email field value box, and then type **f.ramos@example.org** for the new email address.

6. Click to place the insertion point at the end of the value in the Phone field value box, press the **Backspace** key to delete everything except the area code and first dash, and then type **637-8841**. The Phone field value is now 860-637-8841. The updates to the record are complete. See Figure 4-12.

Figure 4-12   **Patient record after changing field values**

Next, Cindi asks you to add a record for a new patient. This person signed up to be a patient of the clinic at a recent health fair held by Chatham Community Health Services, but has not yet visited the clinic. You'll use the PatientData form to add the new record.

To add the new record using the PatientData form:

1. In the Records group on the HOME tab, click the **New** button. Record 52, the next available new record, becomes the current record. All field value boxes are empty (except the State field, which displays the default value of CT) and the insertion point is positioned in the Patient ID field value box.

2. Refer to Figure 4-13 and enter the value shown for each field. Press the **Tab** key to move from field to field.

Figure 4-13 Completed form for the new record

Trouble? Compare your screen with Figure 4-13. If any field value is incorrect, correct it now, using the methods described earlier for editing field values.

3. After entering the Phone field value, press the **Tab** key. Record 53, the next available new record, becomes the current record, and the record for PatientID 22565 is saved in the Patient table.

Cindi would like a printed copy of the PatientData form to show to her staff members. She asks you to print one form record.

Previewing and Printing Selected Form Records

Access prints as many form records as can fit on a printed page. If only part of a form record fits on the bottom of a page, the remainder of the record prints on the next page. Access allows you to print all pages or a range of pages. In addition, you can print the currently selected form record.

Cindi asks you to use the PatientData form to print the first record in the Patient table. Before you do, you'll preview the form record to see how it will look when printed.

To preview the form and print the data for record 1:

▶ 1. Click the **First record** navigation button ⏮ to display record 1 in the form. This is the record in which you have entered your first and last names.

▶ 2. Click the **FILE** tab to display Backstage view, click **Print** in the navigation bar, and then click **Print Preview**. The Print Preview window opens, showing the form records for the Patient table. Notice that each record appears in its own form, and that shading is used to distinguish one record from another. See Figure 4-14.

Figure 4-14	Form records displayed in Print Preview

To print one selected record on a page by itself, you need to close Print Preview and then use the Print dialog box.

▶ 3. In the Close Preview group on the PRINT PREVIEW tab, click the **Close Print Preview** button. You return to Form view with the first record still displayed.

▶ 4. Click the **FILE** tab to display Backstage view again, click **Print** in the navigation bar, and then click **Print**. The Print dialog box opens.

> **5.** Click the **Selected Record(s)** option button to print the current form record (record 1).
>
> **Trouble?** Check with your instructor to be sure you should print the form; then continue to the next step. If you should not print the form, click the Cancel button, and then skip to Step 7.
>
> **6.** Click the **OK** button to close the dialog box and print the selected record.
>
> **7.** Close the PatientData form.

After reviewing the printed PatientData form with her staff, Cindi realizes that it would be helpful for staff members to also have a form showing information about both patients and their visits.

Creating a Form with a Main Form and a Subform

Cindi would like you to create a form so that she can view the data for each patient and the patient's visits to the clinic at the same time. The type of form you need to create will include a main form and a subform. To create a form based on two tables, you must first define a relationship between the two tables. In Tutorial 2, you defined a one-to-many relationship between the Patient (primary) and Visit (related) tables, so you can now create a form based on both tables.

When you create a form containing data from two tables that have a one-to-many relationship, you actually create a **main form** for data from the primary table and a **subform** for data from the related table. Access uses the defined relationship between the tables to join them automatically through the common field that exists in both tables.

Cindi and her staff will use the form when discussing visits with the clinic's patients. The main form will contain the patient ID, first and last names, date of birth, phone number, and email address for each patient. The subform will contain the information about the visits for each patient. You'll use the Form Wizard to create the form.

To create the form using the Form Wizard:

> **1.** On the ribbon, click the **CREATE** tab.
>
> **2.** In the Forms group, click the **Form Wizard** button. The first Form Wizard dialog box opens.
>
> When creating a form based on two tables, you first choose the primary table and select the fields you want to include in the main form; then you choose the related table and select fields from it for the subform.
>
> **3.** If necessary, click the **Tables/Queries** arrow, and then click **Table: Patient**.
>
> Cindi wants the form to include only the PatientID, FirstName, LastName, BirthDate, Phone, and Email fields from the Patient table.
>
> **4.** Click **PatientID** in the Available Fields box (if necessary), and then click the ⟩ button to move the field to the Selected Fields box.
>
> **5.** Repeat Step 4 for the **FirstName**, **LastName**, **BirthDate**, **Phone**, and **Email** fields.

The PatientID field will appear in the main form, so you do not have to include it in the subform. Otherwise, Cindi wants the subform to include all the fields from the Visit table.

6. Click the **Tables/Queries** arrow, and then click **Table: Visit**. The fields from the Visit table appear in the Available Fields box. The quickest way to add the fields you want to include is to move all the fields to the Selected Fields box, and then remove the only field you don't want to include (PatientID).

TIP

The table name (Visit) is included in the PatientID field name to distinguish it from the same field in the Patient table.

7. Click the >> button to move all the fields in the Visit table to the Selected Fields box.

8. Click **Visit.PatientID** in the Selected Fields box, and then click the < button to move the field back to the Available Fields box.

9. Click the **Next** button. The next Form Wizard dialog box opens. See Figure 4-15.

Figure 4-15   **Choosing a format for the main form and subform**

In this dialog box, the section on the left shows the order in which you will view the selected data: first by data from the primary Patient table, and then by data from the related Visit table. The form will be displayed as shown on the right side of the dialog box, with the fields from the Patient table at the top in the main form, and the fields from the Visit table at the bottom in the subform. The selected "Form with subform(s)" option button specifies a main form with a subform. The Linked forms option creates a form structure in which only the main form fields are displayed. A button with the subform's name on it appears on the main form; you can click this button to display the associated subform records.

The default options shown in Figure 4-15 are correct for creating a form with Patient data in the main form and Visit data in the subform.

To finish creating the form:

1. Click the **Next** button. The next Form Wizard dialog box opens, in which you choose the subform layout.

The Tabular layout displays subform fields as a table, whereas the Datasheet layout displays subform fields as a table datasheet. The layout choice is a matter of personal preference. You'll use the Datasheet layout.

▶ **2.** Click the **Datasheet** option button to select it (if necessary), and then click the **Next** button. The next Form Wizard dialog box opens, in which you choose titles for the main form and the subform.

You'll use the title "PatientVisits" for the main form and the title "VisitSubform" for the subform. These titles will also be the names for the form objects.

▶ **3.** In the Form box, click to position the insertion point to the right of the last letter, and then type **Visits**. The main form name is now PatientVisits.

▶ **4.** In the Subform box, delete the space between the two words so that the subform name appears as **VisitSubform**.

▶ **5.** Click the **Finish** button. The completed form opens in Form view. See Figure 4-16.

Figure 4-16	Main form with subform in Form view

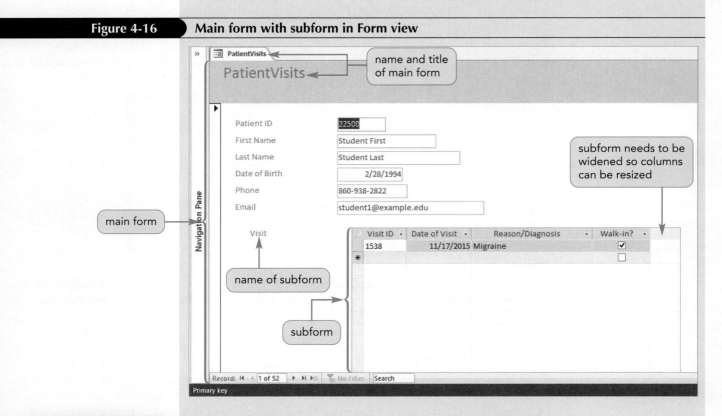

In the main form, Access displays the fields from the first record in the Patient table in a columnar format. The records in the main form appear in primary key order by PatientID. PatientID 22500 has one related record in the Visit table; this record, for VisitID 1538, is shown in the subform, which uses the datasheet format. The main form name, "PatientVisits," appears on the object tab and as the form title. The name of the subform appears to the left of the subform. Note that only the word "Visit" and not the complete name "VisitSubform" appears on the form. Access displays only the table name for the subform itself, but displays the complete name of the object, "VisitSubform," when you view and work with objects in the Navigation Pane.

TIP

The PatientVisits form is formatted with the default Office theme because you applied the Slice theme only to the PatientData form.

The subform designation is necessary in a list of database objects so that you can distinguish the Visit subform from other objects, such as the Visit table, but the subform designation is not needed in the PatientVisits form. Only the table name is required to identify the table containing the records in the subform.

Next, you need to make some changes to the form. First, you'll edit the form title to add a space between the words so that it appears as "Patient Visits." Then, you'll resize the subform. Cindi is concerned that the subform is not wide enough to allow for all the columns to be resized and fully display their field values, especially the Reason/Diagnosis column. To make these changes, you need to switch to Layout view.

To modify the PatientVisits form in Layout view:

1. In the Views group on the HOME tab, click the **View** button to switch to Layout view.

2. Click **PatientVisits** in the blue-gray area at the top of the form. The form title is selected.

3. Click between the letters "t" and "V" to place the insertion point, and then press the **spacebar**. The title on the form is now "Patient Visits."

4. Click in a blank area of the form to the right of the field value boxes to deselect the title. Next, you'll increase the width of the subform.

5. Click the subform. An orange outline surrounds the subform, indicating it is selected.

6. Position the pointer on the right vertical line of the selected subform until the pointer changes to a ↔ shape, and then click and drag to the right approximately two inches. The subform is now wider. See Figure 4-17.

Figure 4-17   **Modified form in Layout view**

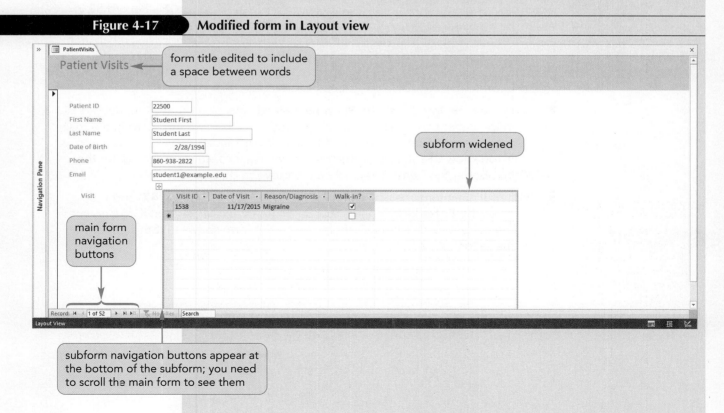

The wider subform will enable you to resize the Reason/Diagnosis column, as necessary, to fully display its field values.

7. On the Quick Access Toolbar, click the **Save** button 🖫 to save both the main form and the subform.

8. In the Views group on the DESIGN tab, click the **View** button to display the PatientVisits form in Form view.

    Trouble? If the fields in the main form are partially out of view, use the vertical scroll bar to scroll to the top of the form and display the fields.

The form includes two sets of navigation buttons. You use the set of navigation buttons at the bottom of the Form window to select records from the primary table in the main form (see Figure 4-17). The second set of navigation buttons is currently not visible; you need to scroll down the main form to see these buttons, which appear at the bottom of the subform. You use the subform navigation buttons to select records from the related table in the subform.

You'll use the navigation buttons to view different records.

To navigate to different main form and subform records:

1. In the main form, click the **Next record** navigation button ▶ six times. Record 7 of 52 total records in the Patient table (for Matthew Weiss) becomes the current record in the main form. The subform shows that this patient made three visits to the clinic. Note that the field values in the Reason/Diagnosis column are not fully displayed.

2. Double-click the pointer ↔ on the right vertical line of the Reason/Diagnosis column in the subform to resize this field to its best fit and display the complete field values.

3. In the main form, click the **Last record** navigation button ▶|. Record 52 in the Patient table (for Alex Cronin) becomes the current record in the main form. The subform shows that this patient currently has no visits; recall that you just entered this record using the PatientData form. Cindi could use the subform to enter the information for this patient's visits to the clinic, and that information will be updated in the Visit table.

4. In the main form, click the **Previous record** navigation button ◀. Record 51 in the Patient table (for Daniel Shaw) becomes the current record in the main form. The subform shows that this patient has made one visit to the clinic. If you know the number of the record you want to view, you can enter the number in the Current Record box to move to that record.

5. In the main form, select **51** in the Current Record box, type **47**, and then press the **Enter** key. Record 47 in the Patient table (for Isobel Kirk) becomes the current record in the main form. The subform shows that this patient made four visits to the clinic.

6. In the subform, resize the Reason/Diagnosis column to its best fit to fully display its field values, if necessary.

7. If necessary, use the vertical scroll bar for the main form to scroll down and view the bottom of the subform. Note the navigation buttons for the subform.

8. In the subform, click the **Last record** navigation button ▶|. Record 4 in the Visit table, for Visit ID 1679, becomes the current record in the subform.

9. Save and close the PatientVisits form.

10. If you are not continuing to Session 4.2, click the **FILE** tab, and then click **Close** in the navigation bar to close the Chatham database.

Both the PatientData form and the PatientVisits form you created will enable Cindi and her staff to view, enter, and maintain data easily in the Patient and Visit tables in the Chatham database.

Session 4.1 Quick Check

REVIEW

1. Describe the difference between creating a form using the Form tool and creating a form using the Form Wizard.
2. What is a theme and how do you apply one to an existing form?
3. A(n) _____ is an item on a form, report, or other database object that you can manipulate to modify the object's appearance.
4. Which table record is displayed in a form when you press the Ctrl+End keys while you are in navigation mode?
5. Which wildcard character matches any single alphabetic character?
6. To print only the current record displayed in a form, you need to select the _____ option button in the Print dialog box.
7. In a form that contains a main form and a subform, what data is displayed in the main form and what data is displayed in the subform?

Session 4.2 Visual Overview:

The report object's name is displayed on the tab for the report.

The report title appears at the top of the report. By default, the report object name is used as the report title, but you can edit the title to display the text you want, as done here, with spaces added between words for readability.

Fields from the primary Patient table appear first in the report.

Fields from the related Visit table appear below the fields from the primary table.

For a **grouped report**, the data from a record in the primary table (the Patient table in this report) appears as a group, followed on subsequent lines of the report by the joined records from the related table (the Visit table in this report).

The navigation buttons allow you to display the first, last, next, or previous page in the report, or to enter a specific page number and move to that page.

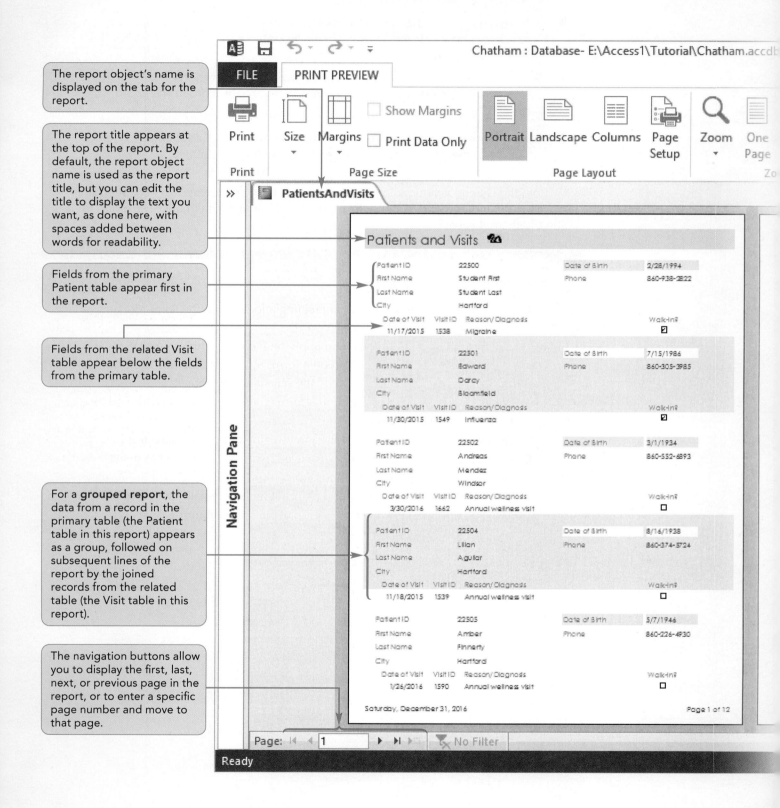

Report Displayed in Print Preview

Click this button to close Print Preview and return to the report in the previously displayed view.

The PatientsAndVisits report was created using the **Report Wizard**, which asks you a series of questions and then creates a report based on your answers. This report is based on data in both the Patient and Visit tables, which are joined in a one-to-many relationship through the common PatientID field.

This report uses **portrait orientation**, where the page is taller than it is wide; you can also format a report in **landscape orientation**, where the page is wider than it is tall.

The set of field values for each record in the related table is called a **detail record**. These three detail records are the Visit table records related to the Patient table record for Matthew Weiss.

Shading is used to distinguish one Patient record from another, and one Visit record from another.

Creating a Report Using the Report Wizard

As you learned in Tutorial 1, a report is a formatted printout or screen display of the contents of one or more tables or queries in a database. In Access, you can create your own reports or use the Report Wizard to create them for you. Whether you use the Report Wizard or design your own report, you can change a report's design after you create it.

Creating a Report Based on a Query

You can create a report based on one or more tables or queries. When you use a query as the basis for a report, you can use criteria and other query features to retrieve only the information you want to display in the report. Experienced Access users often create a query just so they can create a report based on that query. When thinking about the type of report you want to create, consider creating a query first and basing the report on the query, to produce the exact results you want to see in the report.

Ethan Ward, who handles marketing and outreach efforts for Chatham Community Health Services, wants you to create a report that includes data from both the Patient and Visit tables, as shown in the Session 4.2 Visual Overview. Like the PatientVisits form you created earlier, which includes a main form and a subform, the report will be based on both tables, which are joined in a one-to-many relationship through the common PatientID field. You'll use the Report Wizard to create the report for Ethan.

To start the Report Wizard and select the fields to include in the report:

1. If you took a break after the previous session, make sure that the Chatham database is open and the Navigation Pane is closed.

2. On the ribbon, click the **CREATE** tab.

3. In the Reports group, click the **Report Wizard** button. The first Report Wizard dialog box opens.

   As was the case when you created the form with a subform, initially you can choose only one table or query to be the data source for the report. Then you can include data from other tables or queries. You will select the primary Patient table first.

4. Click the **Tables/Queries** arrow, scroll up the list (if necessary), and then click **Table: Patient**.

   You select fields in the order you want them to appear on the report. Ethan wants the PatientID, FirstName, LastName, City, BirthDate, and Phone fields from the Patient table to appear on the report, in that order.

5. Click **PatientID** in the Available Fields box (if necessary), and then click the ⟩ button. The field moves to the Selected Fields box.

6. Repeat Step 5 to add the **FirstName**, **LastName**, **City**, **BirthDate**, and **Phone** fields to the report.

7. Click the **Tables/Queries** arrow, and then click **Table: Visit**. The fields from the Visit table appear in the Available Fields box.

The PatientID field will appear on the report with the patient data, so you do not need to include it in the detail records for each visit. Otherwise, Ethan wants all the fields from the Visit table to be included in the report.

8. Click the >> button to move all the fields from the Available Fields box to the Selected Fields box.

9. Click **Visit.PatientID** in the Selected Fields box, click the < button to move the field back to the Available Fields box, and then click the **Next** button. The second Report Wizard dialog box opens. See Figure 4-18.

Figure 4-18   **Choosing a grouped or ungrouped report**

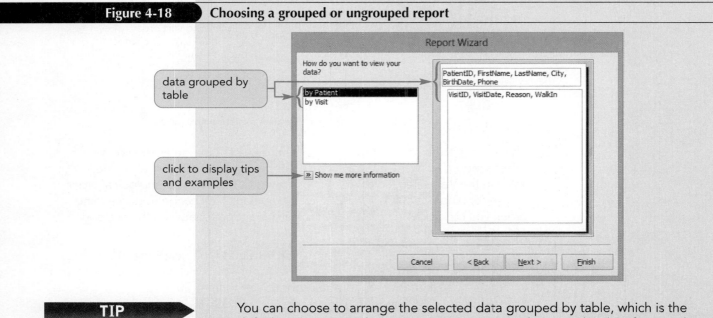

data grouped by table

click to display tips and examples

TIP

You can display tips for creating reports and examples of reports by clicking the "Show me more information" button.

You can choose to arrange the selected data grouped by table, which is the default, or ungrouped. You're creating a grouped report; the data from each record in the Patient table will appear in a group, followed by the related records for that patient from the Visit table.

The default options shown on your screen are correct for the report Ethan wants, so you can continue responding to the Report Wizard questions.

To finish creating the report using the Report Wizard:

1. Click the **Next** button. The next Report Wizard dialog box opens, in which you choose additional grouping levels.

   Currently the report contains only one grouping level, which is for the patient's data. Grouping levels are useful for reports with multiple levels, such as those containing monthly, quarterly, and annual totals, or for those containing city and country groups. Ethan's report requires no further grouping levels, so you can accept the default options.

2. Click the **Next** button. The next Report Wizard dialog box opens, in which you choose the sort order for the detail records. See Figure 4-19.

Figure 4-19 **Choosing the sort order for detail records**

The records from the Visit table for a patient represent the detail records for Ethan's report. He wants these records to appear in ascending order by the value in the VisitDate field, so that the visits will be shown in chronological order. The Ascending option is already selected by default. To change to descending order, you click this same button, which acts as a toggle between the two sort orders. Also, you can sort on multiple fields, as you can with queries.

3. Click the **arrow** on the first box, click **VisitDate**, and then click the **Next** button. The next Report Wizard dialog box opens, in which you choose a layout and page orientation for the report. See Figure 4-20.

Figure 4-20 **Choosing the report layout**

4. Click each layout option and examine each sample that appears.

You'll use the Outline layout for Ethan's report. Also, most of the fields in both the Patient and Visit tables contain relatively short field values, so you'll keep the portrait page orientation. This should provide enough space across the page to display all the field values; you will confirm this when viewing the report created by the wizard.

5. In the Layout section, click the **Outline** option button, and then click the **Next** button. The final Report Wizard dialog box opens, in which you choose a report title, which also serves as the name for the report object in the database.

   Ethan wants the report title "Patients and Visits" at the top of the report. Because the name you enter in this dialog box is also the name of the report object, you'll enter the report name as one word and edit the title on the report later.

6. In the box for the title, enter **PatientsAndVisits** and then click the **Finish** button. The Report Wizard creates the report based on your answers, saves it as an object in the Chatham database, and opens the report in Print Preview.

   To view the entire page, you need to change the Zoom setting.

7. In the Zoom group on the PRINT PREVIEW tab, click the **Zoom button arrow**, and then click **Fit to Window**. The first page of the report is displayed in Print Preview.

8. At the bottom of the window, click the **Next Page** navigation button ▶ to display the second page of the report.

   When a report is displayed in Print Preview, you can use the pointer to toggle between a full-page display and a close-up display of the report.

9. Click the pointer ⊕ at the center of the report. The display changes to show a close-up view of the report. See Figure 4-21.

| Figure 4-21 | Close-up view of the report |

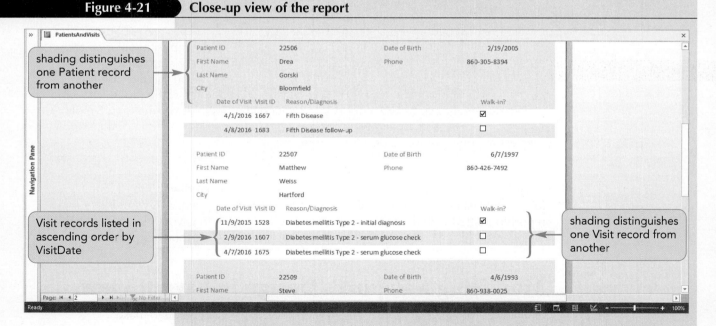

Shading is used to distinguish both one Patient record from another and, within a group of each patient's Visit records, one Visit record from another.

Trouble? Depending on your computer settings, the shading and colors used in your report might look different. This difference should not cause any problems.

The detail records for the Visit table fields appear in ascending order based on the values in the VisitDate field. Because the VisitDate field is used as the basis for sorting records, it appears as the first field in this section, even though you selected the fields in the order in which they appear in the Visit table.

▶ **10.** Use the vertical scroll bar to scroll to the bottom of the second page, checking the text in the report as you scroll. Notice the current date and page number at the bottom of the page; the Report Wizard included these elements as part of the report's design.

Trouble? Depending on your computer's settings, the text of the page number might not be completely within the page border. If so, you'll see blank pages every other page as you complete Steps 11 and 12. You'll fix this problem shortly.

▶ **11.** Click the pointer 🔍 on the report to zoom back out, and then click the **Next Page** navigation button ▶ to move to page 3 of the report.

▶ **12.** Continue to move through the pages of the report, and then click the **First Page** navigation button ◀ to return to the first page.

INSIGHT

Changing a Report's Page Orientation and Margins

When you display a report in Print Preview, you can easily change the report layout using options on the PRINT PREVIEW tab (refer to the Session 4.2 Visual Overview). For example, sometimes fields with longer values cause the report content to overflow onto the next page. You can fix this problem by clicking the Landscape button in the Page Layout group on the PRINT PREVIEW tab to switch the report orientation to landscape, where the page is wider than it is tall. Landscape orientation allows more space for content to fit across the width of the report page. You can also use the Margins button in the Page Size group to change the margins of the report, choosing from commonly used margin formats or creating your own custom margins. Simply click the Margins button arrow to display the menu of available margin options and select the one that works best for your report.

Earlier, when meeting with Cindi, Ethan viewed and worked with the PatientData form. He likes how the form looks with the Slice theme applied, and would like his report formatted with the same theme. You need to switch to Layout view to make this change. You'll also make other modifications to improve the report's design.

Modifying a Report's Design in Layout View

Similar to Layout view for forms, Layout view for reports enables you to make modifications to the report's design. Many of the same options—such as those for applying a theme and changing the color of text—are provided in Layout view for reports.

Applying a Theme to a Report

The same themes available for forms are also available for reports. You can choose to apply a theme to the current report object only, or to all reports in the database. In this case, you'll apply the Slice theme only to the PatientsAndVisits report because Ethan isn't certain if it is the appropriate theme for other reports in the Chatham database.

To apply the Slice theme to the report:

▶ 1. On the status bar, click the **Layout View** button ⊞. The report is displayed in Layout view.

▶ 2. In the Themes group on the DESIGN tab, click the **Themes** button. The "In this Database" section at the top of the gallery shows both the default Office theme and the Slice theme. The Slice theme is included here because you applied it earlier to the PatientData form.

TIP

When you point to the Slice theme, a ScreenTip displays the names of the database objects that use the theme—in this case, the PatientData form.

▶ 3. At the top of the gallery, right-click the **Slice** theme to display the shortcut menu, and then click **Apply Theme to This Object Only**. The gallery closes and the theme is applied to the report.

The larger font used by the Slice theme has caused the report title text to be cut off on the right. You'll fix this problem and edit the title text as well.

▶ 4. Click the **PatientsAndVisits** title at the top of the report to select it.

▶ 5. Place the pointer on the right vertical line of the orange outline surrounding the title, and then click and drag the ↔ pointer to the right until the title is fully displayed.

Trouble? You might need to repeat Step 5 more than once in order for the text to appear correctly.

▶ 6. Click between the letters "s" and "A" in the title, press the **spacebar**, change the capital letter "A" to **a**, place the insertion point between the letters "d" and "V," and then press the **spacebar**. The title is now "Patients and Visits."

▶ 7. Click to the right of the report title in the shaded area to deselect the title.

Ethan views the report and notices some other formatting changes he would like you to make. First, he doesn't like how the BirthDate field values are aligned compared to the Phone field values. You'll fix this next.

Changing the Alignment of Field Values

The FORMAT tab in Layout view, one of the REPORT LAYOUT TOOLS contextual tabs, provides options for you to easily modify the format of various report objects. For example, you can change the alignment of the text in a field value. Recall that Date/Time fields, like BirthDate, automatically right-align their field values, whereas Short Text fields, like Phone, automatically left-align their field values. Ethan asks you to change the alignment of the BirthDate field so its values appear left-aligned, which will improve the format of the report.

To change the alignment of the BirthDate field values:

▶ 1. On the ribbon, click the **FORMAT** tab. The ribbon changes to display groups and options for formatting the report. The options for modifying the format of a report are the same as those available for forms.

▶ 2. In the report, click the first **BirthDate field value box**, which contains the date 2/28/1994. The field value box is outlined in orange, indicating it is selected. Note that the other BirthDate field value boxes are outlined in a lighter orange, indicating they are selected as well. Any changes you make will be applied to all BirthDate field values throughout the report.

> 3. In the Font group on the FORMAT tab, click the **Align Left** button ▤. The text in the BirthDate field value boxes is now left-aligned, and the birth dates are aligned with the phone numbers. See Figure 4-22.

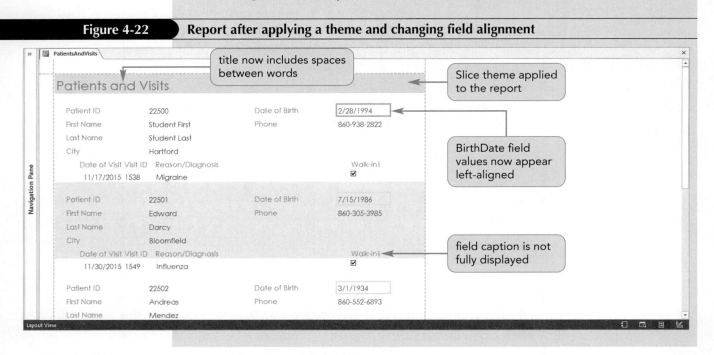

Moving and Resizing Fields on a Report

Working in Layout view, you can resize and reposition fields and field value boxes to improve the appearance of a report or to address the problem of some field values not being completely displayed. In the PatientsAndVisits report, you need to move and resize the WalkIn field label so that the complete caption, Walk-in?, is displayed. Ethan also thinks the report would look better with more room between the VisitDate and VisitID fields, so you'll move the VisitDate field label and associated field value box to the left.

You can select one or more objects on a report and then drag them to a new location; or, for more precise control over the move, you can use the arrow keyboard keys to move selected objects. Ethan asks you to move the WalkIn field's label to the left so it appears centered over its check box, and also to make the label larger.

To move and resize the WalkIn field label:

> 1. In the report, click the first occurrence of the **Walk-in?** field label. All instances of the label are selected throughout the report.

> 2. Press the ← key repeatedly until the label is centered (roughly) over its check box.

> 3. Place the pointer on the right vertical line of the orange outline surrounding the label, and then click and drag the ↔ pointer to the right until the label text is fully displayed.

Next, you need to move the VisitDate field label (Date of Visit) and field value box to the left, to provide more space between the VisitDate field and the VisitID field in the report. You can select both objects and modify them at the same time.

To move the VisitDate field label and field value box:

▶ **1.** In the report, click the first occurrence of the **Date of Visit** field label, press and hold the **Shift** key, and then click the first occurrence of the field value box, which contains the date 11/17/2015. Both the field label and its associated field value box are selected and can be moved. See Figure 4-23.

Figure 4-23	Report after moving and resizing field label

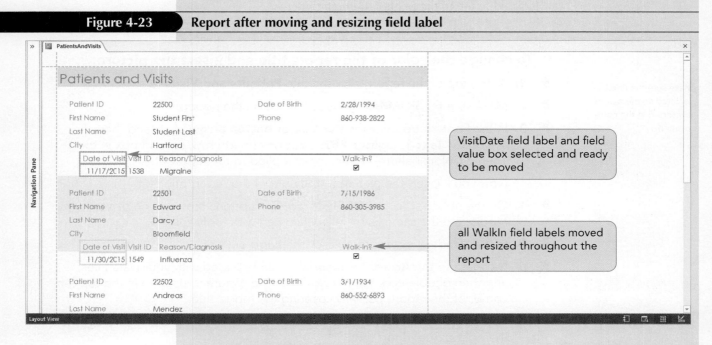

▶ **2.** Press the ← key four times to move the field label and field value box to the left.

> **Trouble?** Once you press the left arrow key, the report might jump to display the end of the report. Just continue to press the left arrow key to move the label and value. Then scroll the window back up to display the beginning of the report.

> Ethan is pleased with the changes to the report format, but he is concerned that the larger font size of the theme might have caused other text in the report to be cut off—especially some of the Reason/Diagnosis field values, which are lengthy. You need to check the report for such problems. First, you'll save the design changes you've made.

▶ **3.** On the Quick Access Toolbar, click the **Save** button 🖫 to save the modified report.

▶ **4.** At the top of the report, click to the right of the report title in the shaded area to deselect the VisitDate field label and field value box.

▶ **5.** Scroll through the report, checking the field labels and field values as you go to make sure all text is fully displayed. When finished, scroll back up to display the top of the report.

Next, Ethan asks you to enhance the report's appearance by inserting the same picture on the PatientsAndVisits report as you included on the PatientData form, and to change the color of the report title to the same darker color used on the form.

Changing the Title Font Color and Inserting a Picture in a Report

You can change the color of text on a report to enhance its appearance. You can also add a picture to a report for visual interest or to identify a particular section of the report. Because Ethan plans to print the report, he asks you to change the report title color to the darker black you applied earlier to the PatientData form and to include the Medical picture to the right of the report title.

To change the color of the report title and insert the picture:

Make sure the title is selected so the picture is inserted in the correct location.

1. At the top of the report, click the title **Patients and Visits** to select it.

2. Make sure the **FORMAT** tab is still active on the ribbon.

3. In the Font group, click the **Font Color button arrow** [A ▾], and then click the **Black, Text 1, Lighter 25%** color box (fourth row, second box in the Theme Colors palette). The color is applied to the report title.

   Now you'll insert the picture to the right of the report title text.

4. On the ribbon, click the **DESIGN** tab. The options provided on this tab for reports are the same as those you worked with for forms.

5. In the Header/Footer group, click the **Logo** button.

6. Navigate to the **Access1 ▸ Tutorial** folder provided with your Data Files, and then double-click the **Medical** file. The picture is inserted in the top-left corner of the report, partially covering the report title.

7. Position the pointer on the selected picture, and then click and drag it to the right of the report title.

8. Click in a blank area of the shaded bar to deselect the picture. See Figure 4-24.

Figure 4-24   **Report after changing the title font color and inserting the picture**

Trouble? Don't be concerned if the picture in your report is not in the exact same location as the one shown in the figure. Just make sure it is to the right of the title text and within the shaded area.

Ethan is pleased with the report's appearance and shows it to Cindi. She also approves of the report's contents and design, but has one final suggestion for the report. She'd like to draw attention to patient records for children and teenagers by formatting their birth dates with a bold, red font. Chatham Community Health Services is planning a special event specifically geared to children and teenagers regarding healthy diets, so this format will make it easier to find these patient records in the report. Because Cindi doesn't want all the birth dates to appear in this font, you need to use conditional formatting.

Using Conditional Formatting in a Report

Conditional formatting in a report (or form) is special formatting applied to certain field values depending on one or more conditions—similar to criteria you establish for queries. If a field value meets the condition or conditions you specify, the formatting is applied to the value.

Cindi would like the PatientsAndVisits report to show any birth date that is greater than 1/1/1997 in a bold, dark red font. This formatting will help to highlight the patient records for children and teenagers. Cindi plans to review this report in a planning meeting for the upcoming special event.

To apply conditional formatting to the BirthDate field in the report:

▶ **1.** Make sure the report is still displayed in Layout view, and then click the **FORMAT** tab on the ribbon.

To apply conditional formatting to a field, you must first make it the active field by clicking any field value in the field's column.

TIP

You must select a field *value box*, and not the field *label*, before applying a conditional format.

▶ **2.** Click the first BirthDate field value, **2/28/1994**, for PatientID 22500. An orange outline appears around the field value box, and a lighter orange outline appears around each BirthDate field value box throughout the entire report. The conditional formatting you specify will affect all the values for the field.

▶ **3.** In the Control Formatting group on the FORMAT tab, click the **Conditional Formatting** button. The Conditional Formatting Rules Manager dialog box opens. Because you selected a BirthDate field value box, the name of this field is displayed in the "Show formatting rules for" box. Currently, there are no conditional formatting rules set for the selected field. You need to create a new rule.

▶ **4.** Click the **New Rule** button. The New Formatting Rule dialog box opens. See Figure 4-25.

Figure 4-25   **New Formatting Rule dialog box**

specify the condition in these boxes

a preview of the conditional format will appear here

use these options to specify the formatting

The default setting for "Select a rule type" specifies that Access will check field values and determine if they meet the condition. This is the setting you want. You need to enter the condition in the "Edit the rule description" section of the dialog box. The setting "Field Value Is" means that the conditional format you specify will be applied only when the value for the selected field, BirthDate, meets the condition.

▶ **5.** Click the **arrow** for the box containing the word "between," and then click **greater than**. Cindi wants only those birth dates greater than 1/1/1997 to be formatted.

▶ **6.** Click in the next box, and then type **1/1/1997**.

▶ **7.** In the Preview section, click the **Font color button arrow** ⓐ ▾ and then click the **Dark Red** color box (first color box in the last row of Standard Colors).

▶ **8.** In the Preview section, click the **Bold** button ⓑ. The specifications for the conditional formatting are complete. See Figure 4-26.

Figure 4-26	Conditional formatting set for the BirthDate field

condition specifies that the selected field value must be greater than 1/1/1997

preview shows the bold, dark red font that will be applied to field values that meet the condition

Bold button selected

dark red font color selected

▶ **9.** Click the **OK** button. The new rule you specified appears in the Rule section of the dialog box as Value > 1/1/1997; the Format section on the right shows the conditional formatting (dark red, bold font) that will be applied based on this rule.

▶ **10.** Click the **OK** button. The conditional format is applied to the BirthDate field values. To get a better view of the report and the formatting, you'll switch to Print Preview.

▶ **11.** On the status bar, click the **Print Preview** button 🔳.

▶ **12.** Move to page 2 of the report. Notice that the conditional formatting is applied only to BirthDate field values greater than 1/1/1997. See Figure 4-27.

Figure 4-27   Viewing the finished report in Print Preview

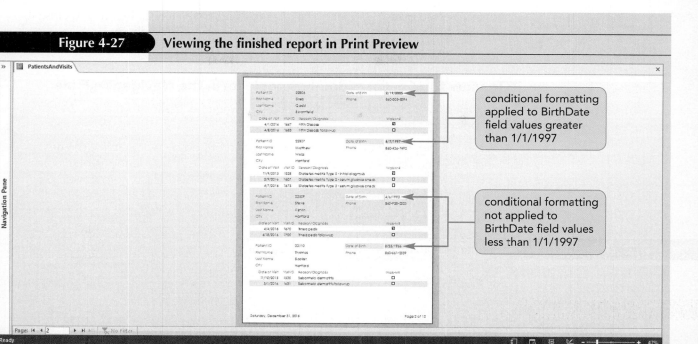

conditional formatting applied to BirthDate field values greater than 1/1/1997

conditional formatting not applied to BirthDate field values less than 1/1/1997

PROSKILLS

Problem Solving: Understanding the Importance of Previewing Reports

When you create a report, it is a good idea to display the report in Print Preview occasionally as you develop it. Doing so will give you a chance to find any formatting problems or other issues so that you can make any necessary corrections before printing the report. It is particularly important to preview a report after you've made changes to its design to ensure that the changes you made have not created new problems with the report's format. Before printing any report, you should preview it so you can determine where the pages will break and make any necessary adjustments. Following this problem-solving approach will not only ensure that the final report looks exactly the way you want it to, but will also save you time and help to avoid wasting paper if you print the report.

The report is now complete. You'll print just the first page of the report so that Cindi and Ethan can view the final results and share the report design with other staff members before printing the entire report. (*Note:* Ask your instructor if you should complete the following printing steps.)

To print page 1 of the report:

1. In the Print group on the PRINT PREVIEW tab, click the **Print** button. The Print dialog box opens.

2. In the Print Range section, click the **Pages** option button. The insertion point now appears in the From box so that you can specify the range of pages to print.

3. Type **1** in the From box, press the **Tab** key to move to the To box, and then type **1**. These settings specify that only page 1 of the report will be printed.

4. Click the **OK** button. The Print dialog box closes, and the first page of the report is printed.

5. Save and close the PatientsAndVisits report.

You've created many different objects in the Chatham database. Before you close it, you'll open the Navigation Pane to view all the objects in the database.

To view the Chatham database objects in the Navigation Pane:

▶ **1.** Open the Navigation Pane and scroll down, if necessary, to display the bottom of the pane.

The Navigation Pane displays the objects grouped by type: tables, queries, forms, and reports. Notice the PatientVisits form. This is the form you created containing a main form based on the Patient table and a subform based on the Visit table. The VisitSubform object is also listed; you can open it separately from the main form. See Figure 4-28.

Figure 4-28 **Chatham database objects in the Navigation Pane**

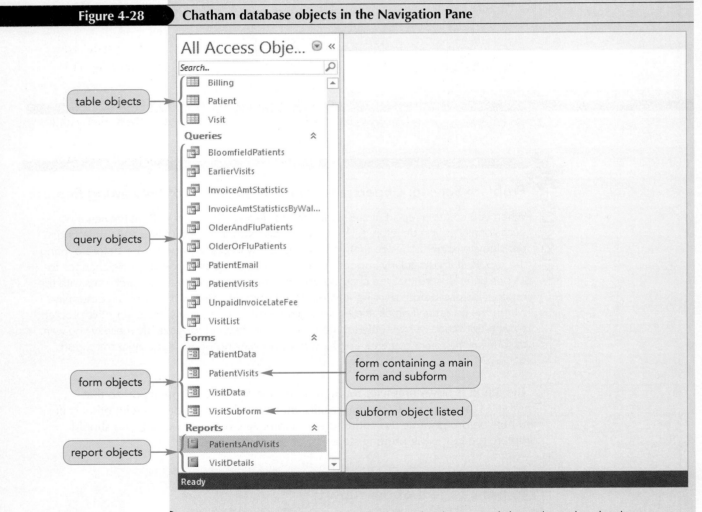

▶ **2.** Compact and repair the Chatham database, and then close the database.

Cindi is satisfied that the forms you created—the PatientData form and the PatientVisits form—will make it easier to enter, view, and update data in the Chatham database. The PatientsAndVisits report presents important information about the clinic's patients in an attractive and professional format, which will help Ethan and other staff members in their community outreach efforts.

REVIEW

Session 4.2 Quick Check

1. In a(n) _____ report, the data from a record in the primary table appears together, followed on subsequent lines by the joined records from the related table.

2. When you create a report based on two tables that are joined in a one-to-many relationship, the field values for the records from the related table are called the _____ records.

3. Identify three types of modifications you can make to a report in Layout view.

4. Describe the process for moving a control to another location on a report in Layout view.

5. When working in Layout view for a report, which key do you press and hold down so that you can click to select multiple controls (field labels, field value boxes, and so on)?

6. _____ in a report (or form) is special formatting applied to certain field values depending on one or more conditions.

ASSESS

SAM Projects

Put your skills into practice with SAM Projects! SAM Projects for this tutorial can be found online. If you have a SAM account, go to www.cengage.com/sam2013 to download the most recent Project Instructions and Start Files.

PRACTICE

Review Assignments

Data Files needed for the Review Assignments: Vendor.accdb *(cont. from Tutorial 3)* **and Supplies.bmp**

Cindi asks you to enhance the Vendor database with forms and reports. Complete the following steps:

1. Open the **Vendor** database you created and worked with in Tutorials 1 through 3, and then click the Enable Content button next to the security warning, if necessary.

2. Use the Form Wizard to create a form based on the Product table. Select all fields for the form and the Columnar layout; specify the title **ProductData** for the form.

3. Apply the Facet theme to the ProductData form *only*.

4. Insert the Supplies picture, which is located in the Access1 ▸ Review folder provided with your Data Files, in the ProductData form. Remove the picture from the control layout, and then move the picture to the right of the form title.

5. Drag a bottom corner of the image to increase its size until the items in the picture are all clearly visible. Continue to resize and reposition the image until it is in the location you want, making sure to keep it within the shaded area of the title and to the right of the title.

6. Edit the form title so that it appears as "Product Data" (two words), and change the font color of the form title to the Blue-Gray, Text 2, Darker 25% theme color.

7. Resize the Weight in Lbs field value box so it is the same width (approximately) as the Units/Case field value box above it.

8. Change the alignment of the Price, Units/Case, and Weight in Lbs fields so that their values appear left-aligned in the field value boxes.

9. Save your changes to the form design.

10. Use the ProductData form to update the Product table as follows:

   a. Use the Find command to search for the word "test" anywhere in the ProductName field, and then display the record for the mononucleosis test (ProductID MO269). Change the Price in this record to **49.50**.

   b. Add a new record with the following field values:

   Product ID: **EG400**
   Supplier ID: **SAN481**
   Product Name: **Non-Latex exam gloves**
   Price: **4.75**
   Units/Case: **80**
   Weight in Lbs: **2**
   Temp Controlled?: **no**
   Sterile?: **no**

   c. Save and close the form.

11. Use the Form Wizard to create a form containing a main form and a subform. Select all fields from the Supplier table for the main form, and select ProductID, ProductName, Price, TempControl, and Sterile—in that order—from the Product table for the subform. Use the Datasheet layout. Specify the title **SuppliersAndProducts** for the main form and **ProductSubform** for the subform.

12. Change the form title text to **Suppliers and Products**.

13. Resize the subform to the right, increasing its width by approximately three inches, and then resize all columns in the subform to their best fit, working left to right. Navigate through each record in the main form to make sure all the field values in the subform are completely displayed, resizing subform columns and the subform itself, as necessary. Save and close the SuppliersAndProducts form.

14. Use the Report Wizard to create a report based on the primary Supplier table and the related Product table. Select the SupplierID, Company, City, Category, ContactFirst, ContactLast, and Phone fields—in that order—from the Supplier table, and the ProductID, ProductName, Price, and Units fields from the Product table. Do not specify any additional grouping levels, and sort the detail records in ascending order by ProductID. Choose the Outline layout and Portrait orientation. Specify the title **ProductsBySupplier** for the report.

15. Change the report title text to **Products by Supplier**.

16. Apply the Facet theme to the ProductsBySupplier report *only*.

17. Resize and reposition the following objects in the report in Layout view, and then scroll through the report to make sure all field labels and field values are fully displayed:

    a. Resize the report title so that the text of the title, Products by Supplier, is fully displayed.

    b. Move the ProductName label and field value box to the right a bit (be sure not to move them too far so that the longest product name will still be completely visible).

    c. Resize the Product ID field label on its right side, increasing its width slightly so the label is fully displayed.

    d. Move the Units/Case label and field value box to the right a bit; then resize the label on its left side, increasing its width slightly so the label is fully displayed.

    e. Select the field value boxes *only* (not the field labels) for the following four fields: SupplierID, Company, City, and Category. Then move the four field value boxes to the left until their left edges align (roughly) with the "S" in "Supplier" in the report title.

    f. Resize the Company field value box on its right side, increasing its width slightly so that all company names are fully displayed.

18. Change the color of the report title text to the Blue-Gray, Text 2, Darker 25% theme color.

19. Insert the Supplies picture, which is located in the Access1 ▶ Review folder provided with your Data Files, in the report. Move the picture to the right of the report title. Drag a bottom corner of the image to increase its size until the items in the picture are all clearly visible. Continue to resize and reposition the image until it is in the location you want, making sure to keep it within the shaded area of the title and to the right of the title.

20. Apply conditional formatting so that the Category field values equal to Service appear as dark red and bold.

21. Preview each page of the report, verifying that all the fields fit on the page. If necessary, return to Layout view and make changes so the report prints within the margins of the page and so that all field names and values are completely displayed.

22. Save the report, print its first page (only if asked by your instructor to do so), and then close the report.

23. Compact and repair the Vendor database, and then close it.

Case Problem 1

Data Files needed for this Case Problem: Gopher.accdb *(cont. from Tutorial 3)* and Tasks.bmp

GoGopher!   Amol Mehta uses the Gopher database to track and view information about the services his company offers. He asks you to create the necessary forms and a report to help him work with this data more efficiently. Complete the following:

1. Open the **Gopher** database you created and worked with in Tutorials 1 through 3, and then click the Enable Content button next to the security warning, if necessary.

APPLY

2. Use the Form Wizard to create a form based on the Member table. Select all the fields for the form and the Columnar layout. Specify the title **MemberData** for the form.

3. Apply the Wisp theme to the MemberData form *only*.

4. Edit the form title so that it appears as "Member Data" (two words); resize the title so that both words fit on the same line; and then change the font color of the form title to the Dark Red, Accent 1, Darker 25% theme color.

5. Use the Find command to display the record for Marco Krukonis, and then change the Street field value for this record to **75 Woodfield Ave**.

6. Use the MemberData form to add a new record to the Member table with the following field values:

   Member ID: **1261**

   Plan ID: **306**

   First Name: **Taylor**

   Last Name: **Byrne**

   Street: **318 Coolidge Dr**

   City: **Jamestown**

   State: **CO**

   Zip: **80455**

   Phone: **303-751-3152**

   Date Joined: **10/1/2016**

   Expiration Date: **4/1/2017**

7. Save and close the MemberData form.

8. Use the Form Wizard to create a form containing a main form and a subform. Select all the fields from the Plan table for the main form, and select the MemberID, FirstName, LastName, Expiration, and Phone fields from the Member table for the subform. Use the Datasheet layout. Specify the title **MembersByPlan** for the main form and the title **MemberSubform** for the subform.

9. Change the form title text for the main form to **Members by Plan**.

10. Resize all columns in the subform to their best fit, working from left to right; then move through all the records in the main form and check to make sure that all subform field values are fully displayed, resizing the columns as necessary.

11. Save and close the MembersByPlan form.

12. Use the Report Wizard to create a report based on the primary Plan table and the related Member table. Select all the fields from the Plan table, and then select the MemberID, FirstName, LastName, City, Phone, DateJoined, and Expiration fields from the Member table. Do not select any additional grouping levels, and sort the detail records in ascending order by MemberID. Choose the Outline layout and Landscape orientation. Specify the title **MemberPlans** for the report.

13. Apply the Wisp theme to the MemberPlans report *only*.

14. Resize the report title so that the text is fully displayed; edit the report title so that it appears as "Member Plans" (two words); and change the font color of the title to the Dark Red, Accent 1, Darker 25% theme color.

15. Change the alignment of the Plan Cost field so that its values appear left-aligned in the field value boxes.

16. Resize and reposition the following objects in the report in Layout view, and then scroll through the report to make sure all field labels and field values are fully displayed:

    a. Move the FirstName label and field value box to the right a bit (be sure not to move them too far so that the longest first name will still be completely visible).

    b. Resize the MemberID field label on its right side, increasing its width until the label is fully displayed.

    c. Move the Phone label and field value box to the left; then move the DateJoined label and field value box to the left.

    d. Resize the Expiration Date label on its left side, increasing its width until the label is fully displayed.

e. Scroll to the bottom of the report; note that the page number might not be completely within the page border (the dotted vertical line). If necessary, select and move the box containing the text "Page 1 of 1" until the entire text is positioned to the left of the dotted vertical line marking the right page border.

17. Insert the Tasks picture, which is located in the Access1 ▸ Case1 folder provided with your Data Files, in the report. Move the picture to the right of the report title. Drag a bottom corner of the image to increase its size slightly. Continue to resize and reposition the image until it is in the location you want, making sure to keep it within the shaded area of the title and to the right of the title.

18. Apply conditional formatting so that any Expiration field value less than 9/1/2016 appears as bold and with the Red color applied.

19. Preview the entire report to confirm that it is formatted correctly. If necessary, return to Layout view and make changes so that all field labels and field values are completely displayed.

20. Save the report, print its first page (only if asked by your instructor to do so), and then close the report.

21. Compact and repair the Gopher database, and then close it.

Case Problem 2

CREATE

Data Files needed for this Case Problem: OBrien.accdb *(cont. from Tutorial 3)* and Tests.bmp

O'Brien Educational Services   Karen O'Brien is using the OBrien database to track and analyze the business activity of her educational consulting company. To make her work easier, you'll create a form and report in the OBrien database. Complete the following:

1. Open the **OBrien** database you created and worked with in Tutorials 1 through 3, and then click the Enable Content button next to the security warning, if necessary.

2. Create the form shown in Figure 4-29.

Figure 4-29   Completed ContractsByTutor form

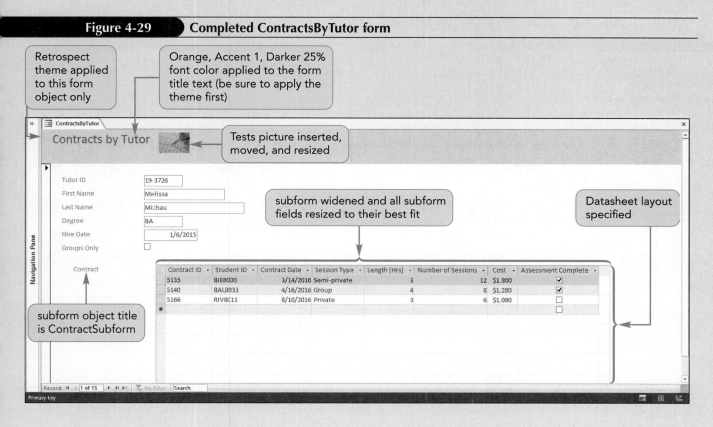

3. Using the form you just created, navigate to the second record in the subform for the third main record, and then change the Assessment Complete field value to **yes**.

4. Use the Find command to move to the record for Samuel Glick, and then change the value in the Groups Only field to **no**.

5. Use the appropriate wildcard character to find all records with a Hire Date field value that begins with the month of March (3). Change the Hire Date field value for Alameda Sarracino (Tutor ID 51-7070) to **3/27/2016**. Save and close the form.

6. Create the report shown in Figure 4-30.

Figure 4-30   **Completed TutorsAndContracts report**

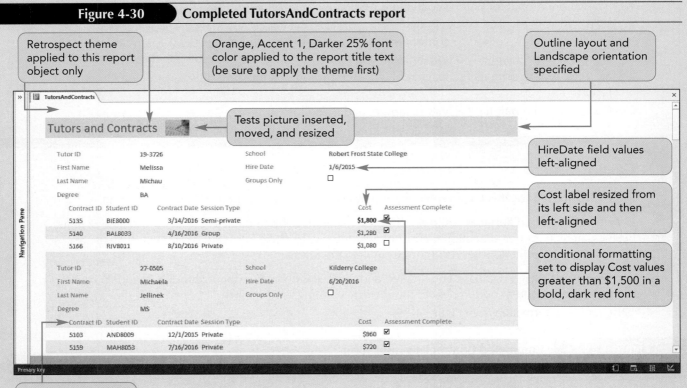

Retrospect theme applied to this report object only

Orange, Accent 1, Darker 25% font color applied to the report title text (be sure to apply the theme first)

Outline layout and Landscape orientation specified

Tests picture inserted, moved, and resized

HireDate field values left-aligned

Cost label resized from its left side and then left-aligned

conditional formatting set to display Cost values greater than $1,500 in a bold, dark red font

detail records sorted by ContractID in ascending order

7. Scroll to the bottom of the report; note that the page number might not be completely within the page border (the dotted vertical line). If necessary, select and move the box containing the text "Page 1 of 1" until the entire text is positioned to the left of the dotted vertical line marking the right page border.

8. Preview each page of the report, verifying that all the fields fit on the page. If necessary, return to Layout view and make changes so the report prints within the margins of the page and so that all field names and values are completely displayed.

9. Save the report, print its first page (only if asked by your instructor to do so), and then close the report.

10. Compact and repair the OBrien database, and then close it.

CHALLENGE

Case Problem 3

Data Files needed for this Case Problem: Shelter.accdb *(cont. from Tutorial 3)* and Animals.bmp

Rosemary Animal Shelter   Ryan Lang uses the Shelter database to track, maintain, and analyze data about his shelter's patrons, donations, and animals. You'll help Ryan by creating a form and a report based on this data. Complete the following:

1. Open the **Shelter** database you created and worked with in Tutorials 1 through 3, and then click the Enable Content button next to the security warning, if necessary.
2. Use the Form Wizard to create a form based on the Animal table. Select all the fields for the form and the Columnar layout. Specify the title **AnimalInfo** for the form.
3. Apply the Ion theme to the AnimalInfo form *only*.
4. Edit the form title so that it appears as "Animal Info" (two words), and change the font color of the form title to the Green, Accent 4, Darker 25% theme color.
5. ⊕ **Explore** 5. Use the appropriate button in the Font group on the FORMAT tab to underline the form title. Save the form.
6. Use the AnimalInfo form to update the Animal table as follows:
   a. Use the Find command to search for records that contain "beagle" anywhere in the Description field. Display the record for the dog named Gus (AnimalID R98), and then change the Age field value for this record to **3**.
   b. Add a new record with the following values:
      Animal ID: **T80**
      Patron ID: [leave blank]
      Animal Name: **Tessie**
      Age at Arrival: **1**
      Gender: **Female**
      Animal Type: **Dog**
      Description: **Terrier mix**
      Arrival Date: **4/9/16**
      Adopted: **no**
      Adoption Date: [leave blank]
   ⊕ **Explore** c. Find the record with AnimalID S35 (for Roggie), and then delete the record. (*Hint:* After displaying the record in the form, you need to select it by clicking the right-pointing triangle in the bar to the left of the field labels. Then use the appropriate button in the Records group on the HOME tab to delete the record. When asked to confirm the deletion, click the Yes button.) Close the form.
7. Use the Form Wizard to create a form containing a main form and a subform. Select all the fields from the Patron table for the main form, and select all fields except PatronID from the Donation table for the subform. Use the Datasheet layout. Specify the name **PatronsAndDonations** for the main form and the title **DonationSubform** for the subform.
8. Apply the Ion theme to the PatronsAndDonations form *only*.
9. Edit the form title so that it appears as "Patrons and Donations." Resize the form title so that the text fits on one line. Change the font color of the title to the Green, Accent 4, Darker 25% theme color.
10. Insert the Animals picture, which is located in the Access1 ▶ Case3 folder provided with your Data Files, in the PatronsAndDonations form. Remove the picture from the control layout, and then move the picture to the right of the form title. Resize the picture so it is approximately double the original size.
11. ⊕ **Explore** 11. Use the appropriate button in the Font group on the FORMAT tab to apply the theme color Green, Accent 4, Lighter 80% as a background color for all the field value boxes in the main form. Then use the appropriate button in the Control Formatting group to change the

outline of all the main form field value boxes to have a line thickness of 1 pt. (*Hint:* Select all the field value boxes before making these changes.)

12. Resize the subform to the right, and then resize all columns in the subform to their best fit. Navigate through the records in the main form to make sure all the field values in the subform are completely displayed, resizing subform columns as necessary. Save and close the form.

13. Use the Report Wizard to create a report based on the primary Patron table and the related Donation table. Select all the fields from the Patron table, and select all fields except PatronID from the Donation table. Sort the detail records in *descending* order by DonationValue. Choose the Outline layout and Portrait orientation. Specify the name **PatronsAndDonations** for the report.

14. Apply the Ion theme to the PatronsAndDonations report *only*.

15. Resize the report title so that the text is fully displayed; edit the report title so that it appears as "Patrons and Donations"; and change the font color of the title to the Green, Accent 4, Darker 25% theme color.

16. Move the Donation Value field label and its field value box to the left a bit. Then resize the Donation ID field label on the right to fully display the label. Move the Description field label and its field value box to the right a bit, to provide more space between the Donation Date and Description fields. Finally, resize the Phone field label from its left side to reduce the width of the label box, moving the word "Phone" closer to the phone numbers. Save the report.

17. Insert the Animals picture, which is located in the Access1 ▸ Case3 folder provided with your Data Files, in the PatronsAndDonations report. Move the picture to the right of the report title. Resize the picture so it is approximately double the original size.

✪ **Explore** 18. Use the appropriate button in the Background group on the FORMAT tab to apply the theme color Green, Accent 4, Lighter 60% as the alternate row color for the fields from the Patron table; then apply the theme color Green, Accent 4, Lighter 80% as the alternate row color for the fields from the Donation table. (*Hint:* You must first select an entire row with no background color for the appropriate fields before applying each alternate row color.) Scroll through the report to find a patron record with multiple donations so you can verify the effect of applying the alternate row color to the Donation fields.

19. Apply conditional formatting so that any DonationValue greater than or equal to 250 is formatted as bold and with the Brown font color.

✪ **Explore** 20. Preview the report so you can see two pages at once. (*Hint:* Use a button on the PRINT PREVIEW tab.) Check the report to confirm that it is formatted correctly and all field labels and field values are fully displayed. Save the report, print its first page (only if asked by your instructor to do so), and then close the report.

21. Compact and repair the Shelter database, and then close it.

Case Problem 4

Data Files needed for this Case Problem: Stanley.accdb (*cont. from Tutorial 3*), Hiking.bmp, and Tour.accdb

Stanley EcoTours Janice and Bill Stanley use the Stanley database to maintain and analyze data about the clients, reservations, and tours for their ecotourism business. You'll help them by creating a form and a report in the Stanley database. Additionally, you'll troubleshoot some problems in another database containing tour information. Complete the following:

1. Open the **Stanley** database you created and worked with in Tutorials 1 through 3, and then click the Enable Content button next to the security warning, if necessary.

2. Use the Form Wizard to create a form containing a main form and a subform. Select all the fields from the Guest table for the main form, and select all the fields except GuestID from the Reservation table for the subform. Use the Datasheet layout. Specify the title **GuestReservations** for the main form and the title **ReservationSubform** for the subform.

3. Apply the Organic theme to the GuestReservations form *only*.

4. Edit the form title so that it appears with a space between the two words. Change the font color of the title to the Blue-Gray, Accent 3, Darker 25% theme color.

5. Insert the Hiking picture, which is located in the Access1 ▶ Case4 folder provided with your Data Files, in the GuestReservations form. Remove the picture from the control layout, and then move the picture to the right of the form title. Resize the picture so it is approximately double the original size.

6. Resize all columns in the subform to their best fit so that the subform column titles are fully displayed. Save the form.

7. Use the Find command to search for records that contain "AB" in the State/Prov field. Display the record for Isabelle Rouy (GuestID 417), and then change the Address field value for this record to **15 Brookside Dr**. Close the form.

8. Use the Report Wizard to create a report based on the primary Guest table and the related Reservation table. Select all the fields from the Guest table, and then select all the fields except GuestID from the Reservation table. Do not select any additional grouping levels, and sort the detail records in ascending order by ReservationID. Choose the Outline layout and Portrait orientation. Specify the title **GuestsAndReservations** for the report.

9. Apply the Organic theme to the GuestsAndReservations report *only*.

10. Edit the report title so that it appears as "Guests and Reservations"; then change the font color of the title to the Blue-Gray, Accent 3, Darker 25% theme color.

11. Move the Phone field label to the left, and then resize it from its right side to make the label box smaller. Then move the Phone field value box to the left, and then resize it on its right side to make the box bigger and fully display the field value.

12. Insert the Hiking picture, which is located in the Access1 ▶ Case4 folder provided with your Data Files, in the GuestsAndReservations report. Move the picture to the right of the report title. Resize the picture so it is approximately double the original size.

13. Apply conditional formatting so that any People field value greater than or equal to 5 appears as bold and with the Red color applied.

14. Preview the entire report to confirm that it is formatted correctly. If necessary, return to Layout view and make changes so that all field labels and field values are completely displayed.

15. Save the report, print its first page (only if asked by your instructor to do so), and then close the report.

16. Compact and repair the Stanley database, and then close it.

⚙ **Troubleshoot** 17. Open the Tour database located in the Access1 ▶ Case4 folder provided with your Data Files. Open the CustomerData form in the Tour database. The form is not formatted correctly; it should be formatted with the Ion Boardroom theme and the theme color Plum, Accent 1, Darker 25% applied to the title. There are other problems with the form title's format as well. Additionally, some of the field labels are not properly formatted with regard to spacing between words. Identify and fix the problems with the form's format. (*Hint:* To fix the spacing between words in the necessary field labels, use the same procedure you use to fix the spacing between words in the form title text.) Save and close the corrected form.

⚙ **Troubleshoot** 18. Open the CustomerBookings form, which is also not formatted correctly. Modify the form so that it matches the corrected format of the CustomerData form and has a consistent design, including the correctly placed image (Hiking.bmp). Fix the formatting problems with the subform as well, and then save and close the corrected form with subform.

⚙ **Troubleshoot** 19. Open the CustomersAndBookings report. This report should have a consistent format in terms of theme, color, and so on as the two forms. Additionally, some of the field labels are not properly formatted with regard to spacing between words. (*Hint:* To fix the spacing between words in the necessary field labels, use the same procedure you use to fix the spacing between words in the report title text.) Find and fix these formatting errors. The report also has several problems with field labels and field value boxes, where the labels and values are not fully displayed. Locate and correct all of these problems, being sure to scroll through the entire report. Also, the conditional formatting applied to the People field is supposed to use a bold Red font. Edit the rule to correct the conditional formatting. Save the corrected report, and then preview it to identify and correct any remaining formatting problems. Compact and repair the Tour database, and then close it.

Teamwork

Working with a Team to Create a Database

Teamwork is the collaborative effort of individuals working together to achieve a goal. Most organizations rely on teams to complete work tasks, regardless of whether those teams are formal and ongoing or informally organized to achieve a specific goal. Some teams might even be virtual, such as teams that use telecommunications technologies and social networks to complete tasks from different corporate or geographical locations.

When an organization decides to use a database to manage information, the database is rarely planned, created, and maintained by a single individual. In most cases, a team of individuals is assigned to work on different stages of database development. For example, a team might research the needs of the organization, the best database management system to use to meet those needs, and the skills required of the team members to create, update, and maintain the database. Then another team might take over the task of actually creating the database and its objects, inputting the data, and installing the database on the organization's network. Finally, yet another team might conduct training sessions to teach users how to use the database to extract the data they require to perform their jobs.

Regardless of the type of database being created, the roles that individual team members play when working on a team are similar to what you might expect in any situation that requires a collaborative effort.

The Roles of Team Members

If a team is to be successful, individual members must see the value in their respective contributions and what the team as a whole gets out of each member's contribution. This means two important requirements must be met: task performance and social satisfaction. Task performance usually is handled by one or more members who are task specialists. Task specialists spend a lot of time and effort ensuring that the team achieves its goals. They initiate ideas, give opinions, gather information, sort details, and provide motivation to keep the team on track.

Social satisfaction is handled by individuals who strengthen the team's social bonds through encouragement, empathy, conflict resolution, compromise, and tension reduction. Have you ever been on a team where the tension was high, and someone stepped in to tell a joke or tried to soften the blow of criticism? That person held the role of managing social satisfaction.

Both the task specialist and social satisfaction specialist are important roles on teams. These are not the only roles, however. Other roles include team leaders, work coordinators, idea people, and critics. The roles of individual team members are not always mutually exclusive. For example, the task specialist might also be the team leader, and the idea person might also fill the social satisfaction role. As you begin working with your team in this exercise, watch how these roles are filled and how they change as your team completes its work. Perhaps you'll want to discuss upfront which role each member is comfortable filling to see how complementary your collective skill sets turn out to be. What if your team lacks a role? Then you'll need to figure out, as a team, how to move forward so you can complete your work successfully. The following are tips that everyone should respect as work on a team begins:

- Remember that everyone brings something of value to the team.
- Respect and support each other as you work toward the common goal.
- When criticism or questions arise, try to see things from the other person's perspective.
- If someone needs assistance, find ways to encourage or support that person so the team is not affected.
- Deal with negative or unproductive attitudes immediately so they don't damage team energy and attitude.
- Get outside help if the team becomes stuck and can't move forward.
- Provide periodic positive encouragement or rewards for contributions.

The Importance of Technology in Teamwork

Many teams now depend on technology to accomplish work tasks. For example, corporate intranets and networks, email and voice mail, texting and instant messaging, teleconferencing and software collaboration tools, social networks, and cell phones can support teamwork. Each time you work in a group, decide at the outset how the team will use different technologies to communicate and document work activities. Determine how the team will organize and combine deliverable documents or presentation materials. Use whatever technology tools make the most sense for your team, your task, and your skills.

PROSKILLS

Create a Database

Many organizations use Access to manage business data, but Access can also be a valuable tool to track personal data. For example, you might create an Access database to store information about items in a personal collection, such as CDs, DVDs, or books; items related to a hobby, such as coin or stamp collecting, travel, or family history; or items related to sports teams, theater clubs, or other organizations to which you might belong. In this exercise, you'll work with your team members to create a database that will contain information of your choice, using the Access skills and features presented in Tutorials 1 through 4. As a group, you'll choose something the team is interested in tracking, such as members and activities of a college service organization or recruiters and job opportunities at your school.

Using Templates

Access includes templates for creating databases. A **database template** is a database containing predefined tables, queries, forms, and reports. Using a database template can save you time and effort when creating a database. For example, if the database objects available in one of the database templates are suitable for the data you want to store, you can use the template to quickly create a database with the objects already created for you. You can then modify them, as necessary, to suit your needs. Before you begin to create a database with your team members, review the following steps for using a database template.

To create a database using a database template:

1. Make sure the New screen is displayed in Backstage view.
2. Click one of the available Desktop templates, or use the box at the top of the screen to search for templates online. (Note that templates without the word "Desktop" in their names require Sharepoint, so do not choose one of those.)
3. Specify the name for your database and a location in which to save the database file.
4. Click the Create button.
5. Use the resulting database objects to enter, modify, or delete data or database objects.

Work in a Team to Create a Database

Working with your team members, you can decide to use a database template for this exercise if the template fits the data you want to track. Note, however, that you still need to create the additional database objects indicated in the following steps—tables, queries, forms, and reports—to complete the exercise successfully.

Note: Please be sure *not* to include any personal information of a sensitive nature in the database you create to be submitted to your instructor for this exercise. Later on, you can update the data in your database with such information for your own personal use.

1. Meet with your team to determine what data you want to track in your new Access database. Determine how many tables you need and what data will go into each table. Be sure that the data you choose to track lends itself to at least three groupings of related data, that at least twenty items are available to track within each group, and that you'll be able to track multiple types of data. Sketch the layout of the columns (fields) and rows (records) for each table.

Also discuss the field properties for each field, so that team members can document the characteristics needed for each field as they collect data. Consider using a standard form to help each person as he or she collects the necessary data.

Next, assign data gathering and documentation tasks to each team member and set a deadline for finishing this initial task. Consider using Excel workbooks for this task, as you can use them to import the data later when working in Access. When all the data for the fields is collected, meet again as a team to examine the data collected and determine the structure of the database you will create. Finally, assign each team member specific tasks for creating the database objects discussed in the following steps.

2. Create a new Access database to contain the data your team wants to track.

3. Create two or three tables in the database that can be joined through one-to-many relationships.

4. Using the preliminary design work done by team members, define the properties for each field in each table. Make sure to include a mix of data types for the fields (for example, do not include only Short Text fields in each table).

5. As a team, discuss and specify a primary key for each table.

6. Define the necessary one-to-many relationships between the tables in the database with referential integrity enforced.

7. Enter 20 to 30 records in each table. If appropriate, your team can import the data for a table from another source, such as an Excel workbook or a text file.

8. Create 5 to 10 queries based on single tables and multiple tables. Be sure that some of the queries include some or all of the following: exact match conditions, comparison operators, and logical operators.

9. For some of the queries, use various sorting and filtering techniques to display the query results in various ways. Save these queries with the sort and/or filter applied.

10. If possible, and depending on the data your team is tracking, create at least one calculated field in one of the queries.

11. If possible, and depending on the data your team is tracking, use aggregate functions to produce summary statistics based on the data in at least one of the tables.

12. Create at least one form for each table in the database. Enhance each form's appearance with pictures, themes, title colors, and so on.

13. Create at least one form with a main form and subform based on related tables in the database. Enhance the form's appearance as appropriate.

14. Create at least one report based on each table in the database. Enhance each report's appearance with pictures, themes, color, and so on.

15. Apply conditional formatting to the values in at least one of the reports.

16. Submit your team's completed database to your instructor as requested. Include printouts of any database objects, such as reports, if required. Also, provide written documentation that describes the role of each team member and his or her contributions to the team. This documentation should include descriptions of any challenges the team faced while completing this exercise and how the team members worked together to overcome those challenges.

GLOSSARY/INDEX

TASK REFERENCE

TASK	PAGE #	RECOMMENDED METHOD
Access, start	AC 7	Click the Access 2013 tile on the Windows Start screen
Aggregate functions, use in a datasheet	AC 162	Open the table or query in Datasheet view. in Records group on HOME tab click Totals button, click Total field row, click function
Aggregate functions, use in a query	AC 163	Display the query in Design view, click the Totals button in the Show/Hide group on the DESIGN tab
Calculated field, add to a query	AC 157	*See* Reference box: Using Expression Builder
Column, resize width in a datasheet	AC 18	Double-click ↔ on the right border of the column heading
Compressed folder, extract all files and folders from	FM 27	Click the compressed folder, click the Compressed Folder Tools Extract tab, click the Extract all button
Compressed folder, open	FM 27	Double-click the compressed folder
Data, find	AC 194	*See* Reference box: Finding Data in a Form or Datasheet
Data Type gallery, add fields to a table with	AC 86	Click the FIELDS tab, click More Fields in the Add & Delete group, click the field or Quick Start selection to add
Database, compact and repair	AC 42	*See* Reference box: Compacting and Repairing a Database
Database, create a blank	AC 7	Start Access, click Blank desktop database, type the database name, select the drive and folder, click OK, click Create
Database, open	AC 26	*See* Reference box: Opening a Database
Datasheet view for tables, switch to	AC 75	In the Views group on the DESIGN tab, click the View button
Design view, switch to	AC 73	In the Views group on the FIELDS tab, click the View button
Documents library, open	FM 10	In File Explorer, click ▷ next to Libraries, click ▷ next to Documents
Excel worksheet, import data from	AC 81	Click the EXTERNAL DATA tab, click Excel in the Import & Link group, complete the import dialog boxes
Field, add to a table	AC 69	*See* Reference box: Adding a Field Between Two Existing Fields
Field, define in a table	AC 59	*See* Reference box: Defining a Field in Design View
Field, delete from a table	AC 87	*See* Reference box: Deleting a Field from a Table Structure
Field, move to a new location in a table	AC 69	Display the table in Design view, click the field's row selector, drag the field with the pointer
Field property change, update	AC 91	Click 🗲, select the option for updating the field property
File Explorer, open	FM 10	Click 📁 on the taskbar
File Explorer, return to a previous location	FM 14	Click ⬅
File list, sort	FM 14	Click the column heading button
File, copy	FM 24	Right-click the file, click Copy, right-click destination, click Paste
File, delete	FM 25	Right-click the file, click Delete
File, move	FM 21	Drag the file to the folder
File, open from File Explorer	FM 15	Right-click the file, point to Open with, click an application
File, rename	FM 26	Right-click the file, click Rename, type the new filename, press Enter
File, save with new name in WordPad	FM 18	Click the File tab, click Save as, enter the filename, click Save

TASK	PAGE #	RECOMMENDED METHOD
Files and folders, compress	FM 27	Select the files to compress, click the Share tab, click the Zip button in the Send group
Files, select multiple	FM 24	Press and hold the Ctrl key and click the files
Files, view in Large Icons view	FM 13	Click the View tab, click [icon] in the Layout group
Filter By Selection, activate	AC 136	*See Reference box: Using Filter By Selection*
Folder, create	FM 19	Click the New folder button in the New group on the Home tab
Form Wizard, activate	AC 182	Click the CREATE tab, click Form Wizard in the Forms group, choose the table or query for the form, select fields, click Next
Microsoft Access Help, search	AC 41	Click [?] on the title bar, enter the search text in the search box, press Enter
My Documents folder, open	FM 10	In File Explorer, click [▷] next to Libraries, click [▷] next to Documents, click My Documents
Object, open	AC 22	Double-click the object in the Navigation Pane
Object, save	AC 20	Click [icon], type the object name, click OK
Picture, insert in a form	AC 189	In Layout view, click the DESIGN tab, click the Logo button in the Header/Footer group, select the picture file, click OK
Primary key, specify	AC 67	*See Reference box: Specifying a Primary Key in Design View*
Property sheet, open	AC 159	Make the object current in Design view, click the Property Sheet button in the Show/Hide group on the DESIGN tab
Query, define	AC 125	Click the CREATE tab, click the Query Design button in the Queries group
Query, run	AC 127	Double-click the query in the Navigation Pane or, in the Results group on the DESIGN tab, click the Run button
Query results, sort	AC 133	*See Reference box: Sorting a Query Datasheet*
Quick Start selection, add	AC 86	Click the FIELDS tab, click More Fields in the Add & Delete group, click the Quick Start selection
Record, add new	AC 20	In the Records group on the HOME tab, click the New button
Record, delete	AC 122	*See Reference box: Deleting a Record*
Record, move to first	AC 30	Click [◀|]
Record, move to last	AC 30	Click [▶|]
Record, move to next	AC 30	Click [▶]
Record, move to previous	AC 30	Click [◀]
Records, print selected in a form	AC 199	Click the FILE tab, click Print in the navigation bar, click Print, click Selected Record(s), click OK
Records, redisplay all after filter	AC 138	In Sort & Filter group on HOME tab, click the Toggle Filter button
Report, print	AC 39	*See Reference box: Printing a Report*
Report, print specific pages of	AC 219	In the Print group on the PRINT PREVIEW tab, click Print, click Pages, enter number of pages to print in From and To boxes, click OK
Report Wizard, activate	AC 208	Click the CREATE tab, click Report Wizard button in Reports group, choose the table or query for the report, select fields, click Next
Ribbon, expand in File Explorer	FM 13	Click [˅]

TASK	PAGE #	RECOMMENDED METHOD
Sort, specify ascending in datasheet	AC 132	Click a column heading arrow, click Sort A to Z
Sort, specify descending in datasheet	AC 132	Click a column heading arrow, click Sort Z to A
Table, create in Datasheet view	AC 11	*See* Reference box: Creating a Table in Datasheet View
Table, open in a database	AC 22	Double-click the table in the Navigation Pane
Table, save in a database	AC 19	*See* Reference box: Saving a Table
Text file, import data from	AC 96	Click the EXTERNAL DATA tab, click Text File in the Import & Link group, complete the import dialog boxes
Theme, apply to a form	AC 185	*See* Reference box: Applying a Theme to a Form
View, change in File Explorer	FM 12	*See* Reference box: Changing the View in File Explorer

GOSCINNY AND UDERZO
PRESENT
AN ASTERIX ADVENTURE

ASTERIX AND THE SECRET WEAPON

WRITTEN AND ILLUSTRATED BY ALBERT UDERZO
TRANSLATED BY ANTHEA BELL AND DEREK HOCKRIDGE

HODDER AND STOUGHTON
LONDON SYDNEY AUCKLAND

British Library Cataloguing in Publication Data

A catalogue record for this book is available from
the British Library

  ISBN 0-340-56295-1 (cased)
  ISBN 0-340-56871-2 (limp)

Original edition © Les Editions Albert René, Goscinny-Uderzo, 1991
English translation: © Les Editions Albert René, Goscinny-Uderzo, 1991
Exclusive licensee: Hodder and Stoughton Ltd
Translators: Anthea Bell and Derek Hockridge
Hand-lettering: Stephen Potter

First published in Great Britain 1991 (cased)
This impression 110 109 108 107 106 105 104 103 102

First published in Great Britain 1993 (limp)
This impression 110 109 108 107 106 105 104 103 102

Published by Hodder Children's Books
a division of Hodder Headline plc
338 Euston Road, London NW1 3BH.

Printed in Belgium by Proost International Book Production